MIKE CONNOLLY
*and the Manly Art
of Hollywood Gossip*

MIKE CONNOLLY
and the Manly Art
of Hollywood Gossip

by VAL HOLLEY

McFarland & Company, Inc., Publishers
Jefferson, North Carolina, and London

LIBRARY OF CONGRESS CATALOGUING-IN-PUBLICATION DATA

Holley, Val.
    Mike Connolly and the manly art of Hollywood gossip /
by Val Holley.
        p.   cm.
    Includes bibliographical references and index.

    ISBN 0-7864-1552-5 (softcover : 50# alkaline paper) ∞

    1. Connolly, Mike.   2. Gossip columnists— United States—
Biography.   I. Title.
PN4874.C668H65 2003
070.4'44 — dc21

                                        2003010989

British Library cataloguing data are available

Cover photograph: Mike Connolly, 1952 (Photograph by Wallace
Seawell, courtesy Wallace Seawell and the Wilkerson Archives)

Manufactured in the United States of America

McFarland & Company, Inc., Publishers
  Box 611, Jefferson, North Carolina 28640
    www.mcfarlandpub.com

For Joseph Plocek
and
Ned Comstock

Contents

Acknowledgments

There are many persons to thank in connection with the challenge of resurrecting Mike Connolly from obscurity. First and foremost is Ned Comstock of the University of Southern California's Cinema-Television Library, whose competence, helpfulness, and extraordinary knowledge of his facility's collection are exemplary. Ned always went far beyond the call of duty and unearthed numerous files relating not only to Connolly but also to Rory Calhoun and the film version of *I'll Cry Tomorrow*, none of which I would have thought to ask for.

Another archivist whose helpfulness made a world of difference is James Leyerzapf of the Dwight D. Eisenhower Presidential Library in Abilene, Kansas. My original question to Leyerzapf was whether anything in his library's papers of General Henry S. Aurand, Commander of the Sixth Service Command during World War II, would shed light on Connolly's wartime civilian job. The answer was no, but by the way, we have four letters from Connolly to Eisenhower. Without this nudge, it would never have occurred to me that Connolly might also have written to Richard M. Nixon.

Lester Strong, a writer and historian from New York, opened up the world of his late friend David Hanna to me and shared copies of Hanna's many paperback books about Hollywood that even the Library of Congress does not have. I am also grateful to Hanna's partner, Richard Foster, for his insights on Hanna's years in Hollywood.

Connolly bequeathed his personal library to St. Mary's College in Moraga, California. Linda Wobbe, the college archivist, provided a thirty-six page list of each book in the Connolly Collection.

Among Connolly's surviving colleagues, Frank Liberman, publicist to Bob Hope for over forty years, must certainly be the grandest gentleman in Hollywood. Whenever I encountered an unfamiliar but seemingly significant name in Connolly's columns, I appealed to Frank's total recall; he was my living encyclopedia of Who Was Who in Hollywood. There were very few names that he could not illuminate for me. As well, the late Terrence O'Flaherty of the *San Francisco Chronicle* provided copies of all his columns relating to his trips with the Bob Hope troupes to Alaska in 1956 and the Far East in 1957, both of which Connolly joined. O'Flaherty also facilitated my entrée to Liberman. Two other helpful veterans of these Hope trips were Peggy King Rudofker and Carl Pelleck.

William R. Wilkerson III ("Willie") could not have been kinder or more welcoming in sharing his memories of both his father's and Connolly's legacies at the *Hollywood Reporter*. For his enthusiasm and encouragement toward this Connolly biography I am indebted. I wish him much success on the biographical work he is doing on his father. Other helpful sources who either worked at the *Hollywood Reporter* or were closely connected to those who did were Dan Jenkins, Ed Hutshing, Jim Henaghan, Jr., Frances Henaghan Ehrlich, and William Feeder; Thomas M. Pryor, former editor of *Daily Variety*, was also accommodating and informative. I interviewed or received letters from reporters who were Connolly's contemporaries, including Jack Bradford, Irv Kupcinet, Liz Smith, Bob Thomas, James Bacon, Herb Caen, Robert Osborne, Herman Klurfeld, Morry Rotman, Bill Diehl, and Will Jones; and press agents of the same era, including Beebe Kline, Esme Chandlee, Jerry Pam, and Dale Olson.

Julie Sanges, secretary to Lillian Roth from 1954 to 1980, has my eternal gratitude for sharing every last scrap of material relating to *I'll Cry Tomorrow* in her possession; otherwise, the nature of Connolly's collaboration on Roth's autobiography would have remained unclear. Alan Eichler, Roth's last manager, gave an interview, went to great efforts to obtain and send a videotape of Roth's appearance on *This Is Your Life*, and referred me to Sanges.

Lawrence J. Quirk, longtime publisher and editor of several Hollywood fan magazines and author of thirty Hollywood biographies himself, agreed graciously to half a dozen interviews over a two-year period. I am grateful that he shared unstintingly his vast knowledge of the gay Hollywood networks of Connolly's time.

The Thomas and Alma Connolly family, with whom I had two meetings, was extravagantly generous in sharing the memorabilia relating to "Uncle Mike's" career they have collected over seven decades. The copies of Connolly's *Daily Illini* columns they furnished freed me from having to dig them up myself. (Although I did spend a day sifting through archives and microfilms at the University of Illinois, the bulk of material I relied on was provided by the Connollys.) Mike Connolly was proud of this family when he was alive, and he would be even more proud today of the attractive, accomplished, devoted, and vast family network they have multiplied into.

For their good-natured memories of their experiences with fellow student Mike Connolly at the University of Illinois, I must thank Maryjane Ryan Snyder, Hallie Rives Amiel, Angus Thuermer, Jack Mabley, Ines Caudera Keller, and Sam Abarbanel.

Scott G. Burgh, chief law librarian of the city of Chicago and one of the Windy City's most knowledgeable and enthusiastic boosters, pointed me toward many Chicago archives and repositories of information that I would never have known about, and hosted me while I was there to do research. Also in Chicago, the late Brother Kevin Griffin of De La Salle Institute was my liaison to his institution's archives, the only surviving records of a formative time in Connolly's life.

Among Connolly's good friends, I was lucky to have the cooperation of George Bon Salle, Judy Brubaker, Dick Clayton, Jack Costanzo, James DeCloss, Jack Devaney, Chatty Collier Eliason, Trini Lopez, A. C. Lyles, Dave Peck, William Roy, Wally Seawell, Jack Vizzard, Jerry Wunderlich, and Dana Wynter (for Greg Bautzer).

Fellow biographers Robert Hofler (Henry Willson) and William J. Mann (Billy Haines) lent moral support and passed along tips and valuable nuggets of information. I was also fortunate to have letters or emails from such gentlemen and scholars as Paul Buhle, Larry Ceplair, Dr. Chad Heap, Norris Houghton, Patrick McGilligan, and Dr. William Solberg.

Finally, to my fine partner, Joseph Plocek, who makes me happy and proud, my thanks for all his patience, indulgence, interference-running, encouragement, good sense, and yes, proofreading.

Preface

I am familiar with Dr. Stanley Fish's blistering criticism of biographers ("Just Published: Minutiae Without Meaning," *New York Times*, September 7, 1999) — they "can only be inauthentic, can only get it wrong, can only lie, can only substitute their own story for the story of their announced subject." Even if I were inclined to agree with him (which, with certain reservations, I am), I believe biography is a worthy pursuit.

What really interests me about Dr. Fish's essay is his endorsement of autobiography. "Autobiographers cannot lie because anything they say, however mendacious, is the truth about themselves, whether they know it or not," he wrote.

Although Mike Connolly kept no diary, the thousands of columns he wrote from November 1949 to November 1966 constitute a remarkable de facto autobiography. Even if much of what appeared in Connolly's columns was fabricated, and even though he attended only a fraction of the parties he "covered," every last word was the truth about himself.

I discovered Connolly in the course of research for my earlier biography on James Dean, when I determined to read what all the gossip columnists had written about my subject. Fortunately, Dean's eighteen-month career in Hollywood, 1954–1955, coincided with the height of Connolly's powers as a columnist for film industry sophisticates. After reading only two or three of his columns, it was clear to me that Connolly had been a giant working among ants; here was a virtuoso of the gorgeous properties of the English language. It was also clear that Connolly was gay. Even though he wrote explicitly that he had a girl on his arm as he made his nightly rounds, something about his responses to the stimuli of camera-eroticized images and nightclub entertainment gave him away.

Since other gossip columnists such as Sidney Skolsky and Hedda

Hopper left behind mammoth collections of their private papers, I set out to find where Connolly's papers were housed, hoping to find a smoking gun or two relating to James Dean. To my surprise, no film archive owned up to having any "Connolly Papers." I began writing to various Connolly peers—Gerold Frank, Bill Diehl, and others—asking if they could help, but no one had any idea. At this point, my idea of a Connolly biography began to germinate.

Finally, Kevin Thomas of the *Los Angeles Times* remembered that a late friend of his, John Mahoney of the *Hollywood Reporter*, had said that after Connolly died, boxes full of his correspondence with prominent figures such as Noel Coward remained behind in his office. Eventually, Connolly's partner, Joseph Zappia, admitted that he had given those boxes to Connolly's successor, Jack Bradford, figuring that anyone who was interested would be most likely to contact Bradford. As fate would have it, a basement flood in Bradford's home had destroyed most of the papers.

Much to my regret, Joseph Zappia's participation in this project was minimal. He wrote a few letters and answered a few questions over the phone, but his family advised him against cooperating. Even before his communication dried up, he claimed not to remember much of the information I sought. When I visited Palm Springs in May 2000, he refused to see me. The issuance of a thirty-two cent postage stamp honoring Charlie Chaplin would surely have scandalized Connolly, so all my letters to Zappia, naturally, were sent with that stamp. He had no reaction to it. He died on January 17, 2002.

Several months later, after the deadline for the submission of this manuscript had already passed, Zappia's partner of the last thirty-five years of his life, James Hill, telephoned me from out of the blue and filled me in on many of the historical details I had sought.

One of my most startling discoveries was that Connolly had no FBI file. I had expected the FBI to yield a treasure trove, given that so many other gossip columnists, both conservative and liberal—Hedda Hopper, Herb Caen, Walter Winchell, et al.—were the subjects of files, and that gay Hollywood figures were likely to have been spied on. Bolstering my certainty further was Connolly's mockery and provocation of J. Edgar Hoover in his column. But there was nothing.

I was also surprised pleasantly to realize that Edgar Lustgarten, the MGM cellist for whose firing Connolly was directly responsible, was a splendid presence on many popular music recordings that I already owned. In his last years, Lustgarten teamed up with jazz pianist Roger Kellaway to form the Kellaway Cello Quartet. In the spirit of all that has been done since the late 1990s to restore credit and honor to blacklist victims, I recommend listening to this group. At present, the easiest recording to find is their collaboration with the Singers Unlimited, *Just in Time*. Lustgarten rocks in *Zip-a-Dee Doo-Dah*.

If this book prompts any Hollywood historian to utilize Connolly's columns as a resource, it will have served its purpose.

"Up-&-coming young agent and spouse hosted an
elegant sitdown dinner in their new home: flowers,
candlelight, pheasant under glass— the works.
Midway through the meal the doorbell rang and a
man busted in to serve a summons on the agent,
much to everyone's consternation, for not paying his
rent on his just-vacated apartment."
— *Mike Connolly, August 8, 1957*

"That agent we said was subpoenaed for nonpayment
of rent during an elegant sit-down dinner wants a
retraction … Glad to oblige: it wasn't pheasant under
glass, it was meat loaf."
— *Mike Connolly, August 12, 1957*

Glutton for Publicity

"Actor we know says he's definitely NOT interested in publicity. Now we've heard everything."
— *Mike Connolly, Hollywood Reporter, May 7, 1952*

When Dr. Alfred Kinsey embarked on his 1939 expedition to the gay neighborhoods of Chicago, prospecting for data he would include in his landmark *Sexual Behavior in the Human Male*, he was not prepared for the flourishing homosexual networks, customs, and haunts he would find. That such a world could have existed right under a researcher's nose astonished him. Writing to a colleague, he wondered, "Why has no one cracked this before?"[1]

A comparable degree of amazement could apply to the case of Mike Connolly, the brilliant gay gossip columnist of the *Hollywood Reporter* from 1951 to 1966. Even with a deluge in recent years of gay Hollywood studies, Connolly, the most talented and influential member of the Hollywood press of his time, has received only scant attention from gay historians. His column, for those who knew how to read between the lines, was a remarkable daily chronicle of gay goings-on, and half a century later his cumulative output is a priceless but virtually untapped lode of gay Hollywood history. Why has Mike Connolly not been cracked before?

In his heyday, he was a force to be reckoned with. A critical player in the battle for box office and buzz, he was pegged by *Newsweek*, in 1954, as "probably the most influential columnist inside the movie colony," the one writer "who gets the pick of the trade items, the industry rumors, the policy and casting switches." A prominent press agent said, "I want the

1

By 1964, when he was invited to sign his name in concrete at the New York World's Fair, Connolly was at the height of his fame; his column was syndicated to 191 newspapers. (Photofest)

producer and the casting director to see my clients' names. Maybe only fifty men. Everyone in the industry reads Mike. But not everybody reads [Hedda] Hopper or [Louella] Parsons."[2]

Mike Connolly is not easily pigeonholed into today's rigidly defined, black-and-white gay categories. If he was careful not to flaunt or write publicly about his sexual orientation, as proscribed by Hollywood protocol, he was candid in other ways about where his sexual interests lay. He lived openly with his partner, Joseph Russell Zappia, and put Zappia on his payroll as his legman. Everyone in Hollywood knew what his situation was. With few exceptions, most sources interviewed for this book would interject, after a minimum of small talk, "You know he was gay, don't you?"

Another gaping hole in Hollywood history is the failure of studies on the McCarthy-era blacklist to take into account the contributory role of Connolly and the *Hollywood Reporter*. By virtue of his Irish Catholic background, Connolly was temperamentally suited to become the most strident anti–Communist voice in the Hollywood press, and his role in promoting and enforcing the blacklist, through which suspected Communists were disenfranchised and destroyed, is an integral aspect of it. With the encouragement of the *Hollywood Reporter's* publisher, William R. Wilkerson, Connolly's crusade proceeded without restraint. Where other columnists had merely ranted and wagged fingers, Connolly would hound, harass, and wreck lives.

A great irony of Connolly's "Rambling Reporter" column was that its abundance of cheesecake items, often downright bawdy, spewed from the portable Corona of a gay man. Despite the disingenuousness, he seldom passed up a chance to play the rake when a buxom actress crossed his path, and his lewdness might have made even the bosom-intoxicated but more decorous Earl Wilson of the *New York Post* blush. Trumpeting Sophia Loren's debut in Hollywood, Connolly wolf-whistled, "Lusty, gusty, busty Miss Loren hits you right in the solar plexus. This gal is STRICTLY for the wide screen." Or he might hyperventilate, "Gloria DeHaven lOOks so gOOd in those wOOlen sweaters she wears." In stark contrast, Connolly's chief competitor, the devoted family man Army Archerd of *Daily Variety*, sounded positively vanilla in the rare instances in which he permitted himself a lingering glance at a pretty woman.[3]

It is tempting to assume that Connolly used anti–Communist propaganda and ribald humor to mask his homosexuality, but that does not square with the relatively open way he lived. His emphasis on these items *was* a survival strategy, however, because he was meeting the expectations of his specialized audience. If he satiated Hollywood with talk of Communists and décolletage, he was then free to fill the remainder of the column with whatever he wanted. Much of what suited him was news of gay stars. A perverse analogy is the old story about pornographers who wrote lines into their films such as "I hope he's not a filthy Communist" so a court could not find the films to be *utterly* without redeeming social value.

At times, Connolly would try to sound like the proverbial ink-stained, skirt-chasing newshound. This was the Connolly that attended political conventions and other mammoth events, mixing it up with mobs of Fourth Estaters. He would write of belting back a few with John Steinbeck, or taking a newspapermen's private luncheon with Harry Truman, or flying to New York with the top brass of the *Chicago Sun-Times* in a private plane, conveying an ambience of savoring cigars and brandy with the gents before joining the ladies.

To bolster these chimerical regular-guy credentials, Connolly had a dependable roster of women (often lesbians) to escort to cabarets and premieres. He took pains to tell his readers that his nightclubbing was done with a "girl on our arm." He rendered the same service to other homosexuals, assuring his audience, for instance, that Rock Hudson always referred to Mrs. Hudson as "Dearest," or that Cesar Romero, Sal Mineo, Tab Hunter, Johnnie Ray, Dick Sargent, and other gay actors had been spotted canoodling with opposite-sex dates in dark corners of romantic bistros.[4]

Connolly's pseudo-macho posturing never worked, though, because he would not stay in character. He simply could not muzzle his natural flamboyance in the face of things that genuinely delighted him:

> Ethel Merman blew our color tube trilling *The Trolley Song* straight out of that magnificent meat-grinder larynx of hers on the *Como Show* and nobody — But Nobody! — but the Merm can clang a "clang" like that.

or

> When Mae [West] and her nine musclemen do her "Diamond Lil" sketch you'll come away convinced, as we were, that Las Vegas was made for Mae and vice versa and that this is the rarest, rip-roarin'est saloon act you've ever seen up there or ANYWHERE![5]

Despite the survival strategy that informed Connolly's column, the actual reason for his longevity and power was no smokescreen but sheer talent. He was hands down the best writer in the Hollywood press, infusing movieland love affairs and casting-couch follies with inimitable sizzle and naughtiness. If one can imagine gossip as literature, Connolly achieved it; he was to gossip what H. L. Mencken was to literary criticism. Like Mencken, Connolly was a uniquely inventive stylist.

In *The Fifty-Year Decline and Fall of Hollywood*, a standard work on the film colony, author Ezra Goodman dissected all the major Hollywood columnists, but Connolly was the only one whose news items Goodman deemed interesting enough to quote. He described Connolly as "effusive," "frothy," "chic," and "soigné" (if these made Connolly sound gay, that was the idea), and seconded the opinion that Connolly was the most influential columnist in town. Goodman's examples demonstrated that Connolly's appeal resided in his ability to transform ordinary film industry shop talk into infectious, "hummable" nuggets that would ricochet all day inside a reader's mind.[6]

Readers anticipated Connolly's alliterations with the same eagerness they would later unleash on Al Hirschfeld caricatures, hunting for cleverly camouflaged *NINAs*. In Connolly's hands, a menu at a glittering soirée would boast "candled crêpes suzettes cremated in cognac and curaçao." A clash among titanic egos on the *Suddenly Last Summer* set was refracted through the Connolly prism as "Joe Mankiewicz tiffed with Monty Clift, Clift quarreled with Kate Hepburn, Kate berated Liz Taylor and Liz lashed out at Sam Spiegel." Creative spellings often ran riot, as when a screenwriter with a Communist past "vigorously, virulently invoked the Vth [Fifth Amendment]" or after "Zsa Zsa [Gabor] zstamped her foot and inzsizsted on her own hairdresser for her guezst appearance." (The day after this last item, *Daily Variety's* Army Archerd flattered Connolly sincerely by reporting what Zsa Zsa "zsays" and "zsighs.")[7]

Influenced in some ways by Walter Winchell, Connolly reveled in cooking up ingenious and insinuating new words, phrases, and spellings. But unlike Winchell, he was college-educated and almost impossibly well-read, drawing on a reservoir of literary and linguistic scholarship that Winchell, despite the protests of partisans, lacked. Additionally, Connolly had a knowledge of vaudeville and cinema history second to none.

"Mike was always reading, reading, reading," recalls Jack Bradford, Connolly's successor in the "Rambling Reporter" column. It would be hard to name another Hollywood columnist who could observe the death of a Pope by quoting Phaedo on the immortality of Socrates' soul or compare a roof-raising Frank Sinatra opening in Las Vegas to the first night of *Ralph Roister Doister* at Eton in 1553. He applauded Peggy Cass for being "the only comedienne we know who sprinkles her cocktail chatter with quotes from *The Waste Land*," and he was known for launching into barroom literary discourses on, say, D. H. Lawrence's influence on Lawrence Durrell.[8]

Beyond the erudition, Connolly was the most skillful broker of gossip in town. The *Hollywood Reporter* had to break industry news a day ahead of the regular papers, and to command this high degree of prescience,

Connolly had perhaps the grandest spy network in America outside of the government, with surrogate eyes and ears in studios, talent agencies, trade guilds, Los Angeles society, psychiatric facilities, Alcoholics Anonymous, Rodeo Drive lingerie departments, and most major U.S. cities—even British Customs. One informer was a nurse, who happened to be on duty the night Robert Mitchum had an emergency operation to remove a carrot from his rectum. Connolly cryptically wrote, "Bob Mitchum underwent minor surgery and went on a protein diet." According to Jack Bradford, Connolly even had moles inside the Communist cells of Southern California.[9]

He was more often than not the first to break the news of Hollywood divorces, studio demotions, and talent agency defections—and he never let his readers forget it. "Now they're ALL taking credit for the exclusive on the coming Joan Cohn–Harry Karl nuptials," he once bragged, "but when you read it here first [forty days ago] the same scribblers sneered."[10]

Some of Connolly's scoops grew into legends, while others altered the course of Hollywood history. He claimed throughout his life that the jaw-dropping scoop on Marilyn Monroe's nude calendar photo session was his, but even the most respectable and authoritative Monroe biographies have attributed the calendar scoop to Aline Mosby of the United Press, in her March 13, 1952, syndicated article. A search of Connolly's columns confirms that nearly a month before the Mosby article, he referred casually to a letter from an optical company executive in Muncie, Indiana, requesting "a copy of that calendar with Marilyn in her birthday suit." Retorted Connolly, "We're not in THAT racket, palsy."[11]

Another chain of events set in motion by Connolly began with his March 1952 disclosure of director Elia Kazan's secret testimony before the House Un-American Activities Committee (HUAC) and refusal to identify other former Communists. The immediate consequences to Kazan were the loss of an expected Best Picture Oscar for *A Streetcar Named Desire* and the collapse of a pending deal with Warner Bros. to produce and distribute *Baby Doll*. This overnight reversal of fortune led to Kazan's change of heart and naming of names before HUAC. Half a century later, the long-term consequences of Connolly's item were still painfully evident in the uproar over whether Kazan deserved an honorary Oscar for lifetime achievement. Kazan did get his special Oscar at the 1999 Academy Awards ceremonies, but a large portion of the audience refused to applaud or stand for him.[12]

Born in Chicago in 1913, Mike Connolly was the second of five children of impoverished Irish immigrants. Even in his earliest years he was mad for movies and musical theater. He loved to write as well, distinguishing himself as a student reporter in Catholic high school. At the University of Illinois he became city editor of the *Daily Illini*, spearheading a drive to rid the city of Champaign of its brothels. His college column exuded the same moral outrage that would later bedevil suspected Communists in the movie industry.

Relocating to Hollywood from Chicago in 1946, he joined *Daily Variety* for five years before becoming the star scribe of the *Hollywood Reporter*. Very early on, people learned to exercise caution in what they said within earshot of him. One colleague still marvels at Connolly's ability to converse intently face-to-face with someone while still picking up on all the other conversations in the room. Some felt that Connolly in person was like Dr. Jekyll while Connolly in print was Mr. Hyde. "He would be so sweet," said another colleague, "that people would think, 'How could he be as bad as he is?'" A close friend remembers his voice as "wispy — it wasn't a nelly voice; it was more sweet than anything and Mike used it to charm people. It was a leprechaun voice."

"Mike's face was the map of Ireland — the blue eyes, the black hair of the northern Irish," remembered Mary-jane Ryan, a college friend. Perhaps because Connolly concentrated so intensely on his work and intellectual pastimes, he had little time to fuss about his appearance, and his peers remembered him that way. To Jim Henaghan, a journalist colleague, Connolly's trademark look was his baggy pants. Carl Pelleck of the *New York Post* shied away from him on a press junket to Alaska because "he looked dirty to me. The memory to me is like Nixon's beard. He didn't care about himself." A longtime friend said, "Mike had no identity with clothes. Not until Beverly Hills tailors gave him suits to advertise themselves did he ever dress decently. He would take his office paperwork home in a cardboard box. He owned no briefcase. Mike could've lived happily in a hovel — as long as he was writing, he didn't care about anything else."[13]

In the summer of 1960, Connolly appeared on the talk show *Open End* with five other gossip columnists. He asserted that a movie star is a "ticket seller," someone who could "bring the people in." Denying that he possessed any star-making powers, he insisted that "the public has to make the stars." The panel was asked if recent upheavals in the old studio system had affected press agents' and stars' solicitations of journalistic favors. If anything, Connolly replied, the solicitations had only become more intense. "I'm very glad," he added. "I'm suspicious of people who don't want publicity. They *need* it."[14]

The guiding principle in Connolly's work was precisely that: Publicity was Hollywood's *summum bonum* and justified anything that could be said about someone. To producer Jerry Wald's barrage of complaints about

Connolly's numerous items about him, an exasperated Connolly finally replied that if Wald would review the record he would realize that he could only gain from being mentioned so often. Rita Hayworth scolded the press for writing about her divorce from Aly Khan, insisting it was for discussion in courtrooms only. "Hooey," Connolly blustered. "[Hayworth] thought nothing of spilling everything she knew about herself when she was on her way up and needed it." In the same vein, he maintained, "If the Duchess of Windsor doesn't relish being 'made unhappy by rumors,' she shouldn't give cause."[15]

Denying that he lacked the power to make stars, however, was part and parcel of Connolly's inclination to dissemble, for even if he could not make stars, he certainly believed he could. Many times he upbraided Hollywood for being absent from funerals of publicists who had "made many of them the big names they are," or gloated that a show had turned into a hit because even if the critics did not like it, the columnists did. A has-been actress was no longer getting movie offers, he reported, "unless this item starts something." In liner notes for *Trini Lopez at PJ's*, he wrote that many of the "exhibitionistic" characters at the live recording session were there "not to hear but to be seen ... by columnists such as myself."[16]

Power was the Holy Grail of Connolly's life, and the "Rambling Reporter" was the bully pulpit through which he exercised it. Possession of the keys to the granting or withholding of important favors was Connolly's panacea for the snubs and exclusions he had suffered in his early years. Romps with neighborhood boys in the rough-and-tumble world of South Side Chicago are nowhere to be found in his recounting of childhood memories. What he did mention amounts to a textbook example of a gay boy who found all his role models in the movies rather than on the baseball diamond or in the streets.

Gossip was the means through which Connolly would demonstrate that his importance was on par with or greater than that of other men. The phenomenon of releasing aggression through verbal rather than physical means is a traditional hallmark of gay male life; it was distilled beautifully as "straight men punch, gay men quip" by Daniel Harris in *The Rise and Fall of Gay Culture*. Seen in this light, gossip is no sissified pastime but the province of gladiators, genuinely a manly art.

Chapter 1

Fool for Fellas

"During a story confab at MGM on what to do about
the homosexual theme of *Tea and Sympathy*
somebody suggested, 'Why not make it all a dream?'
Followed by dead silence."
> — *Mike Connolly, Hollywood Reporter,*
> *Sept. 30, 1954*

If there had not been a Mike Connolly, someone would have had to invent him. Although journalism is not a queer profession (as wardrobe and set design came to be), it was essential that a niche in the Hollywood press be reserved for a reporter who was first-rate, homosexual, and male, a niche comparable to George Cukor's among directors. There were things that only a gay male reporter could achieve. The special fawning tone crucial to the promotion of new male talent was second nature to a writer with gay sensibility. The same sensibility was a natural advantage in the development of a top-notch gossip column. Connolly filled the niche perfectly.[1]

Among Hollywood *cognoscenti*, it was understood that the content and tone of the "Rambling Reporter" were at their most lavender early in the week, after Connolly had spent the weekend harvesting brittle, effete one-liners at various gay gatherings. He had a regular circle of gay male friends who in a social setting could be counted on to sharpen the claws, critique couture and coiffure, and engage in one-upmanship over who could quip most outrageously. Because Connolly worked on Sundays, he could not attend the intimate brunches of George Cukor or Cole Porter,

9

but his chums later passed along to him all the most glorious sound bites. The few that were printable would then pop up in the column, unattributed. "If it's Tuesday, it must be gay," was how one old-timer described Hollywood's tacit understanding of Connolly's modus operandi.

Whether the "Rambling Reporter" under Connolly had a gay agenda is a fair question; although the answer is yes, the agenda was anything but radical. It was not to flout the rules but to obey them — to demonstrate that Hollywood's homosexuals were meeting society's requirements. Thus homosexuals were protected instead of flaunted, and this protection was subsumed into the "Rambling Reporter"'s *raison d'être*: defending Dear Old Hollywood.

Obeying the rules was the key to Connolly's getting away with transmitting the gay pulse of Hollywood. The cardinal rule: Writing about who did what at which gay party was taboo. Only anonymous quips from Cukor-Porter–type parties, most often appearing on Mondays and Tuesdays, could hint at what had been going on, and those who had ears to hear monitored the column appropriately to infer who had been where. For years, Connolly was a regular at the Saturday afternoon pool parties hosted by the screamingly gay talent agent Henry Willson. The rules forbade even a suggestion that the parties occurred, let alone who was there. What Connolly *could* do was to tweak Willson in print over Willson's famous rechristenings of his male clients with dashing, Waspy monikers, from Rock Hudson and Tab Hunter to Yale Summers and Race Gentry, to wit: "Hey, Henry Willson, how about these: Plug Ugly, Zoe Watt, Scrap Pyle, Lotsa Luk, and that Oriental star, Su Mi?" One Monday morning Connolly reported a conversation with Willson, obviously conducted at poolside, about actors who had adopted the ultra-macho surnames of Manly and Heman. Willson had replied, "They're all reaching. The name has to fit the person and if it doesn't it has no meaning."[2]

Rule Number Two: If homosexuals were guests at straight parties, or better yet, if a homosexual happened to host a predominantly straight gathering, it was open season for the "Rambling Reporter." Gore Vidal's thirtieth birthday party at the Chateau Marmont was mixed, so Connolly could mention gay writer Christopher Isherwood provided that his name was flanked by those of women guests. Henry Willson's one-year anniversary gala for Rock and Phyllis Hudson, attended by everyone from Buddy Adler to Al Zugsmith, was fair game for details that were previously off-limits. "One of the female guests," Connolly reported, "wandered from Willson's circus-tented garden into his bedroom and gushed, 'Henry, darling, a BLACK telephone — how chic!'" Many of Willson's renamed clients were there, including Rad Fulton, who brought the British actress Diana

Dors. For the first and only time, Connolly allowed that Willson even *had* a pool. It was roped off, he said, "so nobody pushed Diana in, although several would have liked to."[3]

Coverage of straight events was where Connolly's conveyance of gay information became most explicit, no matter that he was documenting the efforts made to *avoid* the appearance of homosexuality. Clannishness among gay men or women was unpalatable to Hollywood society, so it was important for Connolly always to pair a gay name with an opposite-sex escort, even if Hollywood was perfectly aware the coupling was meaningless. Such feeble intimations of romantic attachment could be unintentionally comical, especially if the same beard went out in succession with each half of the same gay couple. Covering the Academy Awards, Connolly noted that British actress Sarah Churchill attended on the arm of publicist Rupert Allan. Some time later he named Churchill as the squeeze of Allan's partner, Fox public relations director Frank McCarthy, while Allan was at the same party with another actress. Then there was the case of Westinghouse spokeswoman and former actress Betty Furness, who seemed to be Hollywood's most beloved and widely circulating fag hag. She had gone out with so many gay men that to be listed as her date was akin to being outed. Even Connolly dated Furness, most notably at the 1956 Democratic Convention in Chicago, calling her "the well-dressed, charming young lady on our arm." (Furness was forty.)[4]

In Hollywood, enormous significance was placed on the proximity of names in a gossip column. Spencer Tracy once kicked Hedda Hopper in the derrière for being so indiscreet as to put his and Katharine Hepburn's names in the same sentence. Edith Gwynn, the original "Rambling Reporter," would signal trouble in a relationship by placing a comma rather than the conjunction "and" between couples' names. When it came to gay partners' names, the only scribe in the Hollywood press who regularly used them in the same sentence was Connolly. For discretion's sake, he usually bifurcated the couple and inserted two or three other guests' names between the halves, but those in the know got the message.[5]

Among the Hollywood gay couples whose names Connolly placed within spitting distance of each other were producer Harriet Parsons and dancer Evelyn Farney, Jacque Mapes and producer Ross Hunter, Tom Hatcher and screenwriter Arthur Laurents, and Frank McCarthy and Rupert Allan. In one item, director Mitch Leisen and singer Billy Daniels were actually adjacent to each other, but as a three-way "date" with Hedda Hopper. Billy Haines and Jimmy Shields got into the same sentence at least four times; since Shields had never been a film industry name, the mere mention of him was meant to convey gay information to insiders, especially when Connolly scooped Shields's secret facelift. The same held true when Connolly applauded writer David Hanna's genial cocktail party "at Ivy Wilson's place"; Wilson had been president of the Hollywood Women's Press Club, but her son Dougie was Hanna's longtime partner, a connection Connolly intended hip readers to understand. On the other hand, if a gay couple was not affiliated with Hollywood, Connolly could relax his rules, as he did with the famous writer Lucius Beebe and his partner Charles Clegg, publishers of the Virginia City, Nevada, *Territorial Enterprise*. When Beebe and Clegg came to town in their ornate private railroad car, the Gold Coast, Connolly wrote about their joint ownership of it and the cocktail party they hosted in it, which he attended, with no compunction.[6]

Rule Three was that gay innuendoes and double entendres had to be couched in jargon that only adult audiences would get. Despite its obvious bent toward the highly sophisticated movie industry, the *Hollywood Reporter* conducted its dissemination of news as a "family newspaper," and Connolly did not breach prevailing tastes. (James Bond's unforgettable girl Pussy Galore became "Kitty" Galore in the column, and "Gosh" was always substituted for "God.") That Connolly could purvey gay information at all was thanks to the wide latitude his boss and publisher, William R. Wilkerson, allowed in what he wrote; to set off alarm bells among Hollywood's parental set would have been foolhardy. After all, Connolly's predecessor had specifically stated that the "Rambling Reporter" was not a clearinghouse for "lavender" information.[7]

Another clue to parsing the "Rambling Reporter" lay in how Connolly distinguished phenomena that would appeal primarily to a straight audience. His code word for heterosexual was "redblooded," which he often used in discussing the presumptive effects of the latest sexpot discovery on male moviegoers. "Every redblooded American reporter and photographer in town," he averred, "was out at MGM yesterday to catch Joan Collins in her *Opposite Sex* bathtub scene." A brief glimpse of Anita Ekberg in bed in *War and Peace* would, he promised readers, "drive all redblooded males out of their redblooded minds!"[8]

To describe phenomena of special interest to gay men, Connolly had to identify the admirer as female rather than male, as in "Anita Ekberg loves guys with hairy chests." Although it could be argued that such items were completely innocent, devoid of hidden meaning, it was a fact that the heterosexual male Hollywood columnists neither printed such observations nor bothered to distinguish items of interest to straight males, red or blueblooded.[9]

Once in a great while, Connolly threw caution to the wind and let loose with a real humdinger (but only after he left *Daily Variety* and was working in the comfort and security of Wilkerson's shop)— such as "[Screenwriter] Jay Dratler eyed a member of the Jewish loose-wrist set on Fairfax and leered, 'Gefulte swish!'" When Connolly asked Walter Winchell why he wore no makeup on television, Winchell said makeup made him look like "an old Shubert nance." Perhaps the most eyebrow-raising item he ever printed in this vein was, "Love the names on some of the camps' houses on [New York's] Fire Island: Sinerama, Boys Town, The Male Box, The Tulle Box, We Three, Drag-Net, etc."[10]

Before one delves into Connolly's wellsprings of intrigue and scuttlebutt, a fourth rule must be given its due: Journalism is not a queer profession and neither may your partner work in a queer profession. Connolly's partner, Joseph Russell Zappia, had owned and operated a beauty salon in Westwood during his first eight years in Hollywood. Because of Connolly's increasing prominence and fame, the couple agreed the stereotypes inherent in a salon could injure the reputations of both Connolly and the *Hollywood Reporter*, so Zappia closed it.

Connolly needed a legman desperately, and his solution was to hire Zappia. Borrowing a page from Henry Willson's manual, Connolly gave his partner a new name. "We're expanding," the column trumpeted on August 26, 1954. "Joe Russell joins this column's staff as legman starting Monday [August 30]." Zappia explained, "When I started working for Mike, I had to give my name to receptionists or secretaries, so I spelled Zappia, which wasn't easy for them. Mike said I should simplify matters and use 'Joe Russell'— which also made it easier for me."[11]

Throughout the previous year, Connolly had been trying to figure out what to do with Zappia. Joe Russell (or even "Joey" Russell), a name unfamiliar to Hollywood, appeared from out of nowhere twice in the column in 1953, as the "date" of actress Hope Emerson or singer Betty Reilly (both lesbians). But for his next three mentions he was reinstated inexplicably as "Joe Zappia," escort to Reilly and actresses Jane Withers and Mary McCarty. In each instance, he had actually been gathering nightlife news for Connolly. Subsequent to the "We're expanding" announcement, of course, he would always be Joe Russell. This new nom-de-gossip appeared in the column whenever Zappia went on location with a film company, as with his week-long tour of duty in Kauai to cover the shooting of *South Pacific*, or when he covered the post-premiere party for *Around the World in Eighty Days* at Madison Square Garden. Connolly entitled Zappia's dispatch from New York "Legman Joe Russell's Notes-at-Large from the Wicked Metropolis." At its end, he added this postscript: "That's enough out of you, Russell! Make tracks!"[12]

The announcement of Zappia's ascendancy was, on one level, Connolly's coming-out manifesto. The rest of Hollywood already knew or would quickly come to understand the private relationship behind this new professional bond. Ezra Goodman, *Time* magazine's Hollywood correspondent in those days, was irked by the arrangement, couching his disapproval in language that was intended to be transparent. Zappia, Goodman wrote, was a "former hairdresser" and "close friend and collaborator of Mike Connolly," which amounted to "no experience whatsoever in writing, reporting, or show business." Goodman also complained that, owing to Connolly's preeminent status in the press, "it automatically followed that [his] assistant also ranked high in the journalistic hierarchy."[13]

Connolly and Zappia were a genuine love match. "Mike was in love with Joe; he needed him," said a friend. "Joe took care of everything. As Mike became more successful, Joe got better houses for them. He would smooth over disturbances Mike stirred up. Once when Mike was supposed to go to Las Vegas to cover Marlene Dietrich, Joe was sick with the flu. Mike got a friend to stay with Joe while he was away. He wouldn't have left Joe otherwise."

However, the conflicts that crop up normally in any couple were exacerbated because the two men worked together. "Joe would sometimes get mad over his work for Mike," said a friend. "He might be at a studio and Mike wouldn't have briefed him properly on what to cover. Or he'd have to take the heat for things Mike had written. And he was always on Mike's case for getting drunk. Mike would just walk away and shut himself up in his room." Another source of occasional tension was absence from each other. "They never went anywhere together, at least after Mike became prominent, unless it was a party at their home. Mike just couldn't as a public figure," said the friend. "They did travel together, but if they were both at the same event, like a wedding, they always had female escorts. Oh, in those days, you always had to have a date."

One reason Connolly possessed so much inside information is that he was the unofficial mouthpiece of Gay Hollywood. It was the community's dirty little secret: the best column in the industry was steered by one of their own, and they shoveled the news to him. His best friends and best sources tended to be the same people. The closest was publicist Stanley Musgrove, whose clients included Mae West, Susan Hayward, Richard Egan, and other luminaries. Agent Bob Raison and costume designer Orry-Kelly were also part of Connolly's inner circle. All three men loved to be "on" and were well known for acid-tongued barbs. Musgrove and Raison were exceedingly close to Cole Porter — the composer had given Raison money to set up his talent agency — and all of the news from Porter's Sunday gatherings was filtered through them.[14]

Other close friends to Connolly were cabaret comedian Bill McArthur, who coached Connolly in elocution for television appearances and was possibly the crowd's most vicious gossip; singer Mike Rayhill and his boyfriend, television director Ralph Levy, who lived together at the Chateau Marmont; Hollywood Bowl artistic director Wynn Rocamora; dancer Tito Renaldo; photographer Wally Seawell; and Lee Graham, a society columnist and neighbor to Connolly on Marlay Drive, married briefly to the dancer Evelyn Farney. Graham, who loved parties (to which he frequently escorted the likes of Gloria Swanson), was one of Connolly's top news sources. Wally Seawell was less successful as a tipster. "Mike said, 'Seawell, you go to all these parties; why don't you bird-dog for me?' So the next day I went to a party and Mike asked what I saw. A blonde actress with big breasts had been there and I was telling Mike about her, but I couldn't remember her name! So Mike said, 'You're no damned good as a bird dog!'"[15]

Many Hollywood women enjoyed periods of close friendship with Connolly over the years. Rosemary Clooney and he were mutual admirers; they went on vacation to Lake Tahoe and Virginia City together. Actress Terry Moore was also a frequent companion and accompanied him when he spoke to a University of Illinois Alumni luncheon in Los Angeles. Moore was just outrageous and ingenuous enough to consider Connolly fun, and as the secret mistress of Howard Hughes, she needed an escort. Both Clooney and Moore were getting almost daily mentions in the "Rambling Reporter" during these years. As the fifties progressed, Connolly became very friendly with actresses Joan Blondell and Barbara Nichols. He liked Nichols, said a friend, because she was "bawdy and boozy." The great Carol Channing was one of his favorites for nearly two decades; he went sailing with her on Long Island Sound during one of her rare days off from *Hello, Dolly!* on Broadway.[16]

Although Connolly had no shortage of female companionship, no one interviewed for this book remembers his ever being interested in a woman beyond the platonic. One Hollywood woman who liked sex with gay men said she racked up the belt notches with many of Connolly's gay male friends over the years, but not Connolly. "The possibility never occurred," she said. "Not even close." Walter Winchell's column once carried the startling revelation that Hollywood press agent Virginia Wicks and Connolly had "shattered diplomatic relations," but none of Connolly's surviving friends ever heard of Wicks.[17]

A number of lesbians rounded out Connolly's inner circle. Singer-

Although Connolly's homosexuality was widely known in Hollywood, like all gay men in the industry he was expected to appear at public functions with an opposite-sex date. Here he escorts actress Barbara Nichols, his most frequent "date" in the late 1950s, to Errol Flynn's September 15, 1959, party at Frascati's. (Photofest)

comedienne Mary McCarty, whom Connolly and Zappia met while she was on Broadway in Irving Berlin's *Miss Liberty*, was highly esteemed. Others were Carole Mathews, who starred in the western television series *Californian*; ex–Ziegfeld Girl Peggy Fears and her companion, Teddy ("The Sexy Weather-Girl") Thurmond; guitar-playing songstress Betty ("the Irish Señorita") Reilly; talent agent Helen Ainsworth; and actress Hope Emerson. "Hope took her dog everywhere," said Dave Peck, a friend, "and once at Mike's, the dog ate a decorative parachute off a cake Joe had ordered."[18]

One of Connolly's most significant friendships began at his forty-first birthday party on July 10, 1954. Stanley Musgrove and Bob Raison persuaded two young women who worked at Technicolor, Bunny Seidman and Vermelle McCarter, to be their dates. "Mike and I latched onto each other immediately," said Seidman. "I wore my ruffled Michael Novarese gown. Everybody was stinking drunk. I took over and did my 'act,' reading all Mike's birthday cards in different voices. Joe was the host. Lee Graham was there, and I hit it off with him; Jane Withers was there, and Louella Parsons, you know, was incontinent so they sat her on a little stool by the fireplace. I'd taken a Dexamyl before I went, and I gave Mike one. He took them like crazy after that. He and Joe and Vermelle and I became tight. I went under duress, but was glad I did."[19]

The following day, Zappia invited Seidman and McCarter to brunch and dinner, and two days after that, Zappia asked Seidman to go shopping with him. Before long Seidman was renting the apartment over Connolly's garage. "We became like family," Seidman remembered. "I was with them every night: Mike, Joe, their roommate Don LaMarr, myself, Stanley [Musgrove], Bob [Raison], sometimes Vermelle, and Marilyn Morgan, who later married the choreographer Gene Nelson." Sometimes the gang would have pot luck dinners at Lee Graham's house, just down the street.

Invitations to Connolly's parties were coveted; his friend Irv Kupcinet of the *Chicago Sun-Times* dubbed him "the Elsa Maxwell of the movie colony." There was always a healthy mixture of male and female, straight and gay; he did not throw gay parties, per se. In his column he made no bones about who his favorite persons in Hollywood were, and they were usually on hand at his soirees: Jayne Mansfield, Oscar Levant, society columnist Cobina Wright, singer Ella Logan, actress Genevieve Aumont, and show business couples Marge and Gower Champion, Richard and Pat Egan, Jean Wallace and Cornel Wilde, and George Burns and Gracie Allen. He also relished the company of those he considered Hollywood's "genuine wits," including Joan Fontaine and Collier Young, Muff and Charles Brackett, and screenwriter Nunnally Johnson.[20]

The life of the party in Connolly's crowd was Roger Davis, well-

Connolly was an admired party-giver in Hollywood. His most widely reported party was held at his home on January 30, 1954, in honor of Tallulah Bankhead's 52nd birthday. Here, Connolly and Bankhead pose in front of Connolly's pride and joy, his personal library. (Photofest)

known as Fanny Brice's best friend and confidante (and portrayed by Roddy McDowall in *Funny Lady*). Many considered Davis the funniest man alive. He once essayed singing *Happy Birthday* to Connolly in six different languages, a comic *tour de force*. According to Dave Peck, spontaneity was Davis's hallmark. "The first time I met Roger, he put a lampshade over his head, pretending to be a woman whose husband was trying to kill her, right out of Hitchcock's *Shadow of a Doubt*. Roger was very well read, and would go off on world events—'I had lunch with the Queen today,' or similar flights of fancy." Davis once phoned Bunny Seidman at Connolly's, claiming to represent a woman in whose flower bed Seidman had allegedly parked her car. He was so convincing that Seidman actually feared she was about to be sued. According to Jack Bradford, "Roger was great at dialogues between himself and 'Mrs. Murgatroyd,' a thinly veiled Beatrice Lillie. He told one story about her at the Garden of Allah, how she fell into the fountain and there were walruses in there."[21]

At Connolly's New Year's Eve bash that saw 1956 to its wet and raucous close, an incident of the only-in-Hollywood variety occurred. Bunny Seidman wore a head-turning red gown designed by her friend Billy Travilla for the *Loretta Young Show*. "Travilla told me to wear it," Seidman says. "He said they didn't need it any more for the rushes." Although Travilla was not at the party, a competitor, Orry-Kelly, was. According to Seidman, Kelly hated Travilla and constantly accused him of stealing Kelly's designs. "Orry would get pissy-assed drunk," she said. "He came over to me and said, 'That's the most gorgeous gown I've ever seen. Did Michael [Novarese] do it?' When I told him Travilla had done it, he spilled his drink all over me. It was a disaster. I called Travilla the next morning to tell him what had happened, and as luck would have it, he said they *did* need the red gown for the rushes. He told me to take it to a specific dry cleaners, but they wouldn't touch it. Finally, Travilla had to send down dressmakers to redo it by ten a.m. Of course, I didn't tell him that I'd also slept in it!"[22]

The apex of Connolly's reign as a party host came with his January 30, 1954, celebration of Tallulah Bankhead's fifty-second birthday. Held at his home at 1512 Marlay Drive, this grand occasion grew out of a cryptic "Aside to Tallulah" he had floated in his column: "Come on out and we'll personally show you eight palm trees that are EACH over thirty years old." *Tout Hollywood*—Mary Pickford, Susan Hayward, Sheree North, Terry Moore, Guy Madison, Sol Siegel, Billy Haines, Carol Channing, Jane Withers with an Iranian prince in tow—seemed to be present. A minor starlet had desperately phoned a succession of single men until she found one with an invitation.

Bankhead held court in a low-cut red dress and a short haircut that was terribly fashionable just then. Jimmy Durante drew near to her for a kiss and exclaimed, "Isn't she dreamy?" The evening's most memorable entrance must have been made by Zsa Zsa Gabor, since every reporter in attendance wrote about it. Dressed to the nines in a white satin gown embroidered in brilliants, with matching coat, Gabor swept in only to collide head-on with a vintage Bankhead put-down. "Dahhhling," Bankhead intoned, "You look so beautiful I thought you were [your sister] Eva." Gabor's stay at the party was understandably brief.

The badinage brimmed with suggestions of questionable parentage, as Marion Davies announced to the crowd that Bankhead was her child by Calvin Coolidge, while Hedda Hopper insisted to Bankhead that Guy Madison was Hopper's son. Not to be upstaged, Bankhead demanded that she and Hopper sing a duet of *Give My Regards to Broadway*. When the cacophony was over, Bankhead guffawed, "Never again will I take any lip from you about how bad my singing is. You're worse."

The consensus was that Connolly's Bankhead bacchanalia resembled the "hilarious" parties thrown in the Roaring Twenties. During a discussion of the do's and don'ts of facelifts, Davies exclaimed to the guest of honor, "Why, Darling, you're an amateur! This kisser of mine's been lifted from head to toe!" Female impersonator Arthur Blake was on hand to burlesque Bankhead, but she stopped him cold. "No one," she huffed, "can give an imitation of me when I'm in the room to give one of myself!" She then proceeded to imitate Blake-imitating-Bankhead. As the festivities dwindled down, Bankhead was heard to mutter, "Thank God Mary Pickford's gone. Now we don't have to curtsy!" After the confetti and party hats were swept away, Connolly deadpanned in a letter to his brother that the Bankhead gala had required much time and work, but it turned out nicely. He believed all had enjoyed themselves, himself included.[23]

Although Connolly was known in mixed company as a hospitable host of lavish, lively parties, another side of him relished the opportunity to let down his guard in all-gay social situations. Lawrence J. Quirk, longtime publisher of movie fan magazines, explained that discretion prevented gay men of prominence from hosting all-gay events. "Famous men only went to gay parties at others' houses," Quirk said. "They were surrounded by nobodies—makeup artists and others—who allowed their houses to be used. Young guys who needed money, or a bit part, or a letter, would show up. But Mike wouldn't have wanted predatory young men coming around his house."[24]

Beginning in 1948, Quirk, who lived in Boston, would spend summers in Hollywood to work on a biography of his uncle, Jimmy Quirk, the founder of *Photoplay* magazine. He met Connolly in 1948, and the following summer, at a gay cocktail cotillion, Connolly remembered him. "He was infatuated with me," Quirk said. "Typically, he would grab my crotch and ask, 'Hey, what's going on down there?' He was coming on heavily, but he wasn't my type. I was very attractive then and I was with a [Boston] Hearst paper. I had a policy of manipulating people into getting rid of me, instead of my having to get rid of them. I told Mike I had venereal disease. Every time he'd see me after that, he'd ask, 'Did you get that taken care of?' Then I went to bed with someone else and he found out about it. But nothing ever happened between us. He was too close to people I knew, and I didn't want gossip. Once he followed me into a men's room at the Beverly Wilshire where he checked me out from an adjoining urinal. He said, 'The mighty oak from a little acorn grows, and if that's the acorn, the oak must be great!'"[25]

Quirk's spurning of Connolly's advances did not preclude a friendship of sorts; Connolly did many favors for him over the years. "He would speak to stars to get them to let me interview them; he would get me around the press agent," said Quirk. "For example, Mike facilitated my interview with Tom Tryon. Mike also took me to key parties. He'd say, 'There are people you should meet at this party.' He did it to pass me on; he was pimping with me. He threw me to the wolves!"[26]

Quirk, who knew the game from his own experience as a journalist, said career advancement was the subtext at these Hollywood parties, and sex was the currency. "An actor would put his dick in the mouth of whoever could do the most for him. Some of Henry Willson's clients catered to Roger Elwood, a fan magazine editor," Quirk explained. "But I didn't want to be gossiped about, so I was careful. Agents deliberately sent gay actors to me and other gay journalists, but I would meet them at bars. Bob Raison took me around to his clients' homes in the fifties and sixties to get publicity for them."[27]

Although Connolly attended gay parties as a recreational pursuit, most gay men considered him a business contact rather than a friend. "Mike knew everybody, but I don't think anyone who knew him well liked him," Quirk recalled. "He was a piece on the Hollywood chessboard, and you *had* to deal with him. He was always pawing everybody; he was curiosity-obsessed. The smart boys would give in to him and then all concerned got over it. I was always hearing guys at parties joking about their Mike Connolly experiences."[28]

Connolly's views on monogamy can be inferred from his actions. He had great respect for the institution of marriage, and his delight in it was reflected in the number of wedding receptions he hosted over the years for couples including Richard Egan and Pat Hardy, choreographer Gene Nelson and Marilyn Morgan, and *Chicago Sun-Times* executive Russ Stewart and Millie Norris. He devoted countless column inches to promoting and glorifying marital bonds. Marilyn Monroe once stated that if she married again, it would be for her own happiness. "We've got news for Marilyn," he retorted. "That isn't why the Lord instituted the sacrament of matrimony." When Gracie Allen died, Connolly eulogized that George Burns had been one of the luckiest men in the world: "George had thirty-seven blissful years with that enchanting woman. How we envy him." He abhorred divorce and would lecture squabbling couples in print. "Why don't Liz and Dan Dailey drop the kid act and admit there's no one else for either of them?" he scolded. Another couple, to his delight, "got sensible, dropped the divorce suit." His views on male-female relations were traditional and conservative: "Joe Castro and Doris Duke, Baron von Cramm and Barbara Hutton, and whatever happened to the old-fashioned notion that the boy should be older than the girl?"[29]

But there was an unspoken belief in Connolly's words and actions that a committed relationship should both assume and forgive extracurricular flings. "Mike was compulsively promiscuous; he wanted to know what every man had in his pants," said Larry Quirk. "He worshipped masculinity and went after the ones whose sexuality you weren't sure of. Uniforms were a turn-on to him." According to Quirk, Connolly would put the make on the most prominent young actors, including Robert Francis, Guy Madison, Anthony Perkins, Nick Adams, and James Dean. Quirk said there was rampant gossip at gay parties regarding not only Connolly's escapades with these actors but also a noteworthy pornography collection he would display to those he favored.[30]

Two men on the gay party circuit who knew Connolly well were Jerry Asher, a fan magazine writer and former MGM publicist, and the director Edmund Goulding. "Jerry and Eddie were the centers of their own gay circles," said Quirk. "Their circles were less uppity than George Cukor's. Mike was often at their parties. Jerry had the biggest mouth in town; he gossiped like crazy. Eddie was quite the gossip himself. Most of my gossip on Mike came from those two. Mike and Jerry socialized, but warily. There was tension between them; Jerry said Mike was a hypocrite who sacrificed everything to please the Establishment while sneaking around on the side. Once Mike wanted to get rid of a young hanger-on, so he tied a pink ribbon around the kid and sent him over to Jerry's, whose birthday party was in progress. Jerry pushed the young guy away from his door, saying, 'I don't need your type around here.' Then Jerry phoned Mike and said, 'I don't need your condescension!' Mike replied, 'You're hardly God's gift to men, Jerry; you're going to have to pay for it!'"[31]

A heterosexual perspective on Connolly's social milieu comes from Ed Hutshing, a fellow trade paper reporter. Circa 1950, Hutshing, his wife-to-be, and another couple were in a restaurant when Dick O'Connor, a *Daily Variety* reporter, greeted them and said he was on his way to a party at the home of Gypsy Gould, the switchboard girl at *Daily Variety*. Back at home, Hutshing and his party were listening to records, "when suddenly there was a racket of a dozen people knocking at my door — Dick O'Connor, Gypsy Gould, Mike Connolly, and others — taking over, half stiff, half of them gay. It was only our second date and I was horrified. She was from Beverly Hills and very refined."

A telephone call came in for the man of the other couple, who had a grave face when he hung up. "That was Eddie Dmytryk," he said, "and I invited him over." Dmytryk, of course, was one of the Hollywood Ten (see Chapter 8) and a pariah. "Everyone is roaring drunk, and the gays are groping each other," Hutshing continued. "Connolly [who was then *Daily Variety's* gossip columnist] was there and I called him into the bedroom — he probably thought it was an assignation because he came in all smiles and dimples — and I said, 'Don't you dare write about Dmytryk being here or I'll call [*Daily Variety* editor] Arthur Ungar and tell him *you* invited Dmytryk!' So Dmytryk arrived and was a perfect gentleman. Mike never wrote about it. Afterward, my wife-to-be gushed about how it was her 'first real Hollywood party'!"[32]

Ironically, the only young man Connolly ever had the hots for over an extended period, an aspiring actor named James DeCloss, was straight. "Mike's sexual preference was his own business and didn't get in the way of our friendship," DeCloss explained. "I respected that and it was fine." They did not meet at a party; DeCloss was visiting Hollywood from his native Salinas, California, and he stopped by the *Hollywood Reporter* to bring lunch to his sister, who worked the switchboard there. "Mike walked by, we shook hands, and he asked if I wanted to have coffee at his desk. I asked him if he could suggest an acting coach; he said Estelle Harman was the best." Two weeks after enrolling with Harman, DeCloss got a job in the television comedy series *December Bride*.

Connolly started saturating the column with shamelessly promotional bullets addressed to key producers and directors. "Dear Mervyn LeRoy: Take time out from [casting] *No Time for Sergeants* today to see Jim DeCloss — and SAY YES" or "Hey, Sam Wiesenthal, look at Jim DeCloss [for *The Jack Dempsey Story*]. The twenty-year-old actor looks like Jack Dempsey at twenty." (DeCloss was actually twenty-three.) Connolly's efforts finally paid off when he persuaded director Joshua Logan to put DeCloss into *South Pacific*. He even took the opportunity to Henry Willsonize the young actor, telling his readers he had changed the young man's name to Jim Stockton. "But that only lasted about a week," DeCloss clarified.[33]

Connolly would give DeCloss and his pal Brook Vincent, an Ohio State diver, stacks of party invitations he had received and tell them to pick out the ones they wanted and go. "So the first time this happened," DeCloss said, "I sat next to Cary Grant at dinner!" DeCloss and Vincent were always properly dressed and knew how to conduct themselves at high-class events. "Mike got calls all the time complimenting us," DeCloss reported. "He'd say, 'Keep going to those parties; they think you work for me!' If we saw things, we'd tell him about them. I remember talking with Lee Remick a lot."

Thus the threat DeCloss posed to Joseph Zappia was minimal, although Zappia would tell friends that Connolly was in love with this protegé. DeCloss did not know Zappia well, but said he "was the health freak of all time, watercress sandwiches, working out, and all that." Connolly had issued an open invitation to DeCloss to use their swimming pool. After one sunbathing session, Zappia phoned DeCloss to complain that his suntan oil had discolored Zappia's new deck chairs. "It was a drunken call, late at night," DeCloss reported. "After he got the deck chair problem off his chest, he then accused me of trying to steal his husband."

Bunny Seidman remembered Connolly's bringing DeCloss to visit when she was married and living in Del Mar. "They had first gone to San Diego, and were already drunk," she said. "Then we had drinks. We put Jim in the guest room, but Mike passed out on my white couch and ruined it, for which I gave him hell. In the morning, I gave them coffee and sent them back to L.A." Even after DeCloss got married, Connolly's invitations kept coming. "On a whim, Mike asked if I wanted to go to Irv Kupcinet's annual Harvest Moon Festival in Chicago. He said, 'Ask Angie,' my then-wife, 'if it's okay.' It was great. I was at the Ambassador East for five days, spending lots of time in the Pump Room. I sat next to Robert Mitchum at dinner one night."

Summing up Connolly's devoted patronage, DeCloss said, "Mike was a rough-hewn, compassionate Irish drunk who lived on cigarettes and booze. He was nice and gregarious and self-deprecating. He had the ability to make you feel your opinions were important to him. The fun of who he was showed in the column. He was a bright guy, but a sartorial disaster. He could seem like a crumpled old curmudgeon."[34]

Seidman said Zappia would have been terribly upset if Connolly had ever kept a lover on the side. "Joe was the insecure one in their relationship," she said. "He got so upset and so jealous—we got such a kick out of it." However, when the tables were turned and Zappia met a younger man with whom he maintained an ongoing intimate relationship, Connolly was actually glad. "It keeps Joe out of my hair," he told Seidman. She was never privy to anything that made her suspect Connolly had sustained affairs, even while Zappia would be out of town.

One of the most charismatic characters to arouse Connolly's affections was Dr. Tom Dooley, the young Navy doctor famous in the 1950s for his work with Catholic Vietnamese refugees and the bestseller he based on it, *Deliver Us from Evil*. Dooley, who found it expedient for his fundraising efforts to work the salons of Hollywood, embodied all the qualifications of a Connolly soulmate: Irish heritage, Catholic, gay, promiscuous, and certifiably anti–Communist. He was young and handsome to boot.

Connolly wrote breathlessly of Dooley's tours of Tinseltown, giving him full paragraphs where most stars would kill for half a line. In April 1956, Dooley held a press conference and endeared himself to Connolly with his "energetic, driving, and yet spiritual quality." Recognizing how useful Connolly might be, Dooley persuaded him to solicit the donation of a movie projector and a few "comic or animal films" for his planned mission to Laos. "This 'little magic box' will do more than a whole army to fight the commies!" exhorted Connolly.

Two years later, Dooley held Connolly spellbound at a cocktail party with stories of the rapt reactions of "Laos jungle natives" to Tarzan movies, shown on a film projector donated—thanks to Connolly's earlier tubthumping—by Walt Disney. By now, Dooley had the aura of a rock star; his compliments to Marilyn Monroe on her "beautiful blonde hair" and his showing up at the wrong theater for the premiere of *Gigi* were avidly chronicled in the "Rambling Reporter." Upon Dooley's untimely death, Connolly eulogized him as "dedicated and serious-minded, but he had his fun side, too, and we had many a walloping night-on-the-town ... till the sun rose and the wine-bottle was empty."[35]

Larry Quirk, who had an affair with Dooley during the latter's 1956 Hollywood stay, revealed, "Tom was not attracted to Mike and Mike resented it. Tom said Mike came on to him and Tom felt there would be repercussions. Mike was vicious when rejected—he never forgave Tom. You can tell from the flippant tone of that obituary he wrote."[36]

Hollywood in Connolly's day was part of a much larger, highly conservative community, willing to wield a police force that tolerated no homosexual hanky-panky. To have business on the East Coast could be like candyland after the forced circumspection of Southern California.

Hollywood men, said David Hanna, "would come to New York and go wild, and nobody paid much attention to them." Connolly had regular business in New York, especially in the late 1950s when the annual Newspaper Publishers Convention allowed him to hawk his syndicated column. Although Bunny Seidman escorted him to the 1956 convention, they stayed in separate hotels. She assumed the reason he was at the Waldorf while she stayed in the relatively drab Hotel Albert was so he would be free to carry on unobserved.[37]

Connolly had a number of noteworthy gay friends in Manhattan, including Hanna, who had relocated there from Hollywood; Allen Porter of the Museum of Modern Art; William Hawkins, drama critic of the *New York World Telegram and Sun*; and the Woolworth heir and unmitigated debauché Jimmy Donahue. During the 1956 Publishers Convention, Hawkins invited Connolly and Seidman to his apartment in the Dakota for a bibulous Sunday brunch. Afterward, Connolly had to pack for his return to Los Angeles. "When we got to the Waldorf," says Seidman, "Jimmy Donahue and Christine Jorgensen [the famous transsexual of the 1950s] were waiting for us. Jimmy was out of his gourd. We got in the room and Jimmy ordered drinks, then started dancing with the bellhop who brought them up. As Mike was packing, Jimmy would grab his clothes from Mike's suitcase and throw them out the window. Then he was putting withered flowers into the suitcase. Mike was too drunk to know the difference. Finally they got Mike into a cab. Jimmy wanted us to go someplace, but Hawkins hated him. So Hawkins and I said, meet us at such-and-such a place, and then we didn't go there."

Connolly's nickname for Donahue was Seamus. He had known Donahue at least since 1955, when both were in Honolulu at the same time, and was apparently one of the few who could tolerate Donahue's aberrant sense of fun. On one of Donahue's visits to Hollywood, Connolly threw a party in his honor. "Jimmy was drunk and accused me of stealing his wallet," Seidman relates. "Don LaMarr [Connolly and Zappia's housemate] got really pissed over that. He told Jimmy, 'Maybe you'd better leave.' Jimmy passed out, and they just left him where he was. Don usually never said anything bad about anybody, but he told Mike, 'Never have him in this house again.'"

Whether on the east coast or the west, Connolly's web of connections generated not only a surfeit of delectable gossip for his column but abundant introductions and opportunities that could escalate beyond mere flirtation. If, however, he imagined that as a columnist he was immune to his own brand of innuendo and threat, he would soon learn otherwise.

Chapter 2

Confidential Confidential

> "Press agent of an actor 'profiled' by one of the scandal mags told his client, 'Forget it — nobody believes that stuff.'
> The actor replied, 'But I do!'"
> — *Mike Connolly, Hollywood Reporter, May 15, 1956*

The audacity of the gay news and jokes in the "Rambling Reporter" was toned way down in the mid-fifties, not because of a vice crackdown by the Los Angeles police or retrenchment by *Hollywood Reporter* management but because of a scourge that threatened Mike Connolly personally — and its name was *Confidential*, the preeminent scandal magazine of its time. Its inaugural issue blazed onto newsstands late in 1952, launching its wildly successful exploitation of public hunger for the unvarnished truth about film personalities. In no time at all, *Confidential* had Hollywood running scared from whatever stories it would dare to print next. One by one, major stars and performers were finding their once-private pecadilloes trumpeted from its salacious pages. Compounding the fun, a dozen or so imitator magazines sprang up as well, with names such as *Top Secret, Whisper, Hush-Hush, Exposed*, and *Lowdown*.

Confidential's terrorizing of the film industry would endure for nearly five years, until the Los Angeles County District Attorney bowed to behind-the-scenes pressure from the movie studios and indicted *Confidential* on charges including conspiracy to commit criminal libel and conspiracy to circulate lewd and obscene material. Joining the prosecutorial team was the California State Attorney General's office. The infamous *Confidential* trial lasted for two months, August and September of 1957. After the jury deadlocked and a mistrial was declared, the criminal libel charges were dropped, but *Confidential* paid a five thousand dollar fine on the obscene material count and publisher Robert Harrison signed an agreement not to print stories injurious to stars' reputations in subsequent issues.[1]

One of the unsung secrets in this mid-century scandal magazine saga involved not the stars, who were merely victims of smear journalism, but the authors and sources of the hatchet job stories, many of whom were respected members of the Hollywood press. As the criminal prosecution of *Confidential* dragged on through the hottest months of 1957, Walter Winchell observed, "Many writers for respectable slick mags are suffering from the jitters hoping their names aren't exposed in the Hollywood slime-light. They have been enjoying a comfortable income (under other names) peddling lowdown on celebrities that their editors deleted."[2]

Moonlighting journalists on *Confidential's* payroll had varying levels of involvement. Some were paid retainer fees, not to write but simply to pass along gossip that their own newspapers deemed too hot to handle. Contributing writers, those on the front lines whose submissions were considered first drafts (or even barely sketched outlines), were paid between two hundred fifty and fifteen hundred dollars. These contributors' drafts rarely resembled the versions that got into print, which appeared under bylines that were with few exceptions fictitious. The real writing was done either by outside writers, paid up to five hundred dollars per article on a piecework basis, or by *Confidential's* in-house staff of four men. Some articles required numerous rewrites, until they achieved what publisher Harrison called *Confidential's* "toboggan ride" style and sound.[3]

Mike Connolly's official stance was that he was in no way, shape, or form associated with *Confidential*. "Rumors that this department writes stories for *Confidential* and other publications of its type have gained momentum," he stated solemnly in his column of May 11, 1955. "For the record: We have never written for, nor supplied news tips to, any of the scandal type magazines. We did set up a *Confidential*–Joan Crawford interview to enable Joan to stop a vicious yarn that was to be printed about her and her children. The interview killed the story."[4]

Hollywood correspondent Ezra Goodman, however, begged to differ with Connolly's denial. In *The Fifty-Year Decline and Fall of Hollywood* (1961), Goodman, who in previous pages had already laid substantial groundwork to get across the message that Connolly was queer, now delivered his *coup-de-grace* in hopes that his readers would put two and two together. "Some of [*Confidential's*] tipsters were even among the press," Goodman snickered. "One of the leading 'male' gossipists in Hollywood was a source for *Confidential*— the magazine used an unpublished story about this columnist's amorous activities as a journalistic sword over his head."[5]

Goodman knew whereof he spoke regarding *Confidential*; he himself had written secretly for the gutter gazette, as had his long-time mistress, the United Press's Aline Mosby. Mosby, in fact, had been in the press gallery of the courtroom covering the *Confidential* trial when the prosecution's star witness, former *Confidential* editor Howard Rushmore, fingered her as one of their free-lancers. A defense attorney further opened that kettle of fish by adding that Mosby had written a grand total of twenty-four stories for them. United Press assigned another reporter to cover the trial while Mosby slipped out of town in disgrace.[6]

A troubled professional relationship between Goodman and Connolly can be inferred, not only from Goodman's potshots in his book at Connolly, but from Connolly's writings. In the early 1950s, Goodman's name appeared regularly, and in a positive light, in the "Rambling Reporter," sometimes even in the same sentence as Mosby's. That came to a halt on March 30, 1956, the day Connolly noted Goodman was shadowing producer Mike Todd for a *Time* story; after that date Connolly never mentioned Goodman again except in late 1960, to warn that Goodman's book was about to be published, and in 1965, to pillory him for his negative views on Hollywood. "A few bars, Maestro, please, of *Fiddle-Faddle*," Connolly hissed. "Ezra Goodman dug us all up, after burying us in a screed called *The Fifty-Year Decline and Fall of Hollywood*, and is now making a *comme-ci-comme-ça* living off of us by writing pieces about us for the Sunday *New York Times [Magazine]*."[7]

Neither man ever said publicly what the falling-out was over. But the beginning of Connolly's embargo on Goodman's name occurred during the final and worst two-year stretch of *Confidential's* reign of emotional terror, when reporters caught in its web had to outmaneuver each other to remain "respectable."

Two events during 1955, in particular, were too close for comfort in Connolly's life. These were the publication of *Confidential's* May 1955 issue, with its cover story of actor Rory Calhoun's sordid early years as a car-stealing juvenile delinquent (the issue would actually have been on newsstands in early March 1955); and the November 9, 1955, marriage of Rock Hudson to Phyllis Gates, the secretary of Hudson's agent, Henry Willson.

The story of Universal-International Studio's negotiations with *Confidential*, offering to furnish a story on Rory Calhoun in exchange for cancellation of an exposé of the gay life of Hudson, the studio's top star, has been widely disseminated. Hudson's subsequent marriage has been interpreted as a reaction to a close call and a strategy to rebut career-ruining stories about his homosexual life. If Hudson could read the tea leaves, so could the seemingly untouchable Mike Connolly, who, owing to the "journalistic sword over his head" revealed by Goodman, began to fear *Confidential* would turn the tables and hang out the dirty laundry of a trafficker in dirty laundry.

The resort to marriage to survive in Hollywood had precedent in an earlier era. Hollywood historian William J. Mann has noted the same phenomenon occurred when the puritanical Production Code was forced on the movie industry in 1932 and 1933. Where gay costume designers and set decorators had earlier enjoyed total freedom to live in as unorthodox a manner as they pleased, the studios' anti-pansy purges impelled many of them to get married suddenly. What had made perfect sense in the thirties held equally true in the fifties—and for a brief time, it seemed to Mike Connolly that what had staved off the wolves for Rock Hudson might work equally well for him.[8]

"When Mike proposed marriage," Bunny Seidman recounted, "it was right after Rock Hudson got married. At that time everyone was scared to death about *Confidential*. People were talking too much about Mike. He and I were getting along well—even if we did fight like hell sometimes. After one weekend we decided we should get married. It was Mike's idea. He said his being older than me was complementary. He was going to set me up in an apartment. But he would've stayed with Joe."

What Connolly knew about Hudson can be pieced together from his column. On September 23, 1954, he wrote, "Rock Hudson is being pushed into a romance." Three weeks later he first linked Phyllis Gates with Hudson. On May 6, 1955, came the news that "a big, big male star is in the hands of blackmailers because of a silly escapade." Still later, he wrote that some of Hudson's "closest advisers" were opposed to his marrying Gates. Three times he alleged that Hudson and Gates were already secretly married.[9]

The Hudson-Gates wedding-bells items were simply part of Connolly's job in Hollywood image-making, which he did with flourish, letting readers know Hudson had presented Gates with a diamond and opal necklace, that she was the "apple of Hudson's eye," that they were planning a large family, and the like. Yet the conflicting signals that crept into the column on Hudson's being "pushed" and even "blackmailed" were rare exposures of Connolly's own judgment. During the same period he even went so far as to attribute to Hudson the humorous bromide that "a bachelor is someone who has the whole *closet* to himself."[10]

As with most everything that went on in Hollywood, Connolly was privy to the factors that made marriage expedient for Hudson, and these factors preyed on his mind. Bunny Seidman continues, "I was sort of nuts in those days. I wanted to be supported. So I called my father to come to Los Angeles and meet Mike. I told him, 'Mike's a lot older, but very successful.' None of the gang — Stanley, Bill, or Joe — wanted us to get married. Joe simply said, 'You two deserve each other.' Meanwhile, my father agreed to come, and we set up a meeting at Romanoff's. But there was a problem.

"While my father was en route, Mike came up to my apartment over his garage and told me, 'We can't go through with it.' He'd heard that another columnist was going to print an item that said [in essence], 'Which columnist with the raised pinkie is going to shock all of Hollywood and get married?' Mike said he would see me and my father later at Romanoff's. But when my father showed up there, the maître d' gave him a message from Mike. He said he had sudden and urgent business in Las Vegas. But dinner would be on him."

Even though the nuptial scheme faltered, Seidman was willing to maintain the charade for awhile. In April 1956, she accompanied Connolly to the annual Newspaper Publishers Convention in New York, stopping off in Chicago en route. "We went to all sorts of parties," she recalled. "At the Ambassador East, he told all the *Chicago Sun-Times* folks that I was his fiancée. Then we flew with all of them to New York in a private plane." Connolly may have felt that, since the *Chicago Sun-Times* was syndicating his Hollywood column, he ought to play it straight. But the *Sun-Times* was not fooled; one of its top men tried to initiate an affair with Seidman, her "engagement" to Connolly notwithstanding.

Connolly did not think Seidman was the type of girl his family in Chicago wanted him to bring home, so she did not accompany him when he visited them. But he did make feeble attempts to maintain a charade for their benefit; the official line with the relatives was that he had simply not yet found the right girl. He was fond of his sister-in-law Alma and told his brother Tom that if he could somehow find a woman who understood his "problems" and was as good a correspondent as Alma, he would tie the knot without delay.[11]

A letter to the University of Illinois written only the week before he and Seidman flew to Chicago shows how he was feeling about the "marriage thing." He had heard, erroneously, that the university's alumni magazine was going to run an item on him, including the assertion that he was married. Although business considerations and the spectre of *Confidential* had prompted his risible betrothal scenario with Seidman for select audiences, his letter to the university, if somewhat disingenuous, was completely honest, which was his preferred policy on the issue. "I not only am not 'an old married man' by now but haven't any prospects currently for being anything but an old UNmarried man," he wrote. "I hope you can [stop the presses] in time. Otherwise, I may find it a little difficult to get a date around these parts. Even in Hollywood it's considered a little out of taste for a newlywed to step out on the town with someone other than the bride."[12]

This, then, was Connolly's state of mind in the weeks following March 30, 1956, when he mentioned Ezra Goodman in his column for the last time. Goodman would have seen Connolly's vehement May 1955 official denial of any connection with *Confidential*, which was as forceful a denial as any public figure caught with his pants down has ever issued. If Goodman had come into possession of information contradicting Connolly's denial, as he implied in his book, his knowledge would have posed a threat to Connolly.

Some of *Confidential's* highest-profile stories could very well have grown out of items that had appeared earlier in Connolly's column. Two years before the May 1955 Rory Calhoun story appeared (with Calhoun's prison mug shot glaring from off the cover), Connolly ran this item: "The Rory Calhoun who flew to Korea [to entertain troops] doesn't seem like the same guy who gave the juvenile authorities so much trouble years ago."[13]

As well, *Confidential's* infamously lurid March 1957 piece, "It Was a Hot Show in Town When Maureen O'Hara Cuddled in Row Thirty-Five," was not news to anyone who had been following the "Rambling Reporter" for the previous five years. The article said O'Hara had been observed in the dark balcony of Grauman's Chinese Theater by an assistant manager, lying across the lap of a "Latin lover" in a state of passion bordering on sexual intercourse. Connolly, who was partial to O'Hara as he was to all Irish actresses, had signalled to her that he knew about her affair with Enrique Parra and was not amused. "Word wafts up from Mexico City that Maureen O'Hara is having a whirrrrl," he frowned. He grew petulant when she did not respond to his hints to dump her paramour. "If Maureen O'Hara has her heart set on that Mexican," he nagged, "she should know (1) he's married and has a seventeen-year-old daughter, (2) Mexicans don't divorce easily in Mexico and (3) he doesn't own that hotel or that bank but merely works for the people who own them." The notion that a *Confidential* exposé would be for O'Hara's own good was congruent with Connolly's philosophy.[14]

When asked if it were true that Connolly supplied stories for *Confi-*

dential, Bunny Seidman (who, after all, rented his garage apartment and often ate dinner with Connolly and Zappia in their home) replied, "I always thought so—I saw some checks." She knew Connolly to be friendly with *Confidential* publisher Robert Harrison "because we went out — Mike took me, and the guys from *Confidential* were there. Harrison came home with me and did a cartoon drawing for me." Connolly always noted Harrison's arrivals in Hollywood in his column, as well as the comings and goings of Marjorie and Fred Meade, the operators of *Confidential's* west coast outpost, Hollywood Research, Inc.[15]

Connolly also knew Polly Gould, who was the unnamed *Confidential* emissary to Joan Crawford mentioned in his official denial. Gould, a lesbian, was a detective who had gathered information on Crawford's sex life. She was also a popular figure at Connolly's parties, where she was famous for the funniest story that some of the regulars, who were of course jaded in the humor department thanks to the court-jester antics of Roger Davis, had ever heard: "Polly was flying to New York as a courier, carrying cash for investment in a Broadway show," said Seidman. "She was on the toilet when the plane hit turbulence, and she sank into the hole. No one could pull her out and the plane had to make an emergency landing in Kansas City. They had to get a torch and it burned her ass. When she finally got to New York, they asked her, 'But what about the money?'" Gould was expected to testify at the *Confidential* trial, but was found dead from a barbiturate overdose just before her day in court. According to Seidman, Gould had murdered her girlfriend before committing suicide.[16]

All of his shoulder-rubbing with *Confidential* dignitaries suggests that Connolly's official denial should be ingested with a grain or two of salt. It is of a pattern with other journalists who were condemning *Confidential* publicly while cozying up to it in private. *New York Mirror* editor Lee Mortimer was, at least in print, one of *Confidential's* biggest antagonists, yet Robert Harrison would meet Mortimer in an innocuous-looking telephone booth to discuss story ideas. Harrison later explained the symbiosis in this arrangement. Mortimer got a lot of journalistic mileage out of the controversy surrounding *Confidential*, while Harrison enjoyed the sleuthing services of a first-rate scandalmonger. After the telephone booth parleys by day, "we'd glare at each other at some nightclub that night," Harrison chortled.[17]

Connolly's dealings with Harrison fit the pattern followed by Lee Mortimer. The public position of the "Rambling Reporter" was that *Confidential* was a nuisance and menace. "You'd upchuck," Connolly would sigh, "over the names of the well-known writers making a fast, lousy buck writing for *Confidential*." Invariably his Lee Mortimer–like tone reflected abhorrence and disapproval: "[Singer] Billy Daniels went up to *Confidential* publisher Bob Harrison at the Mocambo and snapped, 'That's some magazine you publish. I'd like to have a piece of you — a piece of your heart!'" He sounded gratified when he declared that "three of *Confidential's* local tipsters have been spotted and are being given the brushoff by the studios."[18]

However, the attention Connolly paid to Harrison's entrances and exits was nothing short of avid. In an extremely interesting development, he disclosed that Frederick Fell and Company, who had already published Connolly's book, *I'll Cry Tomorrow*, was planning to publish a biography of Harrison. That scheme must have fallen through, because later Connolly said Simon and Schuster was gearing up to bring out the story of Harrison's life. This book never materialized either.[19]

Just as the *Confidential* trial got underway, Connolly dropped a bombshell that showed how intimately tuned in he was to the defendant magazine's inner workings. "A sensational scandal may crack the *Confidential* trial wide open any minute and make the other testimony sound like tittle-tattle tossed off at a Ladies' Aid tea," he wrote. "To be specific: Some time ago a major studio, tipped off that the magazine had a terribly detrimental tale on tap about its top star, contacted the mag and made a deal for it to drop the story in return for a true story about another star on the lot. The mag agreed — whereupon the studio actually had one of its better scripters write the yarn! To continue: Latter star learned he had been double-crossed and immediately demanded a release from his contract. He got it. Soooo — this same star has been subpoenaed to appear in the current hearings, and the studio execs have now made a deal with him to keep his lip buttoned about the way they sold him down the river — deal being the starring role in a pic for four times his former salary!"[20]

The unnamed principals in Connolly's scoop, of course, were Rock Hudson, Rory Calhoun, and Universal-International. Calhoun had in fact been subpoenaed to the trial. The bitter split Connolly described between Calhoun and U-I is borne out in the column. The "Rambling Reporter" carried no items linking Calhoun to that studio after September 8, 1955. By the end of 1955, Connolly reported that an independent production company had "nabbed" Calhoun, and even alleged that Calhoun was going into the "cave [tourist excursions] business." Later, columnist Hedda Hopper would ask Calhoun point blank, "Why did you pull out of a fat Universal-International contract when your bosses had five important pictures in preparation for you?" Calhoun responded cagily that his interest had gravitated to television. Pressed a second time by Hopper for the specifics of how he got out of his U-I contract, he said simply, "It wasn't too difficult.

Do you think I'm moving too early?" Hopper gave his career move her blessing.[21]

Biographies of Rock Hudson repeat the story of how Universal-International rescued him from *Confidential* by offering Calhoun as a sacrificial lamb, but they confess uniformly their inability to substantiate it. However, none of the Hudson biographies cites Ezra Goodman, one of Hollywood's most honest and candid reporters, whose 1961 book lists the episode among similar examples of studios' feeding alternate yarns to *Confidential* specifically to kill off stories they did not want published. Nor were the Hudson biographers aware of Mike Connolly's contemporary blind item on Hudson, Calhoun, and U-I. As for Connolly's claim that U-I bought Calhoun's silence with highly compensated work in another picture, Calhoun did return to U-I to star in *The Saga of Hemp Brown* in 1958. U-I records show Calhoun's earnings from *Hemp Brown* were $47,500, ten thousand more than each of the last several pictures he made before leaving — not the fourfold increase claimed by Connolly, but the biggest raise they ever gave him.[22]

The eight-week period of the *Confidential* trial was one of the quietest times on record in Hollywood. Many stars had skipped town or even the country to avoid being subpoenaed. The *New York Times* observed that the *Hollywood Reporter* and *Daily Variety* had dropped their usual hypersensitivity to all matters cinematic, "keeping almost entirely mum" about the carnival unfolding at the Los Angeles Superior Courthouse. The trade papers' silence extended to the revelations from the witness stand of names of journalists who had worked for *Confidential*. *Time* magazine and the New York dailies published some of the names, but no west coast paper did.[23]

This internecine combination of events presented Connolly with a threatening Catch–22. Facing him on one side was the information on his "amorous activities" held by *Confidential* as a "journalistic sword over his head" to secure his services as a story supplier. His engagement charade with Bunny Seidman shows how seriously he took the potential havoc to his reputation that such a scandal could wreak. But staring at him from the other side was the possibility of exposure during the trial as a *Confidential* source. His escape from the exposure suffered by Aline Mosby, Florabel Muir, and others seems nothing short of miraculous. Yet he remained in town and on the job during the trial, and his column maintained an insouciant attitude toward the proceedings. Just before the trial began, he scoffed at *Confidential* counsel Arthur Crowley's "pre-trial sideshow" and predicted (incorrectly) the judge would not permit any "three-ring circus." His publication three days later of the "sensational" blind item (on

Calhoun, Hudson, and Universal-International) that threatened to "crack the trial wide open" would have taken courage; conceivably he could have been subpoenaed to explain the item. But the court did not take the bait, most likely because neither Connolly nor his trade paper was on trial. On August 23rd, he wrote, "Understand dozens of filmites have ordered helium balloons for a two hundred-mile ascent above the earth, equipped and provisioned to allow them to stay until after That Trial. And it's devoutly to be hoped that SOME of them will throw themselves out!"[24]

As the trial wound down, however, Connolly's rival at *Daily Variety*, Army Archerd, writing in defense of Aline Mosby, said the state of California could do the industry a big favor if it released a list of all known contributors to *Confidential*; he challenged the state "to remove all doubts." Clearly Archerd had information on other contributors out there who had escaped exposure. Perhaps Howard Rushmore, the embittered ex-editor who had spilled the beans on the witness stand, knew only a few of the magazine's shadow contributors, and only publisher Harrison knew all of them. Harrison, who had successfully fought extradition to California for the trial, once overcame writer Harold Conrad's fear of contributing to *Confidential* by saying, "Lots of big-name writers came through here. You never heard their names, did you?"[25]

It could be that Connolly showed no more chutzpah throughout the *Confidential* ordeal than was required ordinarily in his day-to-day existence as a gossip columnist. On any given day he printed many items that had the potential to land him in hot water. He was also a much less sensational personality than the celebrities, party girls, and prostitutes on the witness stand.

Exactly what "amorous activities" might *Confidential* have held as a sword over Connolly's head? The preeminence of his column assured that young actors would forever be throwing themselves at him to get their names in print, said James Hill. Reports of such transactions were precisely what *Confidential* and all magazines of its ilk were seeking. "[W]hen it came to proving so-and-so actor or politician was a homosexual — a curious preoccupation of his—[*Confidential's*] Harrison would spend thousands of dollars, if necessary, to check facts and line up witnesses," reported a former *Confidential* editor.[26]

When Connolly was honored by the Hollywood Masquers Club as "Irishman of the Year" in 1961, some of the "roasters" on the dais alluded in jest to his extracurricular activities. Actor Cornel Wilde teased that priests would draw straws for the diversion of hearing Connolly's confessions. Actor Pat O'Brien joked that when Connolly was in confession, the priest hearing him hissed, "Namedropper!" Whether these friends were just making it up or were basing their jibes on rumors of Connolly's pecadilloes is unknown, but they were uncannily close to the mark. While Connolly's socializing with prominent gays in the film industry was a matter of record, his safaris into the sub rosa world of bathhouses, hustlers, and climbers were kept discreet and largely unobserved — except for the occasional column item such as "Aside to T.S.: You left your motor running, kid." He claimed not to print "honorable" mentions of aspiring actors in exchange for sexual favors, but he did make introductions at parties and arrange interviews with other reporters.[27]

Larry Quirk, Connolly's fellow Hollywood journalist, heard a number of reports of Connolly's "amorous activities." If gossip about Connolly at gay parties was as rampant as Quirk remembered, it could easily have reached the ears of a tipster for *Confidential*. "Eddie Goulding [the director] told me one young actor did something cruel to Mike," Quirk said. "The actor wanted Mike to do something at a studio for him, while Mike wanted to have sex with the actor. He was angry when Mike didn't keep his promise to help him. So to get even he put sneezing powder on his penis in advance and then let Mike go down on him. Mike ended up sneezing and coughing for a week."[28]

"There used to be a place on Wilshire," Quirk continued. "It wasn't a bathhouse because there weren't baths, but a gym with lots of commodious private 'dressing cubicles.' I know Mike went there because I saw him there, leaving someone's cubicle. Another time I was with a young man who told me he had been picked up by Mike on Hollywood Boulevard," said Quirk. "Mike had a masochistic side; he liked danger. His favorite line was, 'Are you an actor? If not, you should be.' Eddie Goulding also told me Mike had a habit of picking up rough trade, and some of the boys would try to blackmail him. Eddie said Mike almost got himself killed once by a scruffy lad who pulled a knife on him. Another guy robbed him. I think he may have been arrested once, but pulled strings to get off or have the record expunged."[29]

If there is no surviving record of Connolly's having been arrested by the vice squad, it is clear from his column that he held a grudge against the Los Angeles police. He often took potshots at them, such as "L.A. vice squad's new theme song: *Hello, Young Lovers, Wherever You Are*," or "Vice squad has put on fourteen extra men and given them a list of all bars on the side streets between Santa Monica and Sunset." Connolly's friend David Hanna said the vice squad (known simply as "vice") was a constant danger to gay men. "The vice squad was there and had to be kept busy," Hanna recollected. "It was aggressive in its pursuit of gay people in any way it could get them because they were so easy to get." Connolly frequently passed along police stories to readers, such as the night "the sheriff chased a covey of customers out of the Interlude" or "Beverly Hills cops are vice-campaigning with a vengeance" or "Vice squadders have drilled tiny peepholes into most of the town's most notorious saloons." These items were all related in neutral language, but in each case it was gay establishments and patrons that were being targeted and raided.[30]

If Connolly needed help to stay out of jail or to keep a scandalous arrest out of the public eye, there were numerous sources of aid. He knew such services existed; when a friend of his who staged annual police shows got a traffic ticket, he asked, "Anybody know a fix?" A number of lawyers in Los Angeles, including Wendy Stewart and Harry Weiss, handled gay cases. Greg Bautzer, the top facilitator of deals in the entertainment industry, was counsel to the *Hollywood Reporter* and would have had the connections to protect Connolly's good name had the need arisen. Connolly dropped Bautzer's name in the column several times per week in an attitude bordering on worship, even though Bautzer was not an entertainer in need of publicity. Other individuals who were not lawyers were also known as someone to see in times of extraordinary need. Singled out in Connolly's column was Kemp Niver, who won a special Oscar in 1954 for inventing a process that converted old paper film into projectable film. Niver had also been a private investigator in Los Angeles, one of the few, according to Connolly, who "has never been corrupted by these scandal magazines" and who "has also acted, for many years, as a 'laundryman' here, helping to keep certain reputations clean. It has cost him plenty of work but he has never learned how to say no to anyone in trouble."[31]

Another possibility was public relations maven Irving Hoffman, who although New York–based wrote a column for the *Hollywood Reporter* for twenty years. Hoffman, according to a 1953 *Esquire* article, saved a studio millions of dollars when one of its male stars, who had two unreleased pictures waiting in the wings, had been caught in a vice raid. Connolly himself wrote about Hoffman's knack for "keeping news OUT of the papers for his clients."[32]

Although the precise details of Connolly's unhappy experiences with *Confidential* are not known, it is a fact that he stopped printing flamboyant items along the lines of "gefulte swish" or "Shubert nances" even before the smoke had cleared from *Confidential's* long siege of Hollywood. There were, however, equally juicy topics to exploit in keeping the column titillating, and where Hollywood's consumption of alcohol was concerned, Connolly could boast the expertise of a battle-scarred veteran.

Chapter 3

I'll Quit Tomorrow

"Ours was the noisiest, wettest table in the Biltmore Bowl."

— *Mike Connolly, Hollywood Reporter, Nov. 21, 1952*

"Having suffered a hangover or three, we like that Regal Pale billboard: 'Good for the Hole in Your Head.'"

— *Mike Connolly, Hollywood Reporter, Mar. 20, 1953*

The single major literary work of Connolly's career, *I'll Cry Tomorrow*, was a highly personal experience for him. The struggles of its heroine, singer and actress Lillian Roth, against the ravages of alcoholism paralleled Connolly's own personal challenges in situations of proximity to liquor.

When Connolly and Roth first met is uncertain, but he had attended at least one of her live shows in Chicago in the early 1930s and was even then a big fan. She faded out of show business for fifteen years as her problems with alcohol addiction worsened. Her recovery came through Alcoholics Anonymous, beginning in 1946. Hand-in-hand with her sobriety was her baptism into the Roman Catholic church on August 14, 1948, in Santa Monica, California. She asked Connolly to be her godfather at that milestone.[1]

As Roth had resumed her career, she was often asked to speak to church groups about her recovery; inevitably her audiences urged her to write a book. By November 1948, Roth had settled on Connolly as her ghostwriter, very likely after much persuasion on his part. He told a reporter he originally approached Roth "for an interview about a fabulous show biz gal who had fallen from grace only to be redeemed by AA [but] instead of gathering only interview material, [I] stayed for a book." Preliminary versions of the title were *Come to Think of It*, which was Roth's idea, and *World on a String*, after the popular song Roth had introduced at the height of her career.[2]

Connolly's family first learned of his blossoming literary venture when his sister-in-law, Alma, pregnant in Chicago with her first child (Michael Connolly, born in the spring of 1950), received a package of crocheted baby items in the mail with a laconic note saying, "Love, Lillian Roth." "I didn't have any idea who she was," said Alma Connolly. "Then Mike explained to us he was writing a book about this woman and she was a Mary Magdalene–type figure." Letters from the proud ghostwriter over the next several months groaned about the countless hours the book required to take shape, due in part to the staggering amount of research necessary to portray correctly the Broadway of the twenties and thirties. But he and Roth were confident that their literary agent, Stanley Rose, was the finest in the business, and that Rose's belief in the project was a sure sign of its merit. Meanwhile, Connolly unleashed a barrage of publicity for Roth, whose career, though rising gradually from the ashes, was not bringing in enough money to live on. He propagated several rumors of imminent movie roles for her, adding that she was "looking like a million."[3]

By the end of 1951, however, what had seemed a natural candidate for a successful book and especially for a movie had been turned down by Henry Holt, Doubleday, and Random House. Roth was working in Hollywood, "knocking 'em off their stools at the Bar of Music," according to Connolly's column, but still could not make ends meet. Connolly hosted a gala dinner for her at his home on March 23, 1952, before she retreated to New York. Society columnist Cobina Wright was so impressed by Roth's singing at Connolly's that she engineered a six-week booking for her at the Deauville nightclub, which delayed her return to New York. Roth even signed with agent Charlie Feldman for movie work. But after the Deauville engagement, she was met with the proverbial deafening silence, with no prospects either for singing or for publication of the book.[4]

The reasons for the major publishing houses' polite refusals have been lost, but Roth decided to hire a new agent, Abner ("Abby") Greshler, best known (and exceedingly well compensated) for having teamed Jerry Lewis with Dean Martin. Abby Greshler peddled the manuscript successfully to a smaller, lesser-known publisher, Frederick Fell and Company of New York. The clinching of the deal happened just in time to surprise Roth when she was the honoree on the February 4, 1953, episode of *This Is Your Life*. In the show's final minutes, Connolly marched out from behind a curtain, manuscript under his arm, to inform Roth of Fell's agreement to buy it. The show's producers, whose time had run out, made a last-minute decision to send Connolly on stage instead of Roth's old friend Milton Berle, who had also been waiting in the wings—"the first time," Connolly crowed, "that anyone ever cut Berle out of a TV show."[5]

The joy of the book deal and television plug may have been short-lived for Connolly. Roth later maintained the sale was "with conditions I could rewrite it." She was not satisfied with Connolly's treatment, and Fell agreed. Whatever harmony had existed between Roth and Connolly up to this point would now be tested severely. "They fought over the book," Bunny Seidman reported. "Lillian wanted complete control." Friends of both say that a protracted struggle over the book between Connolly and Roth was unavoidable. "Lillian had a running battle with almost everyone in her inner circle," said her longtime secretary, Julie Sanges. "In her world, it was the norm."[6]

Fell telephoned Gerold Frank of New York, who had a reputation in publishing circles as a skilled ghost writer and "story doctor," asking Frank to do "a little buttoning up" on Connolly's manuscript. Oddly, Fell did not offer Frank a contract for the work; Frank's wife was flabbergasted at the effrontery of the scheme. Yet something in the essence of Roth's story, especially the primal terror she experienced, appealed mightily to Frank. He felt driven to accept the assignment, taking a six-month leave of absence from his job as an editor at *Coronet*. Shrewdly, he allowed Fell to read his own reworked version of the manuscript only under a trust agreement requiring a satisfactory financial arrangement among all the parties before any publication. "It was possible to predict," said *Life* magazine, "that the first ghost, Mike Connolly, would not share profits without a struggle." At some point, though, Connolly could see he had no choice if he wanted the manuscript he had worked on so diligently to go forward. Once Frank had been fairly dealt in, however, Roth once again grew petulant; she complained about getting "less than fifty percent of my own life!"[7]

More is known about Frank's ghostwriting methods than about Connolly's. Frank began his mission of reclamation with the assumption that Connolly's manuscript needed to be overhauled completely. Using a tape recorder, he coaxed Roth's long and rambling life story out of her. The transcribed pages numbered in the thousands, and once Frank edited these, he submitted long lists of new questions to Roth, resuming the arduous tape-recording process for another round. Roth's emotions were often raw during the questioning; she wept frequently and at one point became hysterical.

Frank's work product was acceptable to Fell and finally, after a few bouts of cold feet on Roth's part, the book, bearing all three names as authors, was published and on the stands in May 1954. Its success was immediate; it would be the sixth best-selling nonfiction book of the year. On August 25, 1954, it was named a winner of the semi-annual Christopher Awards, the top Catholic literary prize, whose credo is "Better to light one candle than to curse the darkness." The Christopher Awards were founded by Father James Keller in 1945. Father Keller was a close friend to Connolly and had been a guest at Connolly's March 1952 buffet dinner for Roth.[8]

The day after the Christopher Awards announcement, a movie rights deal was signed with MGM, netting a sum of $116,500. Fell and Company owned one quarter of the film rights, and the percentage split between Roth, Connolly, and Frank was 40-30-30. Minus agent Greshler's 10 percent, Connolly's and Frank's shares of the film rights sale were roughly $23,000 each.[9]

Such a streak of good luck and fortune seemed to assuage Roth's feelings toward Connolly, and she wrote him a letter in a bury-the-hatchet mode. He answered that he was thrilled to get a letter from the charming Lillian Roth he had known in the good old days. He promised to attend her opening at El Rancho in Las Vegas in October.[10]

However, the adage that three is a crowd certainly applied to the authorial troika on *I'll Cry Tomorrow*, with each having grounds for a feud with the others. When Frank came to Hollywood on business in October 1954, he phoned Connolly ready to do battle, but the ensuing conversation turned out to be so congenial that Frank invited Connolly to meet for cocktails and Connolly invited Frank to an opening at Ciro's. Thus alcohol, which was the catalyst for their association in the first place, smoothed things over temporarily.

Over cocktails, Frank was privately amused to hear Connolly's insistence that his tubthumping of the book in his column was the reason for its brisk sales. Frank believed that all the publicity in the world could not help a book if it were bad; bookstore proprietors had told him that the public was buying *I'll Cry Tomorrow* because they perceived its intrinsic honesty. (In the opinion of a *New York Times* reviewer, both Frank and Connolly had come between Roth and what she had to say, but the story was "sufficiently poignant" to cut through the prose.)[11]

But it suited Connolly to plug the book in the "Rambling Reporter" whether Hollywood needed it or not. He also took to the stump, bending the collective ear of the Hollywood Women's Press Club and other groups. Some of his audiences' reactions were memorable. "If I gotta go through all that horror to get off the stuff," cracked newsman Gene Fowler, "I'm gonna stay on it!" A couple who joked that *I'll Cry Tomorrow* had prompted them to give up drinking pleaded, "Don't EVER write one about a nympho!"[12]

The evening with Frank at Ciro's may have been Connolly's last peaceful occasion with his co-author. In the judgment of both Roth and Fell, after all, Connolly's manuscript had been deemed deficient, and he resented Frank's having been called in. Henceforth, each time he mentioned Frank it would be a put-down, whether to call him a "muckraker" (in connection with Frank's next project, ghosting another alcoholic autobiography, Diana Barrymore's *Too Much Too Soon*) or to deplore "his self-publicizing pranks" (with which Sheilah Graham was said to be "fed up," vis-à-vis her collaboration with Frank on *Beloved Infidel*). In August 1960, Frank gave an interview to Art Buchwald, in which *I'll Cry Tomorrow* was mentioned but Connolly was not. Although Buchwald and not Frank was completely responsible for the content of the piece, Connolly let out all his accumulated bile the next day, writing, "Omigosh, there goes Gerold Frank again, bombastin' (this time to Art Buchwald) about how HE wrote *I'll Cry Tomorrow*, and not so much as a word of thanks to [me] for sending Zsa Zsa Gabor to him ... Look, Gerold, you can take Zsa Zsa but not our *Cry* credit!"[13]

In fact, Frank did co-author *Zsa Zsa Gabor: My Story* (1960). "Mike was supposed to do Zsa Zsa's book," says Bunny Seidman. "But she put the make on him! So she'd be in control. She lied too much. So Mike turned it over to Gerold Frank." Frank did seem to have the magical touch; Gabor said she told Frank more than she would tell her psychiatrist. Given Connolly's attitude (in print) toward both Gabor and Frank, his referral may have been revenge rather than a favor.[14]

From time to time Connolly also printed addenda to the information given in *I'll Cry Tomorrow*, as if to show that, of Roth's two co-authors, *he* was the one with the real story. "It's neither in the book nor the movie but Lillian Roth's mother ... died a Catholic," he revealed. "Lillian herself baptized her mother on her deathbed." He also claimed that an earlier version of the title was *Spit on My Petticoat*, a gesture said to bring luck to showgirls in the days of vaudeville.[15]

On his part, Frank said politely, "I knew Mike as a skilled reporter and a very industrious fellow who had his hand in many projects." Pressed for a full-fledged interview on Connolly, however, Frank clammed up.[16]

As time went on, whatever rapprochement had been forged briefly between Connolly and Roth seemed to unravel, judging from the unkind things Connolly kept saying about her in his column. "In Las Vegas," he snorted, "they're billing Lillian Roth as 'Author.' Haw." Worst of all was his report of columnist Edith Gwynn's wine-tasting at the swank restaurant Chasen's, held to demonstrate that California and French wines were indistinguishable. "Guests were signing their wine-sipping score cards 'Lillian Roth,' 'Diana Barrymore,' etc.," he leered. He must have suffered some fresh offense to hold his good friend and confidante up to public ridicule in such a way.[17]

Perhaps the most callous disregard for Roth's dignity came when Joseph Zappia compiled a scrapbook of nostalgic photographs, each one accompanied by witty or bawdy captions, for Bunny Seidman on the occasion of her wedding. One photo was of Connolly, Roth, and Susan Hayward, who played Roth in the film version of I'll Cry Tomorrow, beaming together at the movie's world premiere. Zappia had cut out a picture of a fifth of Chivas Regal and pasted it inside the grip of Roth's hand.

Since the film version was, after all, a dramatization of Connolly's work product, the December 22, 1955, world premiere of I'll Cry Tomorrow must have been one of the happiest moments in his life, a victory lap after years of diligent work and a tacit acceptance into the film industry fraternity that heretofore he had only observed and written about. He wrote very little about his feelings at the premiere, but he did rent the presidential suite at the Knickerbocker Hotel that night as a treat to himself. (Gerold Frank did not attend.) In honor of the occasion, Roth confided to him, "It seems like twenty years instead of [seven] since you and I started writing I'll Cry Tomorrow. And now, looking at Susan Hayward playing me, it seems like I'm looking at another person's life story. It isn't me. I'm different than I was ten years ago— thank God.'"[18]

As with the book, Connolly seized every opportunity to talk up the movie in his column, mentioning that the screenwriters had sat in on Alcoholics Anonymous meetings to soak up atmosphere or that Susan Hayward had survived nine heroic weeks of vocal coaching to rise to the occasion of belting out Roth's signature songs. He even took poetic license, feigning surprise that Bridge Over the River Kwai was not a sequel to I'll Kwai Tomorrow, or suggesting that Hayward's other landmark film, I Want to Live!, should be called I'll Die Tomorrow.[19]

Connolly never alluded to the probability of common elements in Roth's life story and his own addiction to alcohol, nor is it clear that he ever devoted any introspection to it. In 1957, he turned down a lucrative liquor endorsement offer, not because he disapproved but because he feared it could "hurt the still-booming I'll Cry Tomorrow paperback sales." Paramount producer A. C. Lyles and other sources heard that Connolly quit drinking during the years he worked on the book. "If that is true," said Bunny Seidman, "then he had started in again by the time I met him, at his forty-first birthday party in 1954." That party was two months after *I'll Cry Tomorrow* hit the bookstores. Connolly's only known hint of a possible stretch of sobriety was in a letter he wrote to his brother. To keep himself going through the months of hard work on the book, he said, he was swallowing copious amounts of vitamins. Certainly his columns never suggested that he might have been on the wagon.[20]

He was less reticent about his smoking habit, disclosing in September 1952 that Olivia de Havilland had not only "inspired" him to give it up, but had gone one step further and badgered him to chew raisins instead of candy and gum. Unfortunately, the smoke-out did not last; the following June Connolly tattled that de Havilland had resumed smoking, and one month later confessed, "We've just gotta cut down on cigarettes." Henceforth, references in the column to smoking tended to be cynical. He identified cancer experts who chewed or smoked, or stars who puffed away in defiance of doctors' orders; magazines that published cigarette ads side by side with articles on cancer; and reasons for not taking studies with white mice seriously. When British producer Alex Korda was admonished that he could live ten years longer by giving up smoking, Connolly cited with approval Korda's retort: "If I quit smoking, what fun will there be living ten years longer?"[21]

But if he refused to recognize his own drinking problem for what it was, there were indications that he took Lillian Roth's problem seriously. In an otherwise casual letter, he rejoiced in her booming career but cautioned her that it was worth nothing if it pushed her to start drinking again. When a number of cocktail parties were thrown to celebrate the publication of *I'll Cry Tomorrow*, Connolly could not resist highlighting the irony, but assured his readers that Roth drank only ginger ale. "P.S.," he added, "the co-writers drank Horses' Necks!"[22]

Over the years, Connolly's drinking provoked raised eyebrows in Hollywood. From author Gore Vidal's perspective, "Mike was your average drunk Irish Catholic queen who was pretty venomous when in his cups and good company outside them." Bunny Seidman said she once had to drag Connolly out of the Ambassador Hotel after he began urinating into a potted plant. Willie Wilkerson, the son of Connolly's publisher, said, "As between mean drunks and happy drunks, Mike was a very happy drunk. I remember very well from parties at my mother's house watching him lose his inhibitions gradually as he drank more — not making passes, but his defense mechanisms melting away completely.[23]

Connolly's closest friends were those who were willing to match his drinking, olive by olive. A favorite was actor Gilbert Roland ("Amigo" to Connolly); with Gia Roland, Bunny Seidman, and others in tow, they would motor down to Tijuana to the bullfights. Parking Roland's Cadillac on the U.S. side, they crossed the border on foot (to avoid long waits in U.S. Customs lines coming back), making a beeline for lunch at the Foreign Club Bar. "Every place we went, Mike had a straight shot of tequila with lemon," said Seidman. On the way home, a heavenly abundance of Scotch, bourbon, gin, vodka, and beer was liberated from a handy refrigerator in the Cadillac.[24]

Mexico native Roland, who held that tequila made one feel ten feet tall and six feet wide, once showed his charitable side after learning Connolly was ailing. "Dear Miguelito," he wrote, "I read where you were fighting a cold. Here is the only weapon known to destroy all germs. Drink it, hombre. It will make the heart glad. If the heart is not glad, then there is no remedy."[25]

Another widely circulated story happened in San Francisco, where Connolly traveled ostensibly to market his syndicated column at the California Newspaper Publishers Association conference; in reality he spent more time cocktailing with friends. Joining the beloved local columnist Herb Caen and Buster and Marlie Stevens ("Stevie") Collier at the Valhalla, Connolly attracted the attention of the other customers by making good on a longtime threat and drinking out of Stevie Collier's shoe. Reporting the incident, Caen said the drink had been a highball.

Word of the deed reached *Los Angeles Times* columnist Art Ryon, who broke Caen's story word-for-word for the benefit of Southern California, adding, "Never mind, Mike. They just don't have the Grand Touch up there. And, besides, how were you to know it was an open-toed shoe?" Not one to take needling complacently, Connolly hit back the following day, in an "Aside to Art Ryon: That was not a highball we drank out of a lady's slipper in San Francisco, it was champagne. Let's not be plebeian, pal! ... Furthermore, Art, you can check it with Herb Caen, who was THERE and who is no mean man with a slipperful himself!"[26]

In Hollywood itself, there was the time Connolly escorted Mrs. Horace Dodge, a former showgirl, to a party at Romanoff's for visiting Chicago newspapermen, where they sat with their mutual friend, *Chicago Sun-Times* columnist Irv Kupcinet. When the party was ready to move on to a nightclub, Kupcinet relates, "Mike had gotten loaded and had to be carried out." Kupcinet agreed to see Mrs. Dodge home, but both were arrested en route for drunkenness. Although Kupcinet later beat the charge in court, the arrest and trial were banner headlines and he considered the incident to be the biggest "Oops!" of his career. "When it was all over," he wrote, "I tried to get some satisfaction from Mike by giving him hell. After all, the rambunctious Mrs. Dodge had been *his* 'date.' And if he hadn't gotten so loaded, I wouldn't have had to chaperone her to jail. He just shrugged his shoulders, winked at me, and said, 'Oooops!'"[27]

One cannot have read Connolly's columns without getting the sense that, if he consumed alcohol to excess, so did thoughts of alcohol consume him. Dispatches from his first trip to Europe in the spring of 1953, replete with bulletins of cocktails, cordials, and chasers at all the beloved bistros of Paris and Rome, left the impression that he was drinking his way across the Continent. It was as if the column were his vehicle for working through the issues raised by his drinking. Alone among the Hollywood press, Connolly devoted an inordinate amount of column space to alcohol and its procurement, ingestion, and consequences. He maintained a running guide to new drink recipes, hangover remedies, the acquisition or loss of liquor licenses, the best bartenders, and the boulevards where police were most likely to arrest drunken drivers.

Even as a college reporter in the thirsty thirties, Connolly was doling out ideas for alcoholic concoctions. "You put two jiggers of rock and rye in a glass with sparkling water and shaved ice, and then you sip it through a straw," he suggested to the first generation of post–Prohibition collegiate drinkers. "It'll stand you on your ear." In Hollywood, he passed along recipes for Purple Cows, Hawaiian Dynamite, Bloody Murphys, Coup D'Etats, and drier-than-thou martinis ("serve gin straight, spray the room with vermouth"). His all-time favorite bartender was the Mocambo's Johnny Trebach, who playfully mispronounced his name as "Cannoli" and kept his cigarettes lighted and his Manhattans refreshed. Trebach could mix up a storm and many of his specialties— Monkeywrenches, Winchell Specials, and Debbie Reynolds Old-Fashioneds—found their way into the "Rambling Reporter."[28]

These intimate encounters with liquor were not without consequences; Connolly was well-versed in the agony of hangovers and whined over and over about having to get up in the morning. A number of hangover remedies of the stars found their way into the column over the years, some of them for real —celery with roquefort cheese, bicarbonate of soda diffused in beer — and some tongue-in-cheek: staying drunk, refraining from drinking the night before, or "taking the juice from one quart of Scotch."[29]

The most controversial aspect of the incessant focus on booze was Connolly's frequent mentioning, by name, of persons in Hollywood who had joined twelve-step groups, ignoring in effect the operative principle in Alcoholics Anonymous. "We've been roasted," he admitted, "for writing about newcomers to AA, argument being that printing it embarrasses the newcomers." His justification was wrapped up in his philosophy on publicity: "But the same people never minded at all when their drunken scrapes smeared them across Page One!" He also insisted that individuals in question had asked him to let the industry know that they were sober.[30]

Although it does seem that Connolly was an unofficial Father Confessor to many of the industry's drunks, his excuses for printing recovering alcoholics' names were disingenuous. His public discussion of private drinking problems was voyeuristic and often mean-spirited. (It was also unique in the Hollywood press; none of the rest was printing anything at all in this vein.) While trumpeting the names of new arrivals at Hollywood AA groups may have served some noble purpose, that can hardly hold true for printing names of those who fell off the wagon, as many did. To boot, Connolly often appended snide editorial comments when sharing such news. "[Actress] Gail Russell joined AA, and high time," he wrote; or, "the newest member of AA is well known to Society. HIC!"[31]

There was an essential disconnect between what Connolly saw in other drinkers and what he could not or would not see in himself. He wrote of his own escapades intending them to be funny; as one to whom the rattling off of baseball statistics did not come naturally, he found that lush stories were the next best means of buddy-bonding himself to a sizeable chunk of Hollywood. "We staggered into Ciro's at high noon yesterday — having staggered out just ten hours earlier!" or "How we ever got out of Glendale after that 'fruit punch' we'll never know" were typical comments on his lubricated social life. Once he was at a Sagittarius party where kids were riding a baby elephant. "First time we ever saw an elephant DURING a party!" he joked.[32]

Perhaps the reason he wrote so much about others' libational feats was that their excesses made his own drinking, so he thought, a safe thing in comparison. Vacationing in Florence, Italy, he observed, "Humphrey Bogart and Orson Welles are both belting the bejeepers out of the grape. Eight double brandies in quick succession is nothing for Welles, for instance." In Las Vegas, he sat with Marlene Dietrich in the Sahara's Casbar until five a.m., "watching the lushes go by." He, of course, was no lush, but a reporter who with a straight face could write, "The prayers of her friends have been answered. One of our great stars has joined AA," or "One of our most beautiful stars (married) has become such a lush she's looking twenty years over her age and not all the camera and makeup trickery in Hollywood can hide it."[33]

As to the stereotyping of newspapermen as drunks, he made it clear that he resented it. Pressed into service by Bob Hope in a cameo role in a television skit, he protested that he had been "typecast" as a barfly. Rock

Hudson once turned down a role as a drunken newsman in *If I Should Die*, and a grateful Connolly wrote, "Thanks, Buddy!" Later on, Connolly was sad to report, Jeff Hunter took the sodden part.[34]

Perhaps the most honest comment Connolly ever made about drinking came when he proposed a working definition of an alcoholic: "Someone you hate who drinks as much as you do." "As much" or "as little" carried meanings far different in Connolly's day than half a century later. He observed that Julie London's recipe for her "creamy" renditions of sultry ballads was "two vodkas-mit-tonic before each recording session. But just two." Nowadays, two drinks often reaches the legal standard for intoxication, but to Connolly, two drinks was merely a warmup.[35]

Connolly did go to Alcoholics Anonymous meetings a few times. His hard-drinking friend David Hanna took him to one meeting, but even Hanna would not dry out for good until the 1970s. And Connolly surely would have attended with Lillian Roth while they were working on *I'll Cry Tomorrow*. But the record shows that, despite Connolly's years of sweat and toil on their book, he never absorbed Roth's lesson.[36]

He was always interested in Roth's career, but it is not known if they ever saw each other again after the movie's premiere at the end of 1955. Sadly, the bonds of Roth's once-happy marriage began to fray after she wrote her 1958 book, *Beyond My Worth* (without assistance from Frank or Connolly); her husband wanted to live in California while she favored New York. When they finally split up, Roth fell off the wagon, apparently for the first time since 1946. Luckily, she clawed her way back to sobriety, but she would relapse from time to time until her death in 1980. Various acting colleagues made it harder for her by taunting her about drinking, particularly a few in her road company of *Funny Girl* during the mid–1960s. Inevitably, Connolly would have learned about Roth's resumption of drinking, but he breathed not a word of it when he mentioned that her divorce lawyer was also her former brother-in-law. In the early sixties, he kept Hollywood abreast of her work on the New York stage in *I Can Get It for You Wholesale*, and when she was hospitalized for surgery, he said she "would appreciate hearing from her old pals."[37]

Friends of Connolly believe he would have lived longer had he been a more moderate drinker; they say that during his open heart surgery at the Mayo Clinic in November 1966, the surgeon was taken aback at how "debauched" his internal organs were. Regrettably, even though Lillian Roth had shown him the way to save his life, it was a path Connolly could not bring himself to follow. He inhabited a harder-drinking era than we know today. Both he and the era were molded in large part by that great metropolis of the Midwest: Chicago.

Chapter 4

Prayers for Peace

"With the celestial light of the holy Gospel, St. Patrick drove from Ireland the darkness of ancient superstition and planted Christianity firmly in the hearts of the sturdy Hibernians."
— *Mike Connolly, The Victory, Mar. 13, 1931*

The portrait of Mike Connolly that emerges from his formative years reveals a high-achieving Catholic boy, precocious in literature and composition. In his early years, at least, he seemed to be a true believer in the tenets of the Catholic Church. There is no hint of rebellion against authority, religious or secular, in anything he wrote during his high school years. Pacifism was his most fervently held cause.

Chicago, Connolly's mother told him, was where the Irish came to get work because "the streets were paved with gold." He was born there on July 10, 1913, the second son of Patrick and Margaret Sutton Connolly, hardworking but poor immigrants. Margaret, one of fourteen children, came to America in 1908, taking work as a housekeeper. Patrick, one of eleven children, "chased her over here" two years later. He worked as a painter and decorator of Chicago's elevated subway stations. Both parents were from County Wexford, villages of Campile and Great Island (and only a stone's throw, Connolly would proudly point out, from Dunganstown, native heath of John F. Kennedy's great-grandfather). During his first pilgrimage to Ireland in May 1953, Connolly learned that an Irish secretary made twenty-eight dollars per week, while in America the same secretary would make one hundred per week. "And you wonder why they all want to go to America," he observed.[1]

There were five Connolly children: Dennis, Michael (Mike), Mary, Thomas (Tom), and John. Mary, who lost her hearing as the result of a childhood illness, went to a boarding school for the deaf, returning to the family on weekends. Each of the brothers went to a different Catholic high school. As the oldest son, Dennis was steered toward the priesthood, but dropped out of seminary and went to work. Mike Connolly was extremely close to Mary throughout his life and left no stone unturned in seeing to her well-being. Of his brothers, he was close only to Tom. Whatever the root of his conflicts with Dennis, his older sibling, his rejoinders always boiled down to Dennis's not being an intellectual.[2]

Connolly's childhood was saturated with Catholic belief and activity. He grew up hearing his mother say, "Anyone who says he *is* a good Catholic *ain't!*" Every Sunday after Mass at St. Lawrence's Church, his family's parish, he was allowed to spend the rest of the day seeing double features at movie houses. His eight years at Holy Angels Grammar School on Chicago's South Side, under the watchful eyes of exacting nuns, would sometimes reverberate in Hollywood. Whenever he ran a tip in the "Rambling Reporter" that turned out to be a bum steer, his inevitable reaction was to ask that "whoever stiffed us please come forward and take the full length of the ruler across the knuckles."[3]

Although Connolly never reminisced in print about going to Mass or the religious instruction he received in school, it is clear from his high school writings that he took seriously the Catholic doctrines he was taught. In one of many tributes to the Blessed Virgin, he cited the literary and artistic achievements She inspired, as well as the many geographic names that explorers throughout history conferred in Her honor. He reminded his classmates that May was the month of devotion to the Blessed Virgin, and suggested a means of showing it. Although four decades of the Rosary were said every day in class, he exhorted the other boys to say the extra decade in chapel at noon.[4]

A congenital heart ailment, which ran in the family, kept him out of school for lengthy spells. Notes from his 1942 physical examination for civil service during World War II indicate "chronic rheumatic heart — organic heart disease is present." Under doctor's orders, he would be put to bed for complete rest and tutored privately at home. At age fourteen he was hospitalized for two months. The high maintenance he required during periods of illness magnified the already strong bond between Irish mother and son. As novelist Alice McDermott observes, "The joke is always the Irish bachelor, ever faithful to his dear mother."[5]

In his junior year, Connolly wrote an editorial for his high school newspaper in honor of Mother's Day, noting that most great men owed their character and success to their mothers. A mother's love, he said, is the world's "most constant, most enduring, and uplifting force." Mother's Day would be duly observed and worshipped every year in his Hollywood columns. "Count yourself among the luckiest alive if you can spend this Sunday with your mother!" he wrote, five years after his own mother was in the grave. He commended an actor who broke a golf date because of Mother's Day and waxed enthusiastic over a performance of *Ireland Must Be Heaven for My Mother Came from There*.[6]

While sick in bed, Connolly amused himself by writing fan letters to silent movie stars. "He would tell them," recalled his younger brother, Tom, "that he was a dying boy, and wouldn't they please grant his last wish and send him an autographed picture?" His letters were so persuasive that one silent star, Louise Fazenda, paid a surprise visit to the family home at 3550 South Cottage Grove to bring young Connolly a quantity of Holy Water. (One can only hope the boy was in bed when Fazenda dropped in.) She told him, perhaps with a degree of prescience, that if ever he were in Hollywood to look her up.[7]

The memories of a Chicago South Side boyhood that bubbled to the surface in Connolly's Hollywood columns centered exclusively on the show business of the day — vaudeville, circuses, silent movies: going to Saturday matinees of *The Perils of Pauline*, featuring Pearl White ("the goddess of our youth"); his favorite pugilist actor, Kit Guard, in the *Fighting Blood* series; the circus aerialist Lillian Leitzel's death-defying high wire stunts; and actress Charlotte Greenwood's "rassling that cake of ice on the Keith Circuit."[8]

After completing eighth grade at Holy Angels, Connolly opted to go to high school at De La Salle Institute, because he felt its student newspaper, *The Victory*, was the best. The school was only ten blocks from his home. Cohen and Taylor, biographers of Chicago Mayor Richard J. Daley, wrote that De La Salle, situated in a "poor black neighborhood," was then regarded as the "Poor Boy's College." In 1954, Connolly would refer to De La Salle as "the Builder of Boys, the Maker of Men," the alma mater of statesmen, congressmen, admirals, generals, six bank presidents, four railroad presidents, and two consecutive mayors.[9]

De La Salle gave Connolly a four-year scholarship based on his academic record at Holy Angels Grammar School. In high school, he would earn A-grades in English, journalism, typing, and shorthand. In Latin, every minute of which he hated during his freshman and sophomore years, he earned B-grades. As for geometry, for which he confessed no aptitude, he managed craftily to squeak through by writing a theme entitled "Euclid, Father of Geometry."[10]

Because of racial tensions in their neighborhood, Connolly's family moved in 1930 to 1524 East 74th Street. By this time, he was a junior and turning out to be the whole show at *The Victory*; he was already writing all the paper's editorials. Despite his often pious tone, he could join his classmates in episodes of teenage jocularity. "In the editorial room," he reminisced, "we used to stuff newspapers under the door and glide the galloping dominoes over a stack of desk blotters so the noise couldn't be heard by the proctors out in the halls."[11]

As a young editorial writer, Connolly was already sounding like himself — not in the style that would later be identified with him, but in the topics he chose to harp on. He was too young and too infatuated with a number of literary greats to sound anything but imitative in the course of urging his student audience to earnestness and nobler pursuits. That other great stylist, H. L. Mencken, had confessed to being "Kipling-mad" as a youth, and the charge applied equally to Connolly.

Mencken told his earliest biographer, "I doubt that any human being has ever read more than I did between my twelfth and eighteenth years." Surely Connolly, by the time he came along, would have been stiff competition for Mencken. Connolly had filled his protracted time confined to bed by reading books and newspapers, the beginning of a lifelong habit of insatiable reading, often a dozen books simultaneously. His desire to be a newspaperman was kindled early on, inspired, he said, by the plethora of famous reporters, poets, and critics who first made their names in Chicago: Cark Sandburg (who dubbed it "The City of the Big Shoulders" and "Hog Butcher of the World"), Charles MacArthur, Maxwell Bodenheim, Sherwood Anderson, Harriet Moore, Amy Leslie, Ashton Stevens, Charlie Collins, and Lloyd Lewis. He also had idols among the nationally known columnists of the day, especially Franklin P. Adams (whose "Conning Tower" column was "the joy of [my] youth"), Mark Hellinger, and Gene Fowler. Connolly could turn out a fair imitation of Adams or any other vernacular columnist of the day if he were writing on appropriate topics such as boxing or local politics.[12]

An editorial he wrote on the value of books and literature in one's life opens a window onto the influences on his thought. Although he had no library at home — his brother says there was no money for books — he was positively ravenous in his consumption of books from public and school libraries. Young Connolly's editorial criticized what he felt was poor taste in the kinds of reading matter his fellow students were checking out of the brand new school library, typified by *The Whoozis Laddies in South*

Africa, or How Tom, Dick and Harry Caught a Fuzzy Wuzzy Bear rather
than the more worthwhile tomes of Melville, Stevenson, Kipling, and the
other literary greats on Parnassus' peak. This quibble, however, was merely
a reference point for a subject on which Connolly was only too happy to
expatiate: the ideal library. He assured his comrades that he was not insisting on a literary diet of classics only; rather, he prescribed a healthy bal-
ance of new and old, humor and gravity, buffoonery and the ethereal.
Authors who merited his favor were Mencken, Hergesheimer, Twain,
O'Neill, O. Henry, Whitman, Shakespeare, St. Augustine, and Plato.[13]

As a junior (1929-1930), Connolly, aside from writing editorials, took
charge of the jokes column, for which he adopted "Don Mike" as his byline.
(To take a melodramatic moniker seemed to be a tradition; the next joke-
meister, Guy Petit-Clerc, styled himself "Black Guy.") He became a member of Quill and Scroll and wrote features and news items on his own
Corona portable typewriter, a 1929 Sears special. With his editor, he
attended a conference of the National Scholastic Press Association at
Chicago's Hotel Knickerbocker. The activities included speeches from
Pulitzer Prize winners, a tour of the *Chicago Daily News* building, and the
showing of "talking pictures," still novel enough for the soundtrack to
merit a mention.[14]

During his senior year he continued to rack up accomplishments, all
related to journalism. He attended the Illinois State High School Press
Association convention, was a winner in his school's Gregg Shorthand
one-hundred-words-per-minute transcription contest, and won fifth place
in the National Scholastic Press Association's editorial-writing contest.[15]

Connolly's final editorial for *The Victory* was both sententious and
touching; he sounded as if he were trying to compose his own Gettysburg
Address. Asserting that the "average" high school boy of 1931 (a sly dis-
claimer; "average" would never include Mike Connolly) recalled nothing
about the Great War, he claimed they viewed it as akin to a sports event,
"reeking with the influence of flag-waving, confetti-throwing talkies." He
was trying to impress upon his classmates that doughboys had gone to war
not in response to ticker-tape parade sentiment but fully aware of the consequences they faced. The real issue for them, he said, was "whether or not
their mothers, wives, and sweethearts were to be protected against any
invaders." Abolition of war, he concluded, ought to be the first priority
on the calendar of humankind's unfinished business. He would repeat this
sentiment throughout his life, but never more plainly than after seeing *The
Bridges at Toko-Ri*, a movie that "makes you realize all over again how
much you hate war."[16]

Another area in which Connolly was already sounding like himself was his attempts at humorous poetry. Unlike his mastery of prose, his poetic gifts were marginal, but that may have been the point. His efforts had titles such as "Senior Goes GaGa Over Rubenstein's Melody in F." The rhymes were clever, but he never seemed to master the metric exigencies. Throughout his Hollywood career he returned again and again to this vehicle of dubious humor, as when actress Maureen O'Hara's role as the unclothed dame of Coventry inspired this outburst: "You can bet a fiver that Lady Godiva found her filly rather chilly."[17]

Dovetailing with these poetic pursuits was Connolly's announcement of a "Brickbat and Bouquet Poetry Club," inviting students to submit four-line poems about anything; the only requirement pertaining to content was that each entry must include "the surname of the victim." Poems (and official ballots for voting on the best effort) would be printed in *The Victory*, and the prize would be two dollars and fifty cents cash. Mysteriously, the incoming ballots were all marked in favor of Connolly's classmate Sam Lizzo, setting off a humorous feud between the two pubescent poets. The crossfire began with Connolly's assertion that Lizzo had bought all the votes. In the end, Connolly threw up his hands and exclaimed, as a true son of Chicago, "You can't beat a machine." Lizzo countered with a letter addressed to the "Editor of *The Victory*," claiming credit for saving Connolly's life because he had dissuaded two classmates from avenging his honor with violence upon Connolly. "When you respond with a poem," Lizzo continued, "I will come and place the lily in your pale hand and may God have mercy on your soul."[18]

The Victory paid tribute to Connolly at the conclusion of his senior year. "The editor, 'Mike' himself, always set the pace for the rest of the staff," it proclaimed. "He not only wrote all the editorials but also news items, features, made headlines, edited, proofread and copyread, and did a great deal of typing."[19]

Connolly seemed satisfied with his high school education and with the Catholic indoctrination that went along with it. Honoring the Christian Brothers who operated De La Salle, he commended them for "renouncing worldly pomp" to teach young men and for their keeping intact the daily catechism instruction and hourly meditation. His high regard for De La Salle endured throughout his life. In the 1950s his clout in Hollywood was such that he could recruit top stars to entertain at the school's annual alumni banquets, held at the Chicago Hilton, including Bob Hope, Hildegarde, Pat O'Brien, Debra Paget, and Morey Amsterdam. Connolly himself would act as toastmaster. "The alumni who attended these banquets still talk about them," noted the director of alumni relations. "And keep in mind that the price of admission to the banquet was a mere six dollars then."[20]

Upon graduation there was no money for college, so Connolly went to work for a travel agency, Powers Tours, in downtown Chicago for three years. In 1932, he took and passed a Civil Service examination for a junior typist position but opted to stay at Powers rather than accept the government job. His choice of which college to attend appears to have been in flux. He asked De La Salle to send his transcript to DePaul University in 1933, but ended up waiting another year to start at the University of Illinois.[21]

At Powers, his responsibilities were "arranging itineraries to all parts of the world for vacationists, office work (mail, etc.), writing copy for travel ads and folders, and conducting tours." He may have found the job through De La Salle, since the school's policy was to secure initial positions for its graduates. Cohen and Taylor report that De La Salle's founding premise was to counteract its students' economic disadvantages by giving them the business skills necessary to succeed in the world. The job placements were accomplished, they note, thanks to a remarkable Irish Catholic network of business contacts.[22]

Powers Tours provided Connolly with enough spending money, on top of what he was saving for college, to keep abreast of the lively arts. Some of the musical shows he saw during his three years between high school and college left a vivid impression with him, especially *Walk a Little Faster*, which he said contained the funniest scene in his theater-going experience: Beatrice Lillie's picking her skirts up, following a very serious speech, and roller-skating off the stage. He also loved watching the Clifton Webb–Libby Holman dance numbers in *The Little Show*.[23]

In fact, Connolly's tastes had long since matured from Saturday matinees to musical theater. In November 1929, when he was sixteen, he attended *Hit the Deck* at the Woods Theater. Although Queenie Smith and Charley King were the romantic leads, Connolly was "knocked out of [my] seat" by Trixie Friganza when she sang her big number, *Hallelujah!* He said he fell in love with her and never recovered.[24]

Connolly's fervently held religious beliefs, as expressed in his high school editorials, would eventually fall away. Bunny Seidman said Connolly styled himself a "professional Catholic," by which he meant someone who goes through the motions. "He never went to church on Sunday," she said. "He never went to confession. But he did like to hobnob with Hollywood's Catholic bigwigs at the annual Communion Breakfast for Catholics in the movies. He wanted people to think he was devout." James DeCloss recalled, "Mike thought the Church was a beautiful institution, but he wasn't a believer."[25]

"It's hell to be Irish and Roman Catholic at the same time," he would write, "but it's heavenly too." If Connolly lapsed as a Catholic, his Irish heritage was ultimately a firmer touchstone in his life than his church; he never ceased to be a practicing Irishman. Perhaps the every-day occurrence of Irish items in his Hollywood columns was a function of being free to proclaim his Irishness if not his homosexuality. Singer Gogi Grant was slated to dub Ann Blyth's voice in *The Jazz Age*, but Blyth, he warned, "has her Irish up and is insisting on doing her own singing as Helen Morgan.... And we always bet on the Irish!" He lauded the city of Dublin's election of a Jewish Lord Mayor as a harbinger of world peace. "Leave it to the straightforward, straight-shooting, straight-from-the-shoulder Irish," he exulted. "They don't sit around making idle cocktail chatter about improving interfaith relations, they go right ahead and do it by electing a Jewish Mayor."[26]

If he defended Irish culture, he could laugh at it as well. "Do yourself a favor," he urged, "and read Ed O'Connor's *The Last Hurrah*, a merciless expose of Irish-Americans by one of them. So funny in spots you'll bust a gut." Rumors from a shooting location in the Emerald Isle prompted him to write, "[Director] John Ford should hear what the locals think about him in Galway, where he shot *The Quiet Man*. Even the Irish can't match his profanity!"[27]

Connolly maintained a lifelong passion for Irish literature and would become an expert on James Joyce. Inclined to launch into literary discourses at unlikely places and times (e.g., the Sands lounge at four a.m.), he would often share with laureate drinking companions such as Clifford Odets or Paul Horgan his theories of what Joyce really meant. For example, he was certain the Joyce scholars were all wet when they interpreted the inscrutable *michemiche* from *Finnegans Wake* as a term meaning to pilfer or to skulk, or even (in French slang) derriere. *Michemiche*, Connolly believed, was the same as "Musha, musha" (rhymes with bush), a term of sorrow in his mother's everyday conversation. His imitations of her brogue often included the expression, as in, "Musha, musha, poor Mrs. Kelly just died, and now Mr. Kelly is burthened with bringin' up the foive childerrrn widout a mither." "Musha, musha" was only one of countless Irish expressions that he absorbed across the dinner table during his parents' conversations about their native Ireland. If a scholar were not Irish, Connolly held, he could not possibly comprehend all the glories of the Joycean canon.[28]

Fundraising appeals in Hollywood in the nineteen-fifties for a museum at the Statue of Liberty were met with such indifference that Connolly was moved to chide the industry. "When one reflects," he wrote, "that we have [in Hollywood] so many immigrants and first-generation

Americans in our midst for whom America has proved a dream come true, one would think they [would support the museum]. Alas and alack, they haven't."[29]

Despite the absence of rebellion or discontent in the written documentation Connolly left of his youth, his faith in the Catholic Church was insufficient to make him happy with his lot in life, because faith by itself had not placed him within the mainstream. He was not content to be on the outside looking in at "normal" men who made all the decisions and rules and laws. A rage seemed to simmer within him, but it never manifested in the typical ways that adolescents and young adults act out their grievances against the world. His rage would show itself instead in his utter incapacity to live and let live.

He did not believe in psychotherapy and, as with the issue of alcohol abuse, he was not given to introspection, so he left behind almost no explicit clues as to what made him tick. The closest thing is a cache of letters he wrote from 1956 to 1962 to Richard M. Nixon, on whom he projected all of his fantasies of the kind of man he wished he were. Connolly knew Nixon and his wife, Pat, from Southern California Republican fundraisers, and would report verbatim even the most trivial small talk the Nixons made in his direction. "I wish," Vice President Nixon said to Connolly in 1955, "there were some way of having more people read the *Hollywood Reporter* than those scandal magazines!"[30]

The letters to Nixon began right after Connolly attended the Republican National Convention in 1956, where he cheered the renomination of the Eisenhower-Nixon team for a second term; he congratulated Nixon, begged to be of assistance in the campaign, and repeated some of the plugs he was making for the GOP ticket in his column. Given that Connolly was consistently astute in recognizing son-in-search-of-father themes in the gamut of the world's great literature, it is surprising that he seemed unaware that the same syndrome lay behind his pursuit of Nixon's favor.[31] (Nixon was only six months older than Connolly.)

The event that really opened the floodgates of Connolly's heart was Nixon's famous "kitchen debate" with Soviet Premier Khrushchev in July 1959, at an American exhibition in Moscow of a model ranch house, in which the vice president and Khrushchev squared off in an unscheduled verbal joust on consumer choice in the two countries. In a letter written the following month, Connolly confessed that what he had always loved about the Nixons was their quintessential American-ness and how their integrity and courage had shone through to all peoples of the world. Surely, he said, other nations could not fail to recognize the Nixons' inherent goodness, and out of that understanding would come the seeds of world peace. He went so far as to assert the Nixons' diplomatic excursion had saved the planet from World War Three, a milestone in pacifism for which he was glad.[32]

Connolly began writing birthday letters to Nixon every January; these are the most naked extant expressions of Connolly's feelings (and studded uncharacteristically with typographical errors, too, a probable indication of being composed after a few martinis). They were love letters, in a way; although they did not express direct love for Nixon, the words "love" and "heart" kept popping up. In one missive he spelled out in great detail the contrasts between himself and Nixon; his envy was palpable as he emphasized his Chicago roots and dyed-in-the-wool Democrat origins; his Roman Catholic schooling and strivings to live a good Catholic life; and his "conversion" to the good life in Southern California and the Republican Party, stressing that he had voted twice for Eisenhower. Taken together with his previous gushing letter about Nixon's majestic American-ness, this letter is Connolly's definitive self-expression.[33]

Soon after Nixon lost the 1960 presidential race to John F. Kennedy, Connolly clipped from *Time* magazine a grinning, surprisingly good-looking photo of Nixon and taped it to another birthday letter he was writing. He implied Nixon's tense performance during the debates with Kennedy had cost him the election, and he was angry that the genuine and genial Nixon he knew had not been seen by the country. Mustering his courage, he reminded Nixon of his many years of show business experience and asked if he could offer a suggestion next time they were together on how Nixon could come across better on the medium of television.[34]

Nixon's replies to Connolly's letters were unfailingly polite but highly impersonal, and sent, of course, by a correspondence-handling staff. Invariably they closed by affirming that Pat joined him in sending whatever the good wish of the occasion was. The biggest contrast in the letters of the two men is that Connolly was never free to reply in kind with "Joe joins me in sending you our best wishes."

Nixon probably never saw Connolly's letters. Fortunately, his staff saved them, and from them one can understand the Waspish aspirations of Connolly's heart. That he was a first-generation Irish Catholic working-class homosexual instead of an influential Anglo-Saxon heterosexual was the font of his rage. The first major outbreak of this rage came in his campaign to close down houses of prostitution in his university town of Champaign, Illinois; later it would recur in even more virulent form when there were Communists to be tarred and feathered in Hollywood.

Chapter 5

Battler for Chastity

"Prostitution won't be forgotten as long as one of
those houses is open."
> — *Mike Connolly, Daily Illini, Oct. 28,*
> *1937*

"If there is only one communist working in Hollywood, there is one too many."
> — *Mike Connolly, Hollywood Reporter,*
> *Feb. 20, 1952*

Arriving in Champaign-Urbana for his freshman year at the University of Illinois, Connolly was hired as private secretary to the eminent
Father John A. O'Brien, director of the campus Newman Center and pas-
tor and chaplain to the university's Catholic population, for fifteen dollars per week and room and board at St. John's Catholic Chapel. That
O'Brien would hire Connolly as a freshman bespeaks the favorable impression Connolly made as an upstanding and bright Catholic youth. O'Brien,
in the introduction to *Where Dwellest Thou?*— his anthology of stories of
conversion to the Catholic faith that included Lillian Roth's— noted that
he had felt "a thrill of joy" when he discovered that Roth's co-author on
I'll Cry Tomorrow "was [my] student secretary of years ago."[1]

"Father O'Brien was a man of charisma, charm, compassion, and
understanding, combined with fire and brimstone," recalls Connolly's
friend Mary-jane Ryan. Another friend, Hallie Rives, remembers O'Brien's

"big, booming voice during hymn singing." O'Brien asked students to call him "Father John."[2]

Aside from Connolly's general classwork and journalistic pursuits, most of his time at the university was spent in Catholic-oriented activities. He joined the local chapter of Phi Kappa, the national Catholic social fraternity. He enjoyed inviting non–Catholic friends such as Ryan and Rives to Sunday night suppers and programs at the Newman Center. "I remember Mike as a surprisingly devout Catholic," says Ryan. "He went to Mass regularly. Father O'Brien adored Mike. You could see it at these gatherings. Mike was a protegé. He was Peck's Bad Boy — wherever he was, there was action."[3]

As secretary to O'Brien, responsible for typing all of the priest's correspondence, Connolly was privy to the staggering amount of debt outstanding on the construction of the Newman Center and St. John's Chapel, operations undertaken and overseen by O'Brien. A year after Connolly graduated, in fact, O'Brien's bishop, who abhorred debt during those Depression years, forced O'Brien to resign and forbade him to say Mass or remain overnight in the diocese. Luckily, Notre Dame University was delighted to recruit O'Brien to its faculty, where he remained from 1940 until his death in 1980.[4]

Winton Solberg, professor emeritus at the University of Illinois, says, "I have no doubt that O'Brien exerted a strong influence on Connolly, because he did on generations of students. O'Brien was the Fulton Sheen of his day. He was a man ahead of his time and paid a price for it." Some of the issues on which O'Brien was out in front of the church were birth control and alternatives to sacerdotal celibacy. He was the first in a long series of larger-than-life Catholic figures with whom Connolly would form alliances. His life and example were the principal influences on Connolly's world view during his college years.[5]

The determination to be a reporter Connolly had shown at De La Salle Institute had not been a passing fancy; he enrolled in the School of Liberal Arts and Sciences as a journalism major. "You took liberal arts your first two years and then you entered journalism school — although you were already a 'campus reporter' for the *Daily Illini* as a freshman," said Mary-jane Ryan. "The journalism school was an entity unto itself. There were one hundred-fifty of us out of a student body of eleven thousand. It was not a great journalism school, although we thought it was at the time. We had an inadequate dean."[6]

Most of Connolly's friends were fellow journalists-in-embryo, who, like Ryan and Rives, had become acquainted as freshmen. "You worked your heart out until two a.m., and then you went out with everybody," said Ryan. "Dating was a sort of group affair at the time. Mike was a heavy drinker, but he was also thoughtful, courtly, sensitive, and caring." Connolly's take on himself was that he was "remarkably easy to get along with."[7]

"I knew Mike as a fellow student and wacko," said Hallie Rives. "I was dazzled by him — the first true free spirit I ever met, which I liked, because I hated the hypocrisy around me. People thought of Mike as a con, but he wasn't. He was just a good guy. He was exploring life in every possible way. I stood aside and just watched him go. He was a deeply layered person, while the rest of us were just black-and-white. We were more than friends; we were family. We neglected our other studies to put out that *Daily Illini*."[8]

Many other college friends of Connolly would also go on to achieve varying degrees of fame. Lou Boudreau, who together with Connolly founded a "Blue Pencil" honor society, played professional baseball and later managed the Cleveland Indians. Sam Abarbanel, who hit Connolly in the face with a heaved tomato at a raucous student gathering, became a press agent in Hollywood. Larry Parks became a prominent film actor and husband of actress Betty Garrett, but would find his career derailed because of youthful Communist affiliations.[9]

No history of homosexual Illinois students from that era has been written, and what if anything Connolly knew and acted upon is unknown. Although Mary-jane Ryan assumes there were gay male students on campus in her day, she had no knowledge of any. She was, however, aware of several lesbians. "Mike's sexual orientation didn't emerge until later," she pointed out. "I don't think it was known at the university. I was in that inner circle and I would have heard it — not that it would have made any difference to me."[10]

Hallie Rives echoes Ryan's recollections: "My daddy was an ob-gyn and straightened us out on sex as children, to prepare us for the kinds of people we'd meet. So, the first time I ran into a lesbian, in our dormitory's laundry room, I knew what was going on." But Rives, too, denied knowledge of male homosexuals on campus. She did say Connolly "was so honest that it was startling to people. It's too personal to give an example, but it had to do with teens' sexual lives." She often heard wild stories about Connolly, involving students and faculty alike, but refused to elaborate. Asked if Connolly ever had a girlfriend, she said, "Mike was not anyone's boyfriend. He never pinned anyone — he would never have done that."[11]

Rives did remember that at Newman Center events, "Mike used to pass the collection plate and sing, 'Oh, Lord, I'm Not Worthy,' with this merry, wicked face. I wondered if he was telling us something about his prior evening. He'd put the double entendre on things. Mike was a faithful,

Mike Connolly as a student on the University of Illinois campus. "Note the ever-present cigarette," remarked his friend and fellow *Daily Illini* reporter Mary-jane Ryan. "Once, by accident, he flipped a cigarette down the front of my dress." (Collection of Mary-jane Ryan Snyder)

attending Catholic. He'd make sacrifices to serve — even if he'd been hell-raising the night before."[12]

Showing anything less than ironclad discretion about his homosexuality while at the university could have worked against Connolly in at least two significant ways. First, it could have dismantled the structure of his Catholic-oriented campus life; he likely would have been bounced from both Phi Kappa and his quarters in St. John's Chapel. Second, it would have given his enemies in the city of Champaign, from shady operators of bawdy houses to the police, ammunition to discredit his articles during the high-profile anti-prostitution campaign of his senior year.

Nonetheless, a gay sensibility sometimes peeked out of his writings for the *Daily Illini*. In his "Talk of the Town" column, he reported the local post office had successfully delivered an envelope that bore no name or address, only directions. "One of these days," he joked, "I'm going to address an envelope to 'America's Sweetheart' [with no other information given] ... and pray they don't deliver it to Robert Taylor." He did use the word "gay" several times in its traditional connotation, showing that he had not come to fear it as incriminating or pejorative. (His later Hollywood columns never used "gay.")[13]

At the end of his junior year, Connolly hoped to be picked as managing editor of the *Daily Illini*. "He really wanted that job," said Mary-jane Ryan. "I remember staying up all night at the end of our junior year, waiting for the *Illini* Board of Control to announce their elections." But the job went to another journalism student, Jack Mabley. Connolly was appointed city editor instead. "That assignment was astonishing to Champaign and to Mike," recalled Angus Thuermer, another journalism major. "Mike had been a campus reporter before that, covering campus theater and other things. No one expected that his assignment would shift like that."[14]

The *Daily Illini's* memorable crusade to close down Champaign's numerous houses of prostitution was the defining event of Connolly's journalistic life. Both contemporary and retrospective accounts treat the crusade as if it suddenly sprang up in the fall semester of 1937. In truth, it began even before Connolly first set foot on the campus as a freshman. "The Walnut Street district," he would point out, "has been the butt of many a joke for years. My own mother knew about Walnut Street long before I came to school. A neighbor of ours and her son came down here to live on First Street when the son started to school. She used to tell my mother about walking past the bawdy houses when she went walking in the afternoon."[15]

Typically, "everyone took [the brothels] for granted," said Jack

Mabley. But that was before anyone had reckoned with Mike Connolly. He seems to have regarded the houses with a combination of fascination and loathing from his first awareness of them, but he would have to wait for his senior year to get the green light to pursue the issue. "We wanted the last two editors to start just such a campaign against these conditions which have been getting freer and more disgusting every year since I was a freshman," city editor Connolly explained. He revealed he had been conspiring with the Champaign Ministerial Association — to which his liaison would have been the Reverend O'Brien — and other civic groups on this objective for four years.[16]

Even if his upperclassmen superiors would put neither significant manpower nor editorial policy behind Connolly's anti-vice mission, they okayed a brazen scheme he proposed while only a sophomore: Rather than rely on fraternity house gossip, he would go personally to the dens of iniquity to conduct his own fact-finding tour. Mabley said Connolly's "streetwise" appearance was a natural advantage: "He looked like an investigative reporter — tough, like a detective."[17]

The details of one of Connolly's forays into the tents of wickedness were published in an unbylined article on May 1, 1936. He wrote that he had been sitting in a whorehouse parlor, sharing sections of a newspaper with the madam, who was "evidently not appreciating our visit." After a student customer dropped an ashtray, the madam suddenly waxed loquacious about students who stole bric-a-brac and even furniture from the joint, which she suspected would later turn up in fraternity houses. But then she remembered that "we were just loafers," and turned silent again, Connolly wrote. "So we left."[18]

For the crusade he envisioned, Connolly had the perfect foil in Jack Mabley. If not particularly religious, Mabley was nonetheless a defender of traditional proprieties and somewhat prim. He would be the rational counterpart to Connolly's histrionics. "A lot of students patronized the houses," Mabley recalled. "That's why we went after them. Mike and I talked it over, and that was it. The campaign was all Mike's. I never went to the houses. I editorialized. He made all the visits, wrote all the stories. He was comfortable in investigating."[19]

When Connolly returned to campus as a senior in the fall of 1937, his first liberty was to rename the city editor's column, traditionally called "Town Talk," to "Talk of the Town." (He claimed to make the change in honor of a tavern in Peoria by that name, but more likely he fancied himself a writer for the column of the same name in the *New Yorker*, which he was already toting conspicuously around campus.) His beat comprised the municipal goings-on in Champaign and Urbana. On the new job less than two weeks, he began to drop hints of the *blitzkrieg* to come. One small item asked, "What well-known madam in what well-known house of prostitution owns a car which she sends around to pick up prospective customers?" Another tattled that certain local cab drivers were getting a "rakeoff" for bringing carloads of students to the Walnut Street district.[20]

But with no more warning than that, the *Daily Illini* detonated its initial bombshell with "a short study of [local] gambling and prostitution" in Mabley's editorial column of October 13, 1937. Champaign, Mabley charged, was "the seat of one of the most disgraceful vice conditions existing in the nation today." Connolly's "Talk of the Town" column flanked Mabley's blast with an imagined dialogue between a student reporter and a city official, in which they rehashed the clichéd excuses for not cleaning up the town.

The Connolly-Mabley strategy was ingenious. Realizing that the university was the key to forcing Champaign to take action, they first attacked its long-term complacency in the face of gambling and prostitution operations so close to campus. Once they had shamed the university into mobilization, they would then turn up the heat on lethargic city officials and owners of the Walnut Street district properties who stood to be hurt by publicity.

The frontal assault had exactly the effect Connolly and Mabley envisioned. Mary-jane Ryan said, "All hell broke loose when those columns were printed. It's what everyone on campus was talking about." Stung by the ensuing uproar, the university directed its legal counsel, a former judge named Johnson, to write an indignant letter to the *Illini*, pointing out that the school had no legal authority to enforce the criminal statutes either of Champaign or the state of Illinois. To Mabley's suggestion that the university appropriate a few hundred dollars to ridding the city of vice, Johnson countered, "If four hundred or five hundred be all that is needed to clean up this community, it is incredible that the city of Champaign cannot find this amount. The governing authorities of Champaign have the power and it is their duty to correct the conditions you describe, if they in fact exist."[21]

Mabley's next editorial hit even harder than the first. "Is or is not the university responsible for the welfare of the student body?" he asked. Citing obvious examples of its longstanding regulation of student behavior (e.g., restrictions on automobile use or loitering on campus after dark), he stated that the university was Champaign's principal citizen and chief industry, bringing the city million of dollars each year; why could it not insist that the city enforce the law?[22]

Connolly's column that same day chortled at Judge Johnson's professed skepticism toward the existence of a commercial sex industry in Champaign. He charged that the town's "vice lords" were vassals of a larger "white slave syndicate," and that the "girls sent down from Chicago" were not good-looking because college town customers "aren't particularly choosy." Quoting a U.S. Public Health Service statement that commercial prostitution could only exist where public opinion consented to it, he concluded with, "How about it, public?"[23]

Throughout the week, Connolly kept up the barrage, challenging Judge Johnson, members of the student senate, and "any other skeptics" to allow him to escort them to the red light district "any night of the week." In what sounded like a Starr Report of its day, Connolly described "strip tease dances going on in the windows of the houses that would make Gypsy Rose Lee blush with envy," houses that would sell beer to students "long after every licensed tavern is closed," and the carelessness of whores "after they've had a few beers themselves."[24]

At this point, Connolly and Mabley got an unanticipated windfall: The wire services grabbed their story. Suddenly, newspapers all over Illinois and in neighboring states were playing up the news of the *Daily Illini's* struggle to wipe out vice. "We hadn't figured that the story would make such good copy for the outside papers," Mabley commented.[25]

Things fell into place all at once. The student senate endorsed the anti-vice drive and voted to create an investigative committee. On October 22, university president A. C. Willard convened a meeting with the mayors and police chiefs of Champaign and Urbana and the county sheriff, demanding that they close all houses of prostitution. President Willard also warned that any student caught in a police raid on a bawdy house would be expelled. In less than ten days, Connolly and Mabley had wrestled the university into submission.[26]

An October 23 *Chicago Tribune* article on the "student paper's anti-syphilis fight" quoted Connolly's statement that venereal disease statistics were the prime motivation behind the campaign. It said a U.S. Public Health Service surgeon had completed a survey of conditions in Champaign, and that "Connolly was of the opinion that [the surgeon's] survey substantiated the one he made himself in amassing material for his assault on vice."[27]

Next on the *Illini's* agenda was a three-article series on local whorehouses, which, although it had no byline, was Connolly's. The profiles were of a piece with his May 1936 report from the trenches, except that after the university's edict he could have been expelled had he been caught anywhere near the Walnut Street district. He described three different houses in great detail, from the tunes playing on the nickelodeons to "gaudy" pink and blue walls and "cheap Axminster-type" rugs. When two students got into a fight over a domino game, a madam quipped, "This isn't a gambling joint; it's a decent, respectable bawdy house," which got a big laugh from the hormone-addled customers gathered around.

Connolly quoted another madam as saying, "We had three extra girls down from Chicago for the police convention." Such an assertion would have added considerably to the growing antipathy held toward the *Daily Illini* by the Champaign police. "The *Illini* was a morning paper, three hundred and sixty-five days a year," notes Mabley. "So the city was interested [in what we printed]. Our circulation exceeded that of the *Daily Gazette*, but not the *Champaign-Urbana Courier*. Those were both afternoon papers."[28]

The *Illini* began publishing a daily front page honor roll of campus and municipal organizations pledged to support the "battle to remove the stigma of the red light from Champaign." Among the early groups on the list were Phi Kappa (Connolly's fraternity) and Father O'Brien's Newman Foundation.[29]

The initial euphoria of committing the university lock, stock, and printing press to the fumigation of Champaign began to ebb somewhat when the *Illini* realized that, despite a police raid or two that netted a few miscreant fraternity boys, all fourteen houses of prostitution continued to do brisk business. "Still no action," grumbled Mabley on October 27, attributing Champaign's refusal to clean up to "too many officials and prominent citizens up to their necks in this business." Connolly decided it was time to turn up the heat on the owners and operators of the houses. Throwing down the gauntlet on October 28, he wrote, "The men who are fighting for the vice racket are beginning to find this isn't just another crusade. This one has a lot of foundation — and they are beginning to feel it." He advised readers to "take careful note" that certain landlords in the city were the major figures in the silent opposition to closing the houses.[30]

"Again last night," wrote Mabley on October 29, "the Walnut Street district was running in full blast." Reprinting in full the Illinois statute prohibiting leasing of premises for prostitution, Mabley resorted to "a mild form of blackmail" by promising not to print names of owners of the brothels "if the houses are closed by Sunday [October 31]." This tactic seemed to be effective. On November 3, the *Daily Illini* announced formally that it was suspending its cleanup campaign, because as to outward appearances, the bawdy houses had been shuttered en masse. However, the student newspaper suspected the houses were merely "playing possum while the heat is on" and said it would discontinue its campaign "temporarily" until it got word that they were reopening. Connolly reminded whomever it may have concerned that he was holding the *Illini's* "yet unpublished list of property owners, real, not alleged" like a sword over their heads.[31]

Finally, on November 17, the *Daily Illini* announced with astounding youthful chutzpah that it had called off the dogs. "They are now all closed," editorialized Mabley. "They really are, yet ... there are many, many doubters.... I ask that anyone questioning that statement please see me and personally point out any bawdy house that is open for business. And I will guarantee that immediate action will be taken, and that house will be closed."[32]

In a month's time, then, Connolly and Mabley had mobilized a complacent university administration and brought organized vice in Champaign to heel. "Of course, it was a piece of cake to knock them over," Mabley reminisced decades later. For the remainder of the school year, there were scattered reports of quiet reopenings of sundry bordellos, but the Champaign police force's newfound alacrity in conducting raids seemed to hold at bay Connolly's incriminating list of property owners. During spring semester 1938, Connolly began a new effort to beat back gambling joints that were thriving locally. He held that "by raising cane [*sic*] about gambling we are hitting the remaining bawdy houses.... We're not going to let it drop."[33]

A recurring rumor in connection with the bawdy house campaign is that under Connolly's supervision, a female student reporter pretending to be looking for a "job" called a madam in the Walnut Street district. After being "hired" sight unseen over the telephone, the student wrote a detailed article about the experience in the *Daily Illini*. Mabley downplays the story. "I didn't know about it, and I knew everything that went on," he said. "I suppose it's possible Mike might have had a female make a call, but that's all. I knew every girl on the staff. It was like family."[34]

The "Chicago syndicate" attacked by Connolly throughout the school year was not a figment of his imagination. Like all native Chicagoans, he (and Mabley, too) grew up within earshot of organized crime and gang warfare, fully cognizant of the entrenched alliance between the Windy City's underworld, politicians, and police. "We well remember a day back in the '30s," he later wrote, "when [Roger] Touhy [a second-tier bootlegger] said he'd kill Jake 'The Barber' Factor if he ever got sprung."[35]

There did seem to be an inherent and foreseeable risk in the *Illini* crusaders' determination to upset the longstanding impunity and profitability of local sin shops. On October 27, Mabley, who lived in a fraternity house, alluded to his personal safety by writing, not entirely in jest, "My roommate is moving out on account of his health, and every time a package comes to the house, the brothers put their ears to it to see if it ticks."

The syndicate, however, perceived not Mabley but Connolly as the serious impediment to their ability to conduct business. Back in Chicago, a delegation of five "underworld characters" appeared at the Connolly family home and warned Margaret Connolly that her son "had put his life on the line" and would be smart to cease interfering with their operations. "I wasn't at home at the time," Tom Connolly recounts, "but my mother was so shaken when I saw her that it was clear something very frightening had happened." He says his brother did not let up in the campaign despite his parents' pleading.[36]

Connolly never acknowledged any threats in anything he wrote for the *Daily Illini*. His colleagues at the newspaper seem to have known of the dangers, however. Hallie Rives said, "He did some dangerous stuff covering the red light district. I was concerned; I thought he'd end up dead. He blazed into places the rest of us feared to tread."[37]

Luckily for the Connolly family, no harm came to any of them. To the contrary, Connolly claimed his mother was "tickled to death to hear about the houses being driven out. She doesn't particularly relish the *[Chicago] Tribune's* statement that I personally visited the fourteen houses of prostitution in Champaign to gather evidence, but she, like many others, is glad they are being driven out."[38]

Mabley said neither he nor his family received threats. "The sheriff of Urbana County did advise me to carry a gun," he says. "We always closed the *Illini* offices at two a.m. and I'd walk home. But I never carried a gun. Once I was at the police station and some menacing-looking characters were outside, seeming to be waiting for me. I called the *Illini* office and asked them to send reinforcements. Finally — it was the funniest thing — they sent Dudley McAllister, a scrawny little guy. Luckily, nothing happened to us."[39]

Connolly's exit from Champaign-Urbana was as overwrought as his anti-vice crusade. The single common thread in the various versions of this tale is its context of inebriated pre-graduation revelry. Some sources say he was arrested; some say he threw the police off his trail. The trauma of the experience was sufficient to keep Connolly off the campus for two decades. On the eve of his belated return, in 1956, the *Champaign-Urbana Courier* profiled him, noting, "He was jailed by Champaign police when a report reached them saying Connolly had been seen running around the campus without his trousers." A letter Connolly wrote to the alumni association at the same time claimed, "It will be my first visit to the campus since I got arrested for driving down the Broadwalk blind drunk!" (This was probably a red herring; the campus Broadwalk was never an auto-mobile thoroughfare, said Mary-jane Ryan.)[40]

Angus Thuermer, Connolly's *Daily Illini* colleague, remembered, "I was called in by the assistant dean of men and asked about the festivities on Wright Street the night before [even though I wasn't there]. Mike was observed by the police running in a race *sans culotte*. I did not know whether to be offended or complimented when the dean told me he called me in because 'I thought you would know about things like that.'"[41]

Decades later, Mabley, in a column about the 1970s streaking craze, wrote that the University of Illinois ought to get credit for the first streak-ing down a college street, thanks to Connolly in 1938: "Mike was a thorn in the sides of the police because he kept exposing their shortcomings. They couldn't catch up with him that night but they did swear out a war-rant for his arrest [and were watching for him at the Champaign train sta-tion]. This was just before graduation, and Mike did not join us at the beautiful commencement ceremonies. He sneaked out of town and caught the Illinois Central at Rantoul, a fugitive from the campus he loved…. He had more motivation for speed than today's streakers…. If the Champaign cops had caught up with Mike he'd have gotten one to ten years in prison." This experience was the foundation of Connolly's lifelong disdain for police.[42]

The drive to shut down the town's whorehouses was Connolly's legacy to his university and Champaign; it was a task he had set his sights on and worked for four years singlemindedly to achieve. Certainly it set the stage for the persecution of Communists that he would later consider his supreme accomplishment in Hollywood. Concerns over prostitution would shortly be crowded off Champaign's horizon by far graver considerations of world war; hence few if any took the time to analyze what Connolly had done, and why he had spent so much energy stirring up a situation that had simply been taken for granted by so many previous graduating classes.

Putting aside the rhetoric and hysteria, one sees that Connolly never produced evidence that the "problem" of the bawdy houses had become "worse" than before (aside from his saying it was). His appeal to "statis-tics" was utterly unsophisticated; he did not show that Champaign-Urbana's rate of venereal disease, such as it was, had increased during his college years. Nor did he offer any breakdown of the circumstances under which venereal disease was transmitted in the twin cities, which would have required, of course, the acknowledgment that heterosexual transmission was only one avenue of contagion. What becomes clear is simply that the houses' existence troubled Connolly more than they had troubled previous university students, and he recognized an opportunity in the situation and persuaded Mabley to join him in it.

It was a situation ripe for demagoguery, and Connolly's natural flair for public agitation was polished to brilliance in his year-long crusade. Techniques of inciting or shaming masses into herd-like behavior were widely employed in the 1930s, and Americans themselves seemed more susceptible than in other eras to the persuasion of demagogues. In Hollywood, the censorial Production Code was put into place in 1934 after legions of Catholic priests and Protestant ministers whipped up hysteria among their flocks, convincing them that Hollywood's Jews were purveying immoral material in talking pictures. Connolly's own crusade was contemporary with the zenith of the great rabble-rousers Father Coughlin and Gerald L. K. Smith. In such an era and climate, it is no wonder that forcing the closure of a baker's dozen of hapless whorehouses was a "piece of cake."[43]

The lessons Connolly learned would serve him well in Hollywood, where Communists would be bigger fish to fry. "One method of crusading, I've found, is to deliver sermons in print ... the other is to print facts," he wrote as the end of his senior year approached. "And I'm not sure but that the latter isn't the more effective way." He did print facts, but the reasoning with which he strung them together was often fallacious. In a classic *argumentum ad verecundiam*, he proclaimed, "I know that the houses are going to be closed — and kept closed! Because President Willard demanded it." Willard must have scratched his head to read this statement, as well he might have the previous day, when Connolly admonished "backsliding" campus organizations that they still had time to sign on to "President Willard's campaign." In a clever projection, Connolly had copped the ultimate endorsement in Champaign through what amounted to blackmail.[44]

Another Connolly mannerism was to engage in puzzling semantic quibbles. Just as the Walnut Street offensive began to heat up, he wrote to a reader, "Please don't accuse us of having a campaign. The *Illini* is not a law enforcement organization." A day later he again protested, "We are not having a campaign, merely calling attention of citizens to a number of things that we KNOW are going on." But Mabley inadvertently contradicted his co-conspirator by calling the campaign a campaign several times in the same week. Before long, Connolly himself was dishing the term with abandon in his own column.[45]

Clues to the ultimate motivation behind Connolly's campaign lie in his rhetoric. It was evangelical and rapturous, even a vengeance aria: "IT CAN BE DONE! IT WILL BE DONE! ORGANIZED PROSTITUTION AND

ITS VILE HANDMAIDENS, SYPHILIS AND GONORRHEA, WILL BE
DEALT A DEATH BLOW BY THE LEADING CITIZENS OF CHAMPAIGN
AND URBANA!" His metaphors of victory and transfiguration translate
as, "Have I proved I'm a man yet?"[46]

Finally, the relationship of Connolly's homosexuality to the enmity
he felt toward bawdy houses must be considered. Throughout human history, in order to break down the power of a majority or monopoly, a minor-
ity has had to recognize and exploit some vehicle that the majority has
ignored or wants to delegate. Before Connolly's arrival in Champaign, the
bawdy houses were ignored by the university and community, and an
appropriate disciplinary policy toward students caught in occasional raids
was in place. It was a situation that Connolly realized he could exploit to
make himself someone to be reckoned with — as important as his heterosexual colleagues.

Caught up in his reportorial bluster, Connolly seemed clueless about
the heterosexual reproductive urges at the root of the local commercial sex
industry — despite having quoted one trollop as saying, "The fellows don't
start coming up until later, usually, when ... they take their dates home."
In an era when college women tended by and large to keep their knees
together, they were dropped off before curfew while their dates were left
feeling aroused and seeking release. Connolly's choice of adjectives whenever he referred to the houses—"vile," "ulcerous"— or to the "animal urges"
that students visited the houses to satisfy — revealed a disconnect between
him and the manifestations of opposite-sex attraction.[47]

Having avoided or missed out on the standard varieties of male ado-
lescent initiation rites, Connolly envisioned a personal smelling tour of the
Walnut Street district as a badge of courage. Certainly it did take courage
to make these visits, yet it was not a means to demonstrate courage likely
to be selected by a heterosexual male. Nor was Connolly qualified to make
field visits to whorehouses as a sex researcher or sociologist; bravado was
his only credential. Nor did his articles reporting his visits add anything
beyond extra color to the campaign. Destroying brothels as a means of
bringing home his first scalp was, ironically, the gayest thing Connolly
could have done.[48]

Chapter 6

Nose for News

"Good old Chicago. Visiting exhibitor told Bob
Raison, 'Gee, I miss Chicago.' Said Bob, 'I miss it,
too, every chance I get.'"
— *Mike Connolly, Hollywood Reporter,*
June 23, 1953

The bleak sum of eighteen dollars per week was the top salary a cub
reporter could expect to make in Chicago in 1938. Faced with such inaus-
picious prospects after college graduation, Connolly retreated to the security he had known at Powers Tours, where he could make forty-five per
week. He led tours to Canada in the summers of 1938 and 1940 and to Mexico and Guatemala in October 1941 for the opening of bullfighting season.
Stateside, he guided groups to Alaska, Yellowstone and Glacier national
parks, and to each of the forty-eight states. One of his favorite missions
was the New York World's Fair of 1939–1940, where his group attended a
fairgrounds staging of *The Hot Mikado*, starring the great Bill "Bojangles"
Robinson. New York nightclubs would make deals with Connolly to detour
off the well-beaten tourist circuits and bring his groups to their establishments.[1]

Thus began Connolly's acquaintance with the wonders of Manhattan: his memories of the city on the eve of World War II included *Pal Joey*
(which he saw several times), "Swing Street" on East Fifty-second Street,
and cabaret singer Mae Barnes, a regular performer at the Bon Soir. His
long sojourn (1931–1942) in the travel business made him into a cos-
mopolitan young man; it would even provoke future nostalgic outbursts.

"We'd like to be the travel agent who handles [20th Century–Fox chief] Spyros Skouras' one hundred thousand air miles per year," he wrote.[2]

From the relative safety of Chicago, Connolly kept tabs on the resurgence of the red light district situation in Champaign, which he had pursued only a year earlier. In February 1939, a madam shot and killed a University of Illinois fraternity boy who had broken her front window. The murder set off an unprecedented state of agitation on campus, and a special prosecutor convened a grand jury to investigate malfeasance in office of the mayor and other city officials. Although Connolly's managing editor Jack Mabley was compelled to testify in Champaign on March 3, 1939, Connolly somehow managed to avoid being subpoenaed. Years later, Mabley said, "I told them everything I knew, which wasn't much because I had been the outside man, supplying planning and editorial indignation. [But] the inside man was Mike. Petty police vendettas can obstruct justice, at least in Champaign. Mike couldn't return to Champaign because they had a warrant for his arrest because he had evaded them."[3]

The expanding theater of war in Europe and the new Selective Training and Service Act of September 16, 1940, mandating peacetime conscription for the first time, confronted Connolly as they did all men between the ages of twenty-one and thirty-six. He completed his draft registration card on October 16, 1940; had physical examinations in July 1941 and February 1942; and reported for induction on May 1, 1942, but was rejected the same day due to his rheumatic heart condition.[4]

After the United States entered the war on December 8, 1941, Connolly developed a keen sense of embarrassment in not being physically able to serve. Deeply patriotic by nature, he took pains to persuade later interviewers that he had worn the uniform. "He was with the Sixth Service Command transportation branch, commanded by General Aurand," wrote a star-struck reporter who interviewed Connolly in 1956. His *Variety* obituary stated that he had "enlisted in 1941 in the Army" and served in the Transportation Corps before "being mustered out in 1945." The parallel obituary in the *Hollywood Reporter* said "he served in the U.S. Army, 1941–45." Even *Who Was Who in America 1961–1968* said Connolly "served with AUS [U.S. Army], WWII." Colleagues and chums in Hollywood were given the same impression. "I remember his saying he was in the service," said Larry Quirk.[5]

The truth is that he worked for the Army Transportation Corps in a civilian job from December 16, 1942, to September 15, 1943, a grand total of nine months. This long-suppressed biographical tidbit is interesting in light of what Connolly wrote about former Congressman Doug Stringfellow, Republican of Utah, who in 1954 admitted that he had falsified his war record. "Apparently it pays to be a phony," Connolly clucked. "Doug Stringfellow is making more money lecturing about how sorry he is for lying about his war record, etc., on *This Is Your Life* than he could possibly have made as representative from Utah!"[6]

In going to work for the Transportation Corps, Connolly would be making less money than at Powers Tours. Most likely, the war had put an end to the travel business and he had to find another job. Fortunately, his experience in shuttling groups of tourists around North America was precisely what the Transportation Corps was seeking. He got the job through D. D. White, a captain in the corps. "I have been in contact with a man who has the desired qualifications based on actual experience gained over a considerable number of years," White wrote in response to an authorization for additional personnel. "He is available and desirous of being employed in this Branch."[7]

The Transportation Corps' offices were in the Chicago Civic Opera House. The job description for Connolly's senior clerk position was "know train routes, schedules, depots, and have knowledge of accommodations available on trains." He routed large groups of army personnel within the United States to points of embarkation for overseas. The key was efficiency, so that movements in and out of military reservations made continuous use of railroad equipment. According to *Logistics in World War II*, few officers in the army had transportation experience, so railroad and shipping companies made their workers available to the army to the fullest extent possible. At least once, Connolly was able to add a personal touch to his work. His brother, Tom, briefly stationed in Washington, D.C., was looked up by a soldier fresh off the train from Chicago. "Are you Connolly?" the soldier asked. "Your brother told me to tell you hello!"[8]

Although Connolly's rheumatic heart condition was honest grounds for deferral from military service, his embarrassment prompted him to adopt a more-patriotic-than-thou stance. Year after year he chided his brethren of the press for failing to note the anniversaries of Pearl Harbor or V-E and V-J days. Late in the 1960 presidential campaign, he decried the absence of the flag ("Where was Old Glory?") from the sets of the Kennedy-Nixon debates. Houses purchased on the G.I. bill, he commented, were "the government's revenge on guys who didn't enlist." Draft dodgers merited withering contempt in his column. During the Vietnam War he told his readers that if they did not like his columns, please "clip them and dump them on the Tomb of the Unknown Draft Dodger."[9]

When Connolly resigned from the Transportation Corps after nine months, he listed "entering private industry" as his reason. Once again, his expertise in transportation had opened a door for him, this time as an assistant to the public relations director of the Santa Fe Railroad, Lee Lyles, helping to produce documentary films. His tenure at the Santa Fe, however, was even shorter than at the Transportation Corps. By January 1944, he had moved over to the venerable City News Bureau, a cooperative that supplied municipal news to Chicago's dailies, radio stations, and the Associated Press. At long last, Connolly had become a reporter in what he called "the toughest and best newspaper town in the country, Chicago."[10]

It could be that the war had depleted the male work force to the point where there were suddenly a few rare openings at City News Bureau ("CNB"), where in normal years applications far outnumbered the available slots in the relatively small bureau. The incentive for Connolly's transition could not have been the salary, which was infamously paltry — twenty-six dollars per week for beginners, according to *Newsweek*. Most likely, Connolly had become resigned to the low pay if there were no other way to realize his dream of being a newspaperman. "Mike told me that in his early days in Chicago he wasted a lot of time in bars and wasn't serious about his work," recalls his pal Dave Peck. "But he woke up and stopped that routine — he gave up what wasn't pertinent."[11]

Newsweek labeled the CNB as "one of journalism's roughest obstacle courses" and its bureau chief, Isaac Gershman, as a boss given to "boot-camp discipline." "It's a Marine Corps deal," said Gershman. However, Connolly said *Newsweek* had been "taken in" by Gershman's bluster. He professed the greatest admiration for the bureau chief, whom he described as "nine feet tall as a reporter ... under that tough facade is the gentlest, nicest, courtliest, softest touch on the toughest newsbeat in the world ... the greatest teacher any of us ever had." Connolly bet the chief ten dollars that the January 1944 murder of socialite Adele Williams in Chicago's Drake Hotel, which was the talk of the city all year, would never be solved, and although he turned out to be right, he never collected. Gershman, Connolly said, knew the "wilder-like-wow" inside dirt on the St. Valentine's Day Massacre, Al Capone, John Dillinger, and all of Chicago's notorious underworld.[12]

By the time Connolly made those glowing remarks about Gershman, his memories had likely been tempered. Another cub reporter at CNB, Morry Rotman, characterized the CNB's culture as "ritual drudgery, very low pay, and very unfriendly bosses. One of its maxims was, 'If your mother says she loves you, check it out!'" Rotman said the CNB's "vows of poverty" brought him, Connolly, and the other cub reporters together in a special bond. "We felt specially anointed by that experience, an elite fraternity of hardy souls. We were anonymous. We never got a byline, even on the rare occasion when a paper would reprint our story untouched.

The Chicago papers prided themselves on thorough coverage of all events, so they wouldn't give a byline to a CNB reporter."

Rotman recalled that he and Connolly would work the graveyard shift, writing obituaries and tracking down anecdotes about the dead. If the deceased had no relatives, they would sometimes invent stories. They also worked the police beat and the city desk. Connolly's true feelings about the CNB might be inferred from his inclination to say "or I'll cover the police beat" where others normally would use "or I'll eat my hat."[13]

Connolly indulged in a bit of reminiscing about the police beat experience during the 1953 nationwide media frenzy over the transsexual Christine Jorgensen: "Any newspaperman of any experience knows [Jorgensen] isn't an unusual case ... We've seen numbers of these unfortunates on police beats. In fact, we used to tell the cops not to bother us when they wanted us to look at another one — and police in Chicago back 'em up against a desk, snap a picture and then kick 'em out on the street again."[14]

A less lurid story Connolly handled was the Jackson Park Theater case, an antitrust suit against major movie studios that wound up in the U.S. Supreme Court. At issue was the "Chicago system of release," which dictated that independent theaters such as the Jackson Park could not exhibit a movie until ten weeks after its first showing in studios' large theaters in Chicago's Loop. Connolly said he learned more about the nuts and bolts of the motion picture industry — production, distribution, and exhibition — from Jackson Park than he did in his first year on a Hollywood beat. His personal highlight of the trial came when Florence Bigelow, owner of the Jackson Park, testified, "I don't see why I can't buy pictures like I buy hats."[15]

If journalism was Connolly's aim, keeping up with police blotters and obituaries was not. On October 18, 1944, his first byline (simply "Mike," in truncated in-house style) appeared on two Chicago nightclub reviews in *Variety*. Initially, his *Variety* work was most likely moonlighting, as it often was with other Chicago correspondents. He often took his brother Tom and Tom's fiancée, Alma, with him to opening nights of the variety shows that were still popular at the end of the war. He also gave Tom and Alma a "gold pass," courtesy of *Variety*, which got them in free to any movie in town, and without waiting in line.[16]

When *Variety* became a fulltime job for Connolly is uncertain, but his share of bylines kept growing, and upon the death of his *Variety* colleague Frank Morgan in February 1946, Connolly assumed the lion's share of dispatches from the Chicago entertainment scene, adding radio, theater, and show business news, chatter, and even a few reviews of the infant medium of television to his responsibilities. Once in a great while, *Vari-*

ety carried articles with his byline, on subjects such as new, lucrative possibilities for stars in jingle recording or the need of radio stations in peacetime to find musical-format replacements for hours and hours of wartime news programming.[17]

His early reviews in *Variety* reveal Connolly's considerable confidence in his knowledge of both the Chicago nightspot scene and the rudiments of showmanship, musicianship, and the popular music canon of the day. "Needs plenty [of] coaching" might be a bold statement from a neophyte critic, but he had been a regular for at least a decade at the same cabarets, supper clubs, and theaters he was now reviewing — and he was eager to rub shoulders after the shows with the performers, too. "We knew Helen Morgan well," he would boast. "We had talked to her backstage at the Oriental a few weeks before she died in October of 1941 ... Whenever we saw Helen we felt like Dickens' Mr. Grumpy, who would sit in the theater pit and stare up ... his hand over his heart."[18]

One hallmark of Connolly's show business coverage was his gifts as a music critic — all the more remarkable for his never having had lessons on any musical instrument. Although he often joked that he was tone-deaf, it was not the case. Trini Lopez, one of his favorite musicians, for whose albums Connolly would write liner notes, felt that "Mike was unique in observing and analyzing an artist." Often Connolly would toss out an astute musical insight in a column. "The melodies of the two top *Music Man* hits are identical," he once informed readers. "*Seventy-Six Trombones* is six-eighths tempo and *Goodnight My Someone* is ballad tempo but they're note-for-note." He admired the Lennon Sisters because they had "the most perfectly synchronized vibrato" he had ever heard. "It's as though one voice were singing all four parts at once."[19]

While still in Chicago, Connolly began lengthy associations with several top entertainers. His review of Frank Sinatra's first postwar performance at the Chicago Theater showed he was already wary of the character behind The Voice; his praise was reserved and limited strictly to Sinatra's musical gifts. Bob Hope, at the Coliseum two months later, was another story. Always one of Hope's most enthusiastic boosters, Connolly raved about "the supreme master of the art of punching a line and timing a gag." Very few of the top musical entertainers he later covered in Hollywood — Hildegarde, Patsy Kelly, Arthur Blake, and many others— did not already know him from his years at *Variety's* Chicago bureau.[20]

Perhaps his biggest splash at *Variety* was the issue of April 25, 1945, when his byline was displayed prominently on the lead front-page story, "CHI'S DRAMA SCHOOL RACKET." The war had engendered ideal conditions— jobs and disposable income but few products to buy —for dozens of voice-and-dramatic schools of questionable credentials to spring up in the Windy City, "out to chisel as much 'tuition' as they can from gullible, stagestruck teenagers." Annual business done by these ersatz schools was estimated at five million dollars. Not since the *Daily Illini's* red-light district crusade eight years earlier had Connolly been in such a position to tear into a good scandal. Borrowing a technique he had learned in Champaign, he recruited two female friends, both attractive former singers with small bands, to pose as showbiz hopefuls, make the rounds of the shyster schools, and report back.

In each case, the comely applicant was ushered into a dingy studio where an instructor, who could not readily produce references or display radio equipment, asked her to sing. The critiques invariably centered on "incorrect" techniques she must have picked up from previous instruction. In one school, the professor-boss was accompanied by a "singularly good-looking chap with a very come-hither manner ... as far as I could tell, 'Curly Locks' was the come-on for a lot of thwarted females." Connolly's article proposed no solution, but pointed out that legitimate schools' reputations were suffering because of the unethical practices of the phonies.

While making his way in Chicago show business circles, Connolly forged lifelong friendships with key figures at the *Chicago Times* (now *Sun-Times*). Principal among these was the great Irv Kupcinet, author since 1943 of "Kup's Column." "I helped Mike a lot when he was getting started," Kupcinet recalled. "I gave him advice — told him how to write a column." Over the next two decades Kupcinet's frequent trips to Hollywood, where Connolly hosted many parties in his honor, kept them in touch. They were also together on Christmas-season junkets with Bob Hope to entertain troops in Alaska and the Far East.[21]

Managing editor Russ Stewart (a former publicist for MGM), corporation counsel Lou Spear, and other top brass at the *Chicago Times* were also part of Connolly's inner Fourth Estate circle. When Russ Stewart married his second wife in Palm Springs in April 1960, Connolly hosted their wedding reception at his home.[22]

Other local newsmen Connolly befriended were Herb Lyon, who went on to become Tower Ticker columnist at the *Chicago Tribune*, and Ashton Stevens, the "never malicious ... dean of drama critics" at the *Chicago Daily News*. Connolly also admired "gentle, shy" John Balaban, head of Chicago's Balaban and Katz theater chain, "who went to bat for [me] many times in many a rough spot, as good friends always do."[23]

Since World War II is recognized as a watershed in gay history, allowing unprecedented numbers of small-town homosexuals to come into contact with each other, it offers an appropriate point to consider Connolly's transition from exemplary Catholic boy to a man willing to adopt a same-sex lifestyle contrary to the strictures of his faith. Scholars hold that Chicago during the war was a sexual Alsatia for gay people. "By the summer of 1942," writes Allan Berube in *Coming Out Under Fire*, "fifty thousand soldiers and sailors were pouring into Chicago's downtown 'Loop' each weekend looking for a good time." Even on weekdays, hordes of GIs on passes lined roads between military bases and the city thumbing rides. Propagandists spread the word that it was civilians' patriotic duty to give these men rides. At Thanksgiving time, hundreds of persons would write to Chicago newspapers asking how to invite servicemen for turkey dinner.[24]

The exact details of Connolly's own coming out went with him to his grave. However, while wartime opportunities for gay people, enlisted and civilian, to meet and mingle in Chicago were abundant (and well documented), the Windy City had already had a vibrant and exceedingly visible gay population before the war. Beginning in June 1939, Dr. Alfred Kinsey conducted his early research in gay male sexuality in Chicago, interviewing a group of homosexual men living in a Rush Street rooming house and, thanks to their referrals, collecting scores of similar interviews over the next several months. They escorted him to gay parties, nightclubs, coffee houses, movie theaters, and even to anonymous trysting spots in city parks and restrooms. From the data he amassed, Kinsey interpolated that Chicago must have had three hundred thousand homosexuals.[25]

In the 1930s, the sociology department at the University of Chicago documented extensively a working-class, youth-oriented gay culture thriving in the city's Near North Side. Drawing on these studies, scholar David K. Johnson identified the portion of Michigan Avenue stretching from the Chicago River north to the Oak Street Beach as the axis of the gay community of the 1930s, with Thompson's, an inexpensive eatery at the corner of Michigan and Ohio that stayed open until late, cited as one of the most popular homosexual destinations. State Street in front of Marshall Field's was another "notorious gay cruising area." The most popular gay bar, Waldman's at 164 North Michigan, opened around 1935 and was famous for its two grand pianos visible through picture windows.[26]

Johnson's research unearthed other interesting discoveries. The terms "coming out" and "gay" were already in use in the 1930s. The haunts of gay men were "common knowledge to a wide segment of the city," including Chicago Renaissance writers such as Sherwood Anderson, James T. Farrell, and Floyd Dell, who portrayed those locales in their fiction. A number of gay-themed novels that appeared in the early 1930s, including

Twilight Men, *Strange Brother*, and *A Scarlet Pansy*, were carried by Chicago's commercial rental libraries in working class neighborhoods and worn out from heavy circulation.[27]

The coalescing of a gay community in Chicago is documented even from before the end of the nineteenth century, and a 1908 book pointed out the city's clubs, steam baths, and restaurants with "homosexual atmospheres." By the 1920s, the Near North Side had become home to thousands of single people "living outside traditional societal conventions, including many of the city's aspiring artists and writers." At the tail end of the 1920s, *Variety* would carry a front page story about the "pansy craze" sweeping across Chicago (also a phenomenon in other major cities), which by then had thirty-five gay tearooms in the Near North Side alone, all decorated with fey details.[28]

In short, Chicago had gay networks and neighborhoods decades before Mike Connolly was born. The options to experiment sexually, socialize with other homosexuals, and come out in his home town were available at whatever point he chose to exercise them, whether as a teenager in high school or as a college graduate. His work at Powers Tours could have presented many possibilities for meeting other homosexuals, whether on the road with his travel groups or in dealing with out-of-town visitors to the 1933–1934 Chicago World's Fair, "A Century of Progress." However, Connolly was an active South Side Catholic, and he lived with his parents until past his thirtieth birthday, so he was not part of the Near North Side neighborhood's singles scene. Nor did he show much interest in the working-class culture that pervaded the Near North Side. Although he was working-class himself, he aspired to pursue and live among the refined. Elegant nightclubs and gilded theaters were his métier.

Without the specifics of Connolly's earliest self-identification as homosexual, there is only circumstantial evidence for when and what he knew and did. Johnson notes that in the 1930s, Michigan Avenue, Chicago's axis of gay life, was called "the boulevard." In Connolly's first "Talk of the Town" column at the university, he printed a list of his "Likes"; alongside thousand-dollar bills and big, round, flat English muffins with marmalade, he listed "Michigan Boulevard." He was also familiar with the Rush Street neighborhood that was Dr. Kinsey's gay Chicago beachhead, reminiscing at a later date about "Chicago's Flat-Foot-Floogie-Floydoy cult on Rush Street." Another gay hangout in the Near North Side of the 1930s was the Dill Pickle Club. "Whenever we eat a dill pickle," Connolly wrote years later, "we think of Maxwell Bodenheim, one of the founders of the Dill Pickle Club, a landmark of Chicago's dank Bohemiasma."[29]

The encounter that led to the life partnership of Connolly and Joseph

Zappia likely occurred between Connolly's 1938 graduation from college and his August 1940 Powers Tours trip to Canada (since Zappia was on that trip and remembered Banff National Park and Lake Louise as the most beautiful sights he ever saw). When Zappia first met Connolly, he was working downtown at Famous Permanent Waves and had a boyfriend, Don LaMarr, who was also a hairdresser. As James Hill, Zappia's partner for thirty-five years after Connolly's death, recounts it, Connolly spotted Zappia one night in a gay bar and was instantly intrigued. When he invited Zappia to dinner, Zappia protested that he was already involved with LaMarr. Connolly would not take no for an answer and barraged Zappia with his blandishments until he had stolen him away from LaMarr. Predictably, said Hill, these transitions were emotionally wrenching for both Zappia and LaMarr. Eventually, peace was made; LaMarr would later move to Hollywood to live with the other two until Connolly's death in 1966.[30]

Zappia also joined Connolly's Mexico-bound tour group the following year, where at an Acapulco resort they were intrigued by a mysterious woman who was continually surrounded by bodyguards. Ever the investigative reporter, Connolly made discreet inquiries and learned she was Eva Braun, the mistress of Adolf Hitler, sent temporarily to Mexico for her safety. Connolly and Zappia took several candid photographs of Braun at poolside and on the diving board. Two months later, the United States was at war, and because Zappia's classification was also IV-F (due to poor eyesight), he and Connolly were never separated during the war years. Connolly notified his draft board on January 29, 1945, that he had a new address, 2848 North Burling Street. The Chicago telephone directory for 1945 lists Zappia at the same address. Connolly's late–1944 hiring by *Variety* must have made him financially able to leave his parents' home.[31]

Two of the men's closest friends during these years were Hortense ("Hortie") and Skippy, a lesbian couple. Connolly had known Skippy, whose bibulous tendencies he found endearing, since her days as a showgirl at the Chicago World's Fair. For the next half-century, Zappia would impersonate Skippy's reliance on alcohol as a panacea for drowsiness, sleeplessness, headaches, and most other maladies. Bunny Seidman remembers visiting Hortie and Skippy with Connolly in Chicago in April 1956. Although he promised to pay for Seidman's return trip to Los Angeles, he had failed to deliver the cash and she was stranded in the Windy City, from where, she reports, Hortie and Skippy called Connolly in Hollywood to "give him hell about it." The two women, she said, occasionally houseguested with Connolly and Zappia in California.[32]

After the war, with a greater abundance of gay male friends to pal around with, a small group of regulars coalesced around Connolly and

Zappia. Using a home movie camera that Connolly had purchased, the group filmed a campy takeoff on *Pygmalion* called *The Gilded Lily*, a vehicle for drag roles that drew on Zappia's hairdressing background to document the transformation of an ugly duckling into a great lady of society. Most of the scenes were filmed in a homemade set decorated as a beauty salon, with Chicago's Saks Fifth Avenue store as the backdrop.[33]

Connolly's openness about his relationship with Zappia in Chicago varied from venue to venue. While he could get away with having Zappia in his tour groups — Hill said Zappia paid his own way and blended into the group — he apparently could not take Zappia to nightclubs, relying instead on companions such as his brother and future sister-in-law. And while Connolly never introduced Zappia to Tom and Alma in Chicago, Zappia was acquainted with Connolly's parents and later recalled having "liked Mike's mother." Most likely, Connolly presented Zappia to his parents only as "a friend."[34]

An interesting sidebar to the question of Connolly's relative openness in Chicago is the Office of the Provost Marshal General's December 1942 investigation of him as a prerequisite to his working for the Army Transportation Corps. An inspector interviewed Connolly's employers, neighbors, and acquaintances and sifted through the Chicago Detective Bureau's records. "He associates with a reputable class of young people of this community and he bears a favorable personal reputation as to moral conduct and habits," the inspector concluded. Presumably, any evidence of homosexual association would have mandated a different conclusion, which leads to speculation about the investigation's thoroughness or about Connolly's ability to cover his tracks skillfully.[35]

Long before subtle homosexual allusions began to adorn his Hollywood columns, Connolly's nightclub reviews for *Variety* reflected a gay sensibility — seldom in overt statements, but mainly in reactions unlikely to be expressed by a heterosexual male. "Although nightclub entertainment was never publicly identified as gay, such performers as Hildegarde and Tallulah Bankhead attracted a devoted gay following, sometimes dropping veiled hints or singing lyrics with double meanings directed at their admirers," wrote Berube.[36]

For *Variety*, Connolly reviewed the nightclub acts of a number of gay cabaret stars, including Patsy Kelly and Arthur Blake. Of comedienne Kelly, appearing at the Empire Room, he wrote approvingly that her "peculiar brand of buffoonery ... offset the standard Kelly look of having just gotten off the subway during the rush hour." He said female impersonator Blake, at the Boulevard Room, was "an unusual booking" for such a big room, but "coming on as he does with a Hildegarde item in stroblite, complete with glowing wig and long gloves," flashier acts "have nothing on him ... he also does Carmen Miranda with all the accoutrements."[37]

If a show had gay overtones, Connolly did not shy away from pointing them out, whether from amusement or disapproval. Reviewing a legitimate comedy about a baseball team, *Second Guesser*, he singled out "the swishy interior decorator who can't understand why those silly men get all worked up over a little thing like a baseball" and the "frilly office of the ball club decked out with chintz by the decorator"—also that character's "Franklin Pangbornisms." Connolly would also take "tall, lean monologist" Jan Murray to task for a "bad case of swishitis he'd be much better off without."[38]

When stripper Gypsy Rose Lee played the Oriental, Connolly appreciated her one-liners, but wrote the remainder of his review with a distinct ho-hum feeling. "Down to a strapless gown," he wrote, "she zips that off, accompanied by screams from [a] stooge in [the] aud[ience], and then does a few very minor bumps." Lee's show was a "lusty, he-man session," he acknowledged—what he would later call "redblooded"—"reminiscent of the days when the baldheads down front looked like a field of mushrooms."[39]

In spite of the success Connolly was enjoying at *Variety*, Chicago was not the ultimate prize for a show business reporter. "*Variety* wanted to transfer him to New York," recalled Tom Connolly. "But he said no. He was holding out for Hollywood." According to his obituary in *Variety*, he worked in Chicago "until 1946 when he went to Hollywood on vacation and remained to go on [the] staff of *Daily Variety*." His bylines on Chicago nightclub reviews stopped appearing in *Variety* after Labor Day, 1946.[40]

Lionizing the Chicago News Bureau's Isaac Gershman in 1964, Connolly thanked the bureau chief for "giving [me] the push out this way to Mecca." Gershman, wrote Connolly, was a diehard fan of the movies. If Gershman's encouragement to Connolly was genuinely a factor in Connolly's migration to California, it was a departure from the path followed most often by Chicago newsmen of note—Franklin P. Adams, Ben Hecht, Charles MacArthur, et al.—who set off for New York. The movies were Connolly's favorite mode of entertainment, and he knew he could not write about them anywhere but Hollywood.

Chapter 7

How to Succeed in Gossip-Mongering

"Trouble with being both a fan and a columnist is that you get all bitched up with the people you've been a fan of."
— *Mike Connolly, Hollywood Reporter, Nov. 9, 1951.*

Chicago's streets may have been paved with gold for his parents' generation, but for Mike Connolly, Southern California was the ultimate El Dorado and (oddly enough) the only place in the world to rear children. He said he was so infatuated with California that he could not be pulled away by wild horses. Hollywood had no more ardent defender. "Jerome Robbins smears Hollywood in the *New Yorker*," he once bristled. "Who needs Robbins? He can stay in New York and we'll all be happier."[1]

It would have surprised Hollywood (and embarrassed Connolly) had anyone unearthed his inaugural "Talk of the Town" column for the *Daily Illini*, in which he had listed Los Angeles among his "Dislikes" (with such distinguished company as Stalin, Hitler, Mussolini, and Shirley Temple).[2]

The idyllic climate, the excitement of the motion picture industry, and freedom from the scrutiny of neighbors, relatives, and classmates must have won Connolly over even before he accepted *Daily Variety's* offer of a job. He and Joseph Zappia moved into a house at 2167 Broadview Terrace, which he would soon want to leave because of the hill-climbing required to reach it. Zappia opened his beauty salon, called Paul and Joseph's, in

Westwood, and eventually their Chicago friend Don LaMarr came west and moved in with them.

Connolly's first assignment at *Daily Variety*, the music beat, was short-lived. He was soon shifted to covering the film studios. Ed Hutshing, a city editor at that time, said, "My impression was that Mike was just a leg-man in the studios then." He had a general assignment to cover all phases of show business, from film charity picnics to movie premieres.[3]

Daily Variety's offices were on Vine Street, just north of Hollywood Boulevard; large storefront windows allowed pedestrians to peer in. Every evening at five p.m., the office came alive as busy reporters returned from their beats and pounded out stories for the following morning on ancient typewriters. Presiding over this frenetic scene from a desk at the rear of the city room was editor Arthur Ungar, who had been with *Variety* in New York for several years before being handpicked to found that sheet's west coast edition, *Daily Variety*, in 1933. Connolly's friend David Hanna wrote that Ungar required absolute dedication, loyalty, and honesty from his staff.[4]

Ungar was the kind of editor-in-chief who went through two or three managing editors in a year. Ed Hutshing called him "the biggest son of a bitch in Hollywood." Hutshing stormed out of *Daily Variety* when Ungar rewrote one of Hutshing's reviews, a thumbs-down critique of the stuttering comedian Joe Frisco, who was drunk on stage at Slapsie Maxie's when Hutshing caught his act. "A week later, Ungar went to the same show, and Frisco was fine, so he wrote a review criticizing my review," says Hutshing. "That I could not tolerate."[5]

Connolly's debut as a Hollywood gossip columnist, which came on November 28, 1949, was not intended as a permanent assignment. *Daily Variety's* chatter column, "Just for Variety," had been written by Florabel Muir, whose renowned motto was, "I'm not a lady, I'm a columnist." An editorial note accompanying Connolly's maiden column announced, "Florabel Muir is vacationing. During her absence your old friend Alta Durant will operate in this space." "Alta Durant" was a pseudonym created from two Hollywood street names and had been used "spasmodically" over the years. "It was a masking name, long used by *Daily Variety*," explained Hutshing. "Mike probably had to use it because he was a staff man and they didn't want the staff to be known. Florabel's real name was used because she was brought in from the outside." Arthur Ungar was known for doing things the old way — on Saturday afternoons, he personally handed out pay envelopes containing cash, a remunerative procedure required by New York state law but unheard of in California, because "that was how it was done." The same entrenched mentality was probably behind the Alta Durant byline's being forced on Connolly.[6]

Despite Arthur Ungar's iron-handed rule, the power and prestige that accrued to Connolly through "Just for Variety" were palpable and immediate. Sheilah Graham, who later authored the same column, reminisced rhapsodically on the "lovely power" she enjoyed during her tenure. "Producers and stars supplied me with so much news it was a problem what to discard," she wrote. "Hedda and Louella were eating out of my hand." These observations are equally applicable to Connolly's stature in Hollywood while helming "Just for Variety."[7]

From the first, many of Connolly's fingerprints as a columnist were evident in "Just for Variety." A typical day's output might include Catholic news, Irish tidbits (especially as St. Patrick's Day approached), alliterations ("Jay Flippen flips ..."), scoldings of alcoholics, touting of his own prowess in digging up scoops, exposing vice, retorts from subjects in response to his items, etc. But by and large, these early columns are not much fun to read half a century later. Connolly had no legman and had to do all his own news gathering, so he was inclined in this period to print things that sounded like handouts from press agents and studios. The signature Connolly style was still a work in progress.[8]

One of the things Connolly learned right away was that the scramble to keep an actor's name in the news amounted to natural law in the Hollywood food chain, and the relations between press agents and reporters were high-strung and fraught with recriminations. Judging by his frequent sarcastic comments about press agents ("p.a.'s"), he had little patience with them, to wit: "Bing [Crosby] is older than he looks to his p.a." or "Liz [Taylor]'s baby is the first in years that wasn't forecast as twins by a p.a."[9]

Connolly was officially silent on his labor under Arthur Ungar. He told his brother Tom that he bought a hat when Ungar's aged mother died because he assumed the funeral would be Orthodox Jewish. Then he learned it was not Orthodox, so he lamented buying the hat for naught. Ungar himself died suddenly on July 24, 1950. No sooner had Ungar been laid to rest than Connolly's real name began to adorn "Just for Variety." By now, the notion that Connolly was only pinch-hitting was forgotten; in any case, Florabel Muir had become Hollywood correspondent for the New York Daily News.[10]

The happy news on the byline front coincided with Connolly's and Zappia's purchase of a new house at 1512 Marlay Drive; Connolly rejoiced about both in a letter to his brother. The new home, which would not require hill-climbing, had two bedrooms, two baths, and three fireplaces. For the entertaining Connolly had in mind there was a large reception hall and an enviable view of Los Angeles. Above the two-car garage was a guest apartment which they would fix up and rent out.

Replacing Arthur Ungar as *Daily Variety's* head honcho was Joe Schoenfeld, a former Hollywood agent and Hearst reporter. Although Connolly never mentioned Schoenfeld on record, it is likely that his job under this new administration was scarcely more pleasant than with Ungar. Other occupants of the "Just for Variety" seat, however, were not as reticent about Schoenfeld. Viola Swisher, Connolly's immediate replacement, disclosed that Schoenfeld became "apoplectic with rage" over a harmless item about a producer who was a sacred cow to Schoenfeld. "He greeted me with a shrill scream," complained Swisher. "His attitude was, 'Don't let the facts interfere with my friendship with the producer.' That blow-off led to a parting of the ways for us."[11]

Sheilah Graham, who followed Swisher, lasted a year under Schoenfeld and candidly aired his trespasses against her. "He treated me like an ignorant cub reporter," she groused. "We had fights almost every day, usually over trivial matters." Schoenfeld never consulted Graham about his deletions from or additions to her column. He would also rewrite items, changing their veracity as well as their meaning, and embarrassing Graham in the process.[12]

Meanwhile, down the street at the rival *Hollywood Reporter*, publisher William R. ("Billy") Wilkerson II was, for the second time in 1951, seeking a new "Rambling Reporter" gossip columnist. Herb Stein, the in-house scribe from 1948 through March 1951, had been lured away to Annenberg Publications. Wilkerson then tapped a long-time friend, the hard-drinking Jim Henaghan, for the column, but Henaghan's itinerant nature and desire to get rich writing screenplays got the best of him; he was out the door by September's end.[13]

The "Rambling Reporter" column had been started in 1930 by Edith Gwynn, Wilkerson's then-wife, and piloted by her over the next two decades. Gwynn held onto the column after the marriage ended as part of their divorce settlement agreement. From the first, Gwynn established the column's institutional mannerisms, e.g., credit-seeking and self-touting; the royal We ("we told you of it over a week ago" ... "we said"); and daily reports of celebrity sightings at LaRue, the elegant Sunset Strip restaurant owned by Wilkerson. (It helped that the "Rambling Reporter" could eat for free there.) She resigned in 1937 after Wilkerson blue-penciled an item that, though accurate, offended an advertiser, but came back to the fold in 1942 for another six years. Hollywood insider Ezra Goodman believed the Rambling Reporter to be the best-read gossip column in town, attributing this to its well-established "breezy" tradition, that sometimes made even scandal magazines blush.[14]

The factors that led Wilkerson to offer Connolly the Rambling

Reporter spot are unknown. The *Hollywood Reporter* and *Daily Variety* monitored each other's issues like foreign spies, however, and Wilkerson would have seen Connolly's *Just for Variety* every day. Earlier in 1951, Connolly had tweaked Wilkerson in a clear spirit of rivalry by writing, "W. R. Wilkerson is out of LaRue, Las Vegas, within a few weeks after the opening of the gambling casino-restaurant. This makes the second Las Vegas venture in which he didn't last long, the first being his association with Bugsy Siegel in the Flamingo." As well, Connolly's frequent comments on the depravity of Communists would have had Wilkerson yelling, "Hear, hear!"[15]

Wilkerson's son, Willie, says the recruitment should be viewed in the context of rival publisher relations. "The trade papers were born in the Depression and you fought for every inch of turf. There was no love lost between them. My father knew Mike was good," he observes, "and so he was putting a hole in the competition's valve. Mike was traded like a team player."[16]

It is not possible to understand Mike Connolly's stellar career at the *Hollywood Reporter* fully without knowing how he fit into the organization created by its founder and publisher. William R. Wilkerson was an Alpha male to whom a certain stripe of male homosexual, whose ego would permit a subservient relationship to a boss, could attach himself, like a eunuch to an emperor, benefiting from a secure employer and protector. Wilkerson was a can-do man who envisioned things and made them happen. Aside from his *Hollywood Reporter*, there were his legendary restaurants (including LaRue, Cafe Trocadero, and L'Aiglon), which he founded because he felt Hollywood needed sophistication on par with Paris. There were also Ciro's, the elegant nightclub, and the Flamingo, the first really magnificent casino in Las Vegas. A teetotaler on one hand and a compulsive gambler on the other, Wilkerson seemed unable to imagine that his plans would not materialize.[17]

David Hanna wrote, "In the pre-war depression days when I first joined the *Hollywood Reporter* [years before Connolly's time], Billy had the habit of flying to Las Vegas and gambling the payroll. We often weren't paid until the middle of the following week, but no one complained. Besides the reality of [our] being unable to pick up jobs elsewhere, Billy's gambling kept the paper alive. A winning streak with the payroll could support it for a week or so."[18]

Wilkerson's staff was larded with homosexuals. "My father was surrounded by gays," relates Willie Wilkerson. "While he was not approving of them, they did not make his list of three critical hatreds: people who stole from him, drunks, and Communists." In his daily column, "Trade Views,"

Wilkerson once excoriated a plan to adapt a gay-themed novel for the screen as "lunacy" but stopped short of condemning homosexuality per se. "[This] type of thinking will ALWAYS keep us in hot water with the powers who are continually trying to legislate against us," Wilkerson warned.[19]

Chief among Wilkerson's homosexual courtiers was George H. Kennedy, who gave him a lifetime of faithful service, first as personal secretary and then as business manager. At parties, Wilkerson would imitate Kennedy, who would be devastated when word of the boss's mimicry got back to him. Willie Wilkerson compares his father's relationship with George Kennedy to Duke Ellington and Billy Strayhorn. "It does provoke the question of why he surrounded himself with a group of people he disapproved of," says the son. "The gays I knew at the *Hollywood Reporter* while growing up were very loyal to my dad. They did not fit into the criterion of thieving from him. That was very important to him. One employee was stealing, and my father screamed at him until he dropped dead of a heart attack. Instead of saying what a tragic thing, my father stood over the body and told George, 'Get him out of here! But through the back door — no thief should go out the front.'"[20]

Another valued homosexual employee was David Hanna, who reviewed movies, edited, and wrote the "Rambling Reporter" when it was between columnists. Hanna said the bond between him and Wilkerson was such that there would always be a job for him at the *Hollywood Reporter* if he wanted to come back. "There were posh private offices upstairs which, as man-of-all-work, I often occupied," said Hanna; "one of these lay across the hall from Billy's tasteful executive suite. I enjoyed 'raiding privileges,' hitting his refrigerator for Coke. Billy seldom drank because alcohol, he said, made him belligerent. Cold-sober, however, he would never pass as a kindly, sweet old man. Still he was a Southern gentleman, for all his gruff exterior."[21]

Where Connolly's well-known homosexuality and drinking were concerned, Willie Wilkerson said his father "did a lot of nose-holding. But he knew he wasn't living in a perfect world." George Kennedy recalled, "Mr. Wilkerson's steadfast philosophy had always been 'you get what you pay for.' He believed that if you hired and bought the best, you got the best. It was that simple." Wilkerson's acquisition of Mike Connolly's talent would turn out to be a fortunate move. "Mike is the only one who became bigger than the paper," Wilkerson would observe much later. Connolly would often laud Wilkerson, as well, with compliments such as "an always-on-the-ball boss who keeps things jumpin'."[22]

Thus on October 1, 1951, Connolly began what would be a relatively happy fifteen-year residency at the *Hollywood Reporter*. For the first time,

Like a concert pianist, Connolly often posed for publicity stills at his keyboard. This photograph dates from about 1963. (Photofest)

the name of the "Rambling Reporter" author appeared at the column's beginning instead of the end. Connolly wrote to Hedda Hopper that he would find it hard to follow Jim Henaghan, whom he called a real sweetheart, but otherwise he had no misgivings. "There was a lot less pressure at the *Hollywood Reporter* and it was a happier ship than at *Daily Variety*," recalled Ed Hutshing, who had worked at both. "When I started at the *Hollywood Reporter* in late 1947, Frank Pope, the managing editor, told me, 'This is a swinging door job.' Wilkerson fired me several times and he fired

Pope several times, but he'd always ask me back and I usually managed to get a raise in the process." Luckily, Connolly was sufficiently in sync with the boss never to be fired.[23]

The main difference to Connolly in his new job, he told interviewers, was freedom, both from assignments extraneous to his column and from meddling by Wilkerson. Dan Jenkins, who was television columnist at the *Hollywood Reporter* when Connolly's tenure began, recalled that Wilkerson "never once told [me] what to write or called [me] on the carpet for something already written — a rather remarkably broadminded attitude considering that our particular viewpoints have often differed considerably." There were limits, however. A Jenkins piece that blasted Senator Joseph McCarthy's anti–Communist antics was handed back to him by an editor with no explanation beyond, "We can't print that." Later, Jenkins said, "I came to realize Wilkerson would've stuffed it down my throat. Another time I wrote about MGM's being ridiculous in its hatred for television — not allowing its employees to buy television sets at discount, and so forth. MGM wrote to Wilkerson about it, and he forwarded the letter to me with 'For Your Information' penciled on it. That was the closest he ever came to controlling what I wrote."[24]

On the other hand, the New York–based press agent and *bon vivant* Irving Hoffman, whose "Tales of Hoffman" appeared for two decades in Wilkerson's paper, "roar[ed] like a lion" whenever the publisher altered or cut Hoffman's prose, which was often. *Esquire* reported that Hoffman's views, which ranged widely in topic and were often socially conscious, rarely coincided with those in Wilkerson's own column, "Trade Views." Hoffman finally quit in January 1953 after Wilkerson informed him he was not conducting a forum "for the publication of beliefs and complaints other than whether a picture is good or bad."[25]

Connolly's autonomy probably fell somewhere in between that accorded to Jenkins and Hoffman. This is not surprising, given the premium visibility of the "Rambling Reporter" column. "Mike had free rein in a lot of stuff, but when it came to politics, he was under the watchful eye of my father," said Willie Wilkerson. "George Kennedy was very clear on that; he said, 'If something was important enough, your father was involved.'" Wilkerson's big Las Vegas venture, the Flamingo, is an example of something important enough. David Hanna wrote that during one of his stints as the "Rambling Reporter," rumors of rigged games at the Flamingo were rampant. "Billy contributed to the column and, in fact, was its best legman," Hanna commented. "Among the items he handed me every evening were some dealing with 'big winners' ... 'walking off with a bundle' ... 'nearly breaking the house.'"[26]

The only extant example of Wilkerson's oversight of Connolly stems from a complaint by Warner Bros. mogul Jack L. Warner, who once fired off a petulant letter to Wilkerson after Connolly compared a medical expense dispute between the studio and a contractee to Northwestern and Notre Dame. The publisher simply responded, "I will talk to Connolly and get his version of the story"—adding that Warner and he should have lunch. Six days later, Warner hit the ceiling once again over another seemingly harmless item; this time an indignant telegram was sent zinging to Wilkerson. The publisher was then under doctor's orders to spend fewer hours at his office and the proposed lunch with Warner had to be postponed. There is no record of any consequence to Connolly from Warner's tantrums.[27]

Wilkerson was, in fact, highly pleased with Connolly's work. "The two of them shared a very good professional and personal relationship," Joseph Zappia recalled. "Mike's column was so important to the paper that Billy wouldn't allow them to go to press until someone in the print shop read the column to him or showed him a copy. If Billy left the office early, he had someone call him wherever he was and read the column to him."[28]

Over the years Connolly referred occasionally to his philosophy on journalism in general and his own column in particular. "Get yourself in there, plan it, and start writing a column that'll make their hair stand on end," he advised his successor in the "Rambling Reporter," Jack Bradford. Appearing on the *Open End* talk show, he said his motto was "Get it first, but get it right," with apologies to William Randolph Hearst. Equally important was to be entertaining. "Despite a great ego, [Walter] Winchell at least makes columning amusing to read," he commented approvingly. Where his daily four p.m. deadline was concerned, he preferred to live dangerously. "If I wait until three o'clock, the pitch and the pace will keep it fresh and interesting." Fortunately, he had the option of changing or adding anything until eleven p.m., because the typesetters remained on duty and the printing plant was on the *Hollywood Reporter* premises.[29]

His day at the office (so he told interviewers) began at 9:30 a.m., although this got later and later over the years. Typically, he got things rolling by making and taking calls on two phones that rang continuously. "Our eyesore of a desk," as he called it, was encumbered with several foot-high piles of notes and papers. His work week was Sunday through Thursday, to support the column's Monday-morning-through-Friday-morning publication schedule. He collected an estimated 250 items per day and would then cull out the best fifty or sixty. He would lead off with items calculated to set Hollywood tongues to wagging. Reports from the studios were usually peppered with pithy quotations from stars. High-profile parties, both in Hollywood and in Los Angeles society, might be covered. Since Connolly was a passionate fan of the popular music scene, performers from the Sunset Strip nightclubs of the day — Mocambo, Ciro's, the Cocoanut Grove, Slate Brothers, Crescendo, Interlude — were often played up. Each of the column's three long paragraphs would conclude either with a new joke or an outrageous remark, often scavenged directly from private gay social events.[30]

The office had a nickname for Connolly: The Star. Someone had affixed a five-pointed star to his office door and it remained there. Aside from Wilkerson, Connolly had the largest office at the *Hollywood Reporter*; it even had a private staircase. The walls groaned under an aggregation of autographed photos, mostly of movie stars but a few of politicians such as Richard Nixon and even a World War II photo of Connolly's brother Tom.[31]

George Kennedy said he and Connolly would take "pills" at the office to sustain energy. "It was something along the lines of speed," explained Willie Wilkerson. "George said it was absolutely wonderful, like a magic carpet that carried them through the day." These may have been dexamyls, which Bunny Seidman had introduced to Connolly.

For his secretary, Connolly tapped an ally from the *Daily Illini*, Esther Deutch Hoff, who had graduated two years ahead of him. When she married his good friend, sports editor Dave Hoff, the *Illini* ran their pictures on its front page. Dave Hoff died young, and Connolly asked Esther to move to California to work for him. Despite his good intentions, though, he came to feel she was in the way — "She wasn't all that hip," said Jack Bradford, "and Mike couldn't really 'laugh and scratch' with his phone callers with her sitting just five feet away in the office. So Stanley Musgrove found Esther a job as executive secretary to [director] Robert Wise. That's when Mike decided to hire me."[32]

As with Esther Hoff, Connolly was hiring someone he already knew well. Bradford, like Connolly and Hoff, was a University of Illinois alumnus. He came to Hollywood as an aspiring actor hoping to be in pictures, after a few legitimate credits in New York. Initially, Connolly was quite taken with Bradford and helped his nascent career by mentioning him often in the column. "As early as 1956 I was feeding items to Mike through Joe [Zappia]," said Bradford. "I met Joe at a gym and he introduced me to Mike, and I went to work for Mike in the fall of 1958 [after small roles in *No Time for Sergeants* and *FBI Story*]. I worked only in the mornings. My job was to keep people away from him! I'd be on the phone and Mike would be on his phone. On some days we may have just said hello and goodbye."

After four years on the job, Bradford was deemed ready to substitute for Connolly during vacations. (Before that, Jim Henaghan, Connolly's predecessor, did the pinch-hitting.) "In the beginning I was certainly not 'on the inside of things' as became the case some years later when Mike really began to trust me with some of the innermost secrets," said Bradford. "Mike was a private kind of guy. Very few were allowed 'in.' When I would type out his items, I got to know, basically, what he would do to them; how he was going to change them. The items were typed up one per half-sheet, triple-spaced, so Mike could rearrange them and put the 'Connolly touch' on them. So when I first wrote the column, people said I sounded like Mike." Bradford's first three weeks as Connolly's substitute, in the summer of 1962, coincided with many significant Hollywood events that proved his mettle, such as Marilyn Monroe's death and the Bette Davis–Joan Crawford feuds during the making of *Whatever Happened to Baby Jane?*[33]

Bradford was, even in those days, an avid astrologer. "I once warned Mike that he should not leave for Palm Springs on a Friday. 'What if the motor fell out of your car?' I wondered. But he and Joe set out for Palm Springs. Later on, I got a call from Mike and Joe in Riverside and their motor *had* fallen out! They were flabbergasted. From then on, Mike always consulted with me on astrological aspects of every major move. For instance, he decided against going to the Berlin Festival."[34]

While Bradford was Connolly's morning gatekeeper, Joseph Zappia worked for him in the afternoons, but not at the office. "I was his legman for studio visits and location jaunts. I wrote down pages of notes, or called in daily items from location. Mike used about 10 percent of it — sometimes none," Zappia recalled. To read Connolly's column, one would think he had either incredible stamina or the ability to be at two or more glittering events at once. In reality, he had many stringers on the lookout, supplying him with news. "I would cover a party for him, and then he'd rewrite it brilliantly," said Zappia. An example of Connolly's phantom haunting of the Hollywood circuit is his column of August 14, 1959, which describes a marathon evening (a Wednesday, no less) of taking in the premiere of Disney's *Big Fisherman*, Tommy Sands's opening at the Cocoanut Grove, and the debut of singer Doris Lee at Dino's nightclub. The reality was that Connolly had attended none of those events but spent the evening at the Hollywood Bowl, raptly taking in a Russian dancing troupe of two hundred and ten members, about which he wrote nothing.[35]

"Wherever he is," reported *People Today*, "Connolly keeps a folded sheet of copy paper handy and jots down shorthand notes." Paramount producer and ambassador-at-large A. C. Lyles says, "I can't picture Mike without paper and pencil." However, working a party with a notepad was considered gauche and Connolly's success at discretion was mixed. "Never take notes at a party," Cole Porter once scolded him. Later the same evening, an obnoxious guest prompted someone to wonder out loud, "Should I pour her cyanide or champagne?" To Connolly's great amusement, Porter whipped out his own notepad, and the priceless phrase the composer had just overheard found its way into "I Am in Love," in his 1953 Broadway musical, *Can-Can*.[36]

Although Connolly complained frequently about publicists and agents who sent inanities his way, in some cases he formed solid friendships with them. Frank Liberman, one of Hollywood's finest publicists, was such a person. Amazingly, Liberman could recall verbatim one of Connolly's best alliterations nearly fifty years after it was printed: "Flapping their Florsheims in a fervid fandango." "I don't remember how I met Mike," Liberman said, "But we hit it off. In a rare moment of introspection, he once asked, 'Whaddya think of my column today?' I said, 'I'm not putting it on my bookshelf next to *Moby Dick*.' He liked that. After that I started giving him items. Once when he was pumping me for news, I said, 'Orson Welles and Rita Hayworth are *definitely* through.' They had been divorced for years by then. He liked my sense of humor, and he was a genuinely funny man himself."

Liberman, whose wife was the sister of the *Hollywood Reporter's* Broadway columnist, Radie Harris, said Connolly was very important to his status as a publicist. "He used my material, and free items — that is, not about my clients — as well. We were in almost daily contact for years. I talked to him every day except Saturdays. Once I had eleven items in one of his columns. And Mike was very careful about what plants he took."[37]

In addition to publicists, Connolly made countless friends among out-of-town show business reporters who made regular trips to Hollywood. Bill Diehl, film editor of the *St. Paul Dispatch*, spent one month each year in Hollywood. "I'd drop in on Mike in his cluttered office and enjoy his hospitality between his never-ending phone calls," Diehl reminisced. "He'd rub his eyes, explain he'd been at some Hollywood wingding until three that morning, and then dig into his mountain of work."[38]

On one such visit, publisher Wilkerson burst into Connolly's office to say his wife had just given birth to his son Willie. "Both Mike and I guffawed," said Diehl, "as Wilkerson exclaimed, 'And all these years, I thought I was shooting blanks!'" On another visit, Connolly read aloud to Diehl one of Sheilah Graham's "Just for Variety" columns. "Sheilah's attempts to sound as if she had a scoop were laughable," Diehl said, "and Mike used to cluck his tongue: 'Oh, Sheilah, Sheilah, you can be funny.'"

Connolly had so many friends in Minnesota's twin cities, in fact, that when he flew to the annual Minneapolis Aquatennial in July 1957, he was feted in grand style by Diehl, Will Jones of the *Minneapolis Tribune*, and Cedric Adams of the *Minneapolis Star*. Adams took Connolly and the rest of his Hollywood entourage, consisting of Jimmy Stewart, Eddie Fisher, and Jayne Mansfield, on a delightful boat ride on Lake Minnetonka.[39]

Yet another source for film industry news was referrals passed along by other columnists. Connolly was cordial to the rest of the Hollywood press in his column, publishing occasional good-natured plugs about all of them, even if many of them regarded him warily. Unquestionably his greatest ally was Louella Parsons. "Louella might call Mike and say, 'I don't want to run this story, because it's a dear friend of mine — but *you* can use it!'" remembered Jack Bradford. Such reciprocity was widespread in the Hollywood press. Parsons described Connolly as "my greatest newspaper rival but still one of my greatest friends." Her gentleman friend in her senescence was songwriter Jimmy McHugh, who shared Connolly's July 10 birthday. The three usually celebrated the day together.[40]

Although Connolly had a seemingly infinite number of sources and venues, news was but a single variety of information he purveyed. "Much of the column was filled up with press agents' expectations for their clients. Hence, a lot of what you read never happened," confessed Bradford. A March 20, 1953, item about actress Jane Powell's making the mistake of brushing a stray lock of hair from her forehead at an auction and becoming the owner of a five-thousand-pound antique bed sounded legitimate enough. However, the identical mishap was reported again on February 17, 1956, but this time Susan Hayward had the unruly strand of hair that saddled her with an antique chest of drawers that fit nowhere. The explanation, at least in Hayward's case, is that she had hired Connolly's best friend Stanley Musgrove to mount a publicity campaign to aid her in capturing the Best Actress Oscar for her star turn in *I'll Cry Tomorrow*. Connolly not only was inclined to grant Musgrove favors but desperately wanted Hayward to win and boost sales on the paperback version of his *I'll Cry Tomorrow*; hence he was printing her name almost every day during Oscar season. (Hayward lost to Anna Magnani.)[41]

"His writing," Jack Bradford commented, "is for people to ask, 'What does he mean? No, no, what does he *really* mean?' If he wrote about an actress suffering from mal-de-motorbike, you can bet that only that girl knew 'motorbike,' per se, had nothing to do with it." The actress was Natalie Wood, and Connolly's wacky diagnosis was his discreet way of saying Wood had attempted suicide by swallowing a bottle of prescription pills. The item was quite typical of "Rambling Reporter" style in that only

Connolly and the target were meant to understand the item. Connolly reported that Frank Sinatra "had tears in his eyes" after Connolly congratulated him for a great performance at the world premiere of *The Man with the Golden Arm*. It was intended as a joke; according to Bunny Seidman, Sinatra, who despised the press, had actually repaid Connolly's flattery by giving him the middle finger. In another seemingly innocent bit, Connolly mused, "Why don't Liz [Taylor] and Eddie [Fisher] want it known they're all alone by a plugged telephone in Connecticut?" Most readers would have glossed over the item without a second thought, but not Fisher; he scrambled to clarify Connolly's meaning in a telegram: "Dear Mike — What I actually did was inform my flacks I crave a big time writer-director buildup rather than a producer push. I gave that up yesterday. Tomorrow I may be a singer again."[42]

Another function of the column was for Connolly to assume the role of a Holy Angels Grammar School nun and crack the knuckles of those who trespassed against Hollywood. "When Connolly publicly spanks some misbehaving star, in a way that no studio would dare," declared *People Today*, "the star, knowing his sins are being publicly promulgated, becomes as obedient as Mary's lamb." His edicts over the years might have been compiled and published as the industry's guide to correct behavior; he was like a cop writing tickets for violations. For example, prowling bargains in Bullock's or Saks' was "unmoviestarrish," he decreed. A wayward actress who thought no one noticed prompted him to rant, "Glamorous movie stars don't eat tuna sandwiches at drugstore counters."[43]

In Connolly's demonology, disrespect for Hollywood was the deadliest sin, with weight gain, failure to attend funerals, and letting one's head swell ("believing one's own publicity") ranking high on the list. "Wish Shelley Winters would quit dishing out those anti–Hollywood interviews," he warned. "What did we do to you, Shell, outside of making you a star?" Over the years Connolly fired off a lengthy list of do's and don'ts directed at Winters, dictating that she should not wear tattered shoes and stockings with runs in public, or appear at the Beverly Hills Hotel pool in zinc oxide makeup and rompers, but could she please comb her hair.[44]

Even Judy Garland, whose musical emoting would elicit cascades of Connolly's lavish superlatives, was not exempt from his jabs if she crossed over the line. "That was an ill-advised blast Judy Garland took at Hollywood," he scowled, after a candid slip she made to the press. "Judy won't have to lose more weight for her next role, since she'll be playing a hefty harridan." When Garland's weight threatened to thwart the filming of *A Star Is Born*, Connolly was merciless, sniping that corpulent Mario Lanza should be her leading man and the studio should let them "stay hefty and film it with the widest lens they can find." Garland biographer Gerald Clarke said Garland admitted to friends that Connolly's comments were hurtful.[45]

The flip side to these blows below the belt was Connolly's praise of exemplary conduct in the service of the industry, as with Ann Blyth, who "never lets her public down — always bright and shining in hat, gloves, sharp makeup and Cadillac"; and Anne Baxter, "altogether enchanting with that handspan waist," who could do no wrong. In Phoenix for the world premiere of *Three Violent People*, Connolly reported that Baxter had packed ten Edith Head outfits and wore each one during two days of non-stop promotional appearances. "She was every inch the movie star and we loved her for it."[46]

But all play and no work made Mike a dull boy; press agent puffery, private jokes, and tongue-lashings and demerits were no substitute in the end for news. To give his column its edge, Connolly needed important scoops, and not only was his instinct for them well-honed, but no one could come near his talent for applying to them the perfectly provocative spin. If Shelley Winters was his favorite piñata, Zsa Zsa Gabor was his inexhaustible font of the most delicious gossip. Tallulah Bankhead had once angered Gabor by comparing her devilishly to her sister Eva; when an auctioneer at a charity event in Palm Springs referred to Zsa Zsa as Eva in an honest mistake, Zsa Zsa threw a fit. The auctioneer's retort, to Gabor's boyfriend, businessman Hal Hayes, was recorded gleefully by Connolly: "I wouldn't marry a woman with a temper like that — you're in for a helluva time!"[47]

A few months later, a spy at Merle Oberon's dinner for the Henry Fords gave Connolly a juicy story. Gabor, the spy said, had tried to enlist Ford in persuading Oberon to let Hal Hayes remain for dinner after cock-tails when Oberon had made it clear there were to be no crashers. No one could have related the saga more wickedly than Connolly. "Miss Gabor," he prattled, "wearing non-matching shoes, one gold, one silver, was backed by [Pulitzer Prize–winning playwright] Ketti Frings. Cooed Ketti: 'C'mon, Merle, be a sport' ... Merle: 'I'm the mistress of my home' ... Ketti: 'Okay, if they go, I go' ... Merle (to butler): 'Bring Mrs. Frings' wrap too.'"[48]

Ketti Frings had a significant role in breaking the news that Holly-wood had waited with bated breath for most of 1959 to hear: which actress would be cast in the title role of 20th Century–Fox's *Cleopatra*. Through-out the year Connolly had identified six different "front runners" for the part, including Susan Hayward, Joan Collins, Gina Lollobrigida, and Lee Remick; he never shined the spotlight on Elizabeth Taylor because he said her salary demands would never be met. In early autumn, Ketti Frings invited Connolly, not a regular in her circle, to a dinner-dance at her home. All the major columnists were in attendance. Frings cut in on Connolly while he was on the dance floor. "Do you know why you were invited tonight?" she asked Connolly. "Kurt [her husband, Taylor's agent] is going to announce Liz for *Cleopatra*." Connolly bolted for the telephone, creating a stir among the guests, especially the other columnists. For such a major scoop, delivered in such dramatic fashion, his item the following day was understated: "Liz Taylor is signed and sealed for *Cleopatra* ... in which Liz will make a spectacular first entrance like Aphrodite but without all those doves."[49]

That Ketti and Kurt Frings plotted in advance to spoon-feed the *Cleopatra* scoop to Connolly speaks to his preeminence as a disseminator; they believed that more key filmmakers got their trade news from Mike Connolly than from any other source. The same preeminence is why Connolly could be such a scourge to Hollywood's Communists.

Chapter 8

Indecency

"There's probably dancing in Red Square today. Joe McCarthy was a great American and his death is a loss to all Americans."
— *Mike Connolly, Hollywood Reporter, May 3, 1957*

The Hollywood blacklist began in November 1947 as an alarmed reaction by the Motion Picture Association of America to public fear of subversive Communist influence in the content of movies. In May of that year, the House Committee on Un-American Activities (HUAC) had held hearings in Hollywood, calling on cooperative, or "friendly," witnesses to reveal what they knew about Communist activity. At follow-up hearings held in Washington, D.C., in October, nineteen screenwriters whose hostility to HUAC was well known were subpoenaed to appear. Ten of the "unfriendly" witnesses challenged HUAC's right to interrogate them about their political beliefs and invoked their Fifth Amendment rights rather than answer questions about current or past Communist Party affiliation. This group came to be known as the Hollywood Ten. They were cited for contempt of Congress and ultimately went to jail.

After the contempt citations, a meeting of motion picture producers convened at the Waldorf-Astoria Hotel in New York. The majority agreed that a sea change in public opinion had occurred and the industry was now in danger of box office boycotts and government control of moviemaking. They issued a statement known as the Waldorf Declaration, asserting that the Hollywood Ten had done the industry a disservice, that the Ten would be discharged from employment in the studios, and that the studios would no longer knowingly hire anyone who was a Communist or a member of any group advocating the overthrow of the U.S. government.[1]

In Washington, D.C., parallel purges of suspected Communists in the State Department, army, and most agencies of the federal government were urged onward by the grand inquisitor of the anti–Communist movement, Senator Joseph McCarthy, Republican of Wisconsin. A significant irony of the McCarthy era, as pointed out by author David Ehrenstein, is that "so many of its key figures (Roy Cohn, Whittaker Chambers, J. Edgar Hoover, and McCarthy himself) were closet homosexuals whose anti–Communist zeal was spurred by fear of being found out."[2]

Even if Mike Connolly was not closeted per se, it remains impossible to believe there was no connection between his sense of difference and the compulsion with which he persecuted Communists. Taken together with his 1937–1938 crusade to force Champaign, Illinois, to close down its bordellos, his anti–Communism reflects the need to establish his manhood and to compensate for not being like other men, not propagating his Irish genes, and not having fought in World War II. By espousing orthodox, mainstream viewpoints as his own, Connolly the outsider would confer upon himself the insider status he craved. The phenomenon was all too familiar to playwright Arthur Laurents, who wrote that right-wingers "were born on the wrong side of the tracks [and] thought playing footsie with conservatives would allow them to cross over. Like the homosexuals back in New York who were Republicans because they wanted to belong."[3]

In Champaign, Connolly had cited venereal disease statistics to justify his efforts to quell prostitution; in Hollywood, his official rationale for anti–Communist demagoguery was that, if they were not put down, Communists would destroy the U.S. government. His diatribes brimmed with intolerance of unorthodox political views and employed the same fallacious reasoning he had employed in Champaign. "If all the angry little men who became commies were so eager to 'help the underdog,' why didn't they drop everything and go to darkest Africa to help the underprivileged there?" he snarled. "What was so uplifting about joining an organization aimed at overthrowing the Government?"[4]

As was the case at the University of Illinois, where he maintained disingenuously that he was not running a "campaign," his propensity for semantic quibbles was alive and well in Hollywood, where he would scoff at a Ford Foundation report that used the term "blacklist." "Our more stable citizenry call it an economic freezeout of the three hundred twenty-six people who raised two million for the overthrow of the U.S. Government," he lectured. "They are not entitled to work here." Playwright Tennessee Williams tried to defend director Elia Kazan from Connolly's attacks by protesting, "Why pick on him just because he made a mistake sixteen years ago and joined the communist party when he didn't know what it was all about?" Connolly's response: "So who's PICKING?"[5]

Walter Winchell, Hedda Hopper, and Florabel Muir, the other gossip columnists known to bedevil Communists from time to time, never came close to attaining the exquisite scurrility of Connolly. Hearing that Charlie Chaplin, an open Communist sympathizer, and Chinese premier Chou En-Lai dined together in Geneva, Connolly wrote that the latter "used to be a female impersonator in China"—then, upon further reflection, decided that such a pairing was "not surprising—look how many years Chaplin spent impersonating a man!" Diana Dors, the British actress under contract to RKO, told *Picturegoer* magazine that she disapproved of Connolly's anti–Chaplin posture, provoking his massive retaliation. "Thank you, Miss Dors, for the Valentine," Connolly rebuked. "Up the Hammer and Sickle, girl, and gather ye those good old Yanqui dollars while ye may." Such verbal batterings, however, were mild compared to his seek-and-destroy missions aimed at getting Communists fired; he could be lethal not only to prestigious directors and writers but to unionized cutters, projectionists, and musicians as well.[6]

Because Connolly had been a music critic at *Daily Variety* before switching to the gossip beat, there had been nothing in the body of his writing to alert Hollywood to his views on Communism. But only two days into his tenure on the "Just for Variety" column, he was already inveighing that a local press agent was winning no friends by his "uninvited" praise of the Hollywood Ten as "brilliant intellectuals." Throughout his two years with "Just for Variety," he warned regularly of Communist taint in movies and carried inside scoops from HUAC's 1951 hearings in Hollywood. However, the opinions he expressed did not reflect those of the management. *Daily Variety* pointedly kept its distance from high-decibel red-baiting after World War II.[7]

The *Hollywood Reporter* had the opposite policy; it was labeled "HUAC's staunchest friend" by Dalton Trumbo, one of the Hollywood Ten. With its right-wing orientation rooted in its dependence on movie studio advertising, the *Hollywood Reporter* was regarded as a mouthpiece for the studios. From its founding in 1930, it was solidly pro-producer and anti-writer, due in part to publisher William R. Wilkerson's belief that the Screen Writers Guild was the prime incubator of Communists in Hollywood. Wilkerson had editorialized in his "Trade Views" column against

"Communist takeover" of the guild as early as 1938. During the thirteen-year Screen Writers Guild ban on its members' advertising their services in trade papers, which the *Hollywood Reporter* itself provoked by railing against the guild's alleged Communist tilt, Wilkerson decreed in retaliation that screenplay credits would be omitted from his paper's film reviews. *Daily Variety*, in contrast, did not take up the cudgel and continued to print screenwriter credits during the ban.[8]

Willie Wilkerson explains, "My father was like a relentless pit bull on the Communist issue. There were many things at work here. First, articles on Communism sold papers. Second, as a Catholic, he despised the atheism in Communism. He used Mike Connolly as his mouthpiece on that issue." Indeed, just as the acid-tongued vice president Spiro Agnew came to be known as "Nixon's Nixon," Connolly may be thought of as "Wilkerson's Wilkerson." Within a week of his debut as "Rambling Reporter" on October 1, 1951, terms such as "jerk," "scummie," "rat," and "vermin," which had been off-limits at *Daily Variety*, began to infest his attacks on identified Communists and unfriendly witnesses.[9]

As Wilkerson's business manager, George Kennedy, had noted, when a story in the *Hollywood Reporter* was important enough, Wilkerson would be involved in it. When Connolly reported that director Elia Kazan had confessed previous Communist Party membership to HUAC but refused to supply any evidence on his former comrades, Kazan's good friend, 20th Century–Fox chief Darryl Zanuck, phoned not Connolly but Wilkerson to protest the item. Wilkerson replied that a member of HUAC had leaked to him the minutes of the "confidential" hearing in which Kazan had testified, and disclosed further that Kazan would soon be summoned to an open hearing in any case. Connolly's name did not come up in the exchange; he had simply written the item and led off that day's column with it.[10]

But it would be wrong to assume that Connolly was only a ventriloquist's dummy to Wilkerson. He had proved at the University of Illinois how capable he was of running a cleansing campaign on his own, and his anti-Communist comments for *Daily Variety*, *Screen Stories*, and other publications not controlled by Wilkerson demonstrate that such sentiments were his own. An unidentified but high-level producer once lit into Connolly, calling him a "witchhunter," an exchange that would not have happened if Connolly were only perceived as a Wilkerson puppet. Bunny Seidman said she and Connolly "used to go tooth and nail" over the blacklist issue. "Mike would say, 'They've taken over the industry — you can't have people like that around.' He'd rant and rave and get furious that I'd think in a different way. Once at a party he was very nice to [actor] Sterling Hayden, who had been blacklisted. I said, 'You're such a two-faced bastard.'"[11]

The entire *Hollywood Reporter* shop was of one mind on the Communist issue, said Seidman. "George Kennedy, [editor] Don Gillette, they were all on the anti–Commie bandwagon with Mike," she recalled. Connolly rarely kept company with anyone who did not share his philosophy. An important exception was *Chicago Sun-Times* columnist Irv Kupcinet, Connolly's close friend since the War years. "Kup" had joined the group of liberal actors and actresses who traveled to Washington in October 1947 as moral support for the unfriendly witnesses, and he later lamented the "unbelievable bad taste and sheer stupidity of the HUAC Congressmen." He was proud to have called Senator McCarthy's bluff by examining surreptitiously the papers McCarthy would wave at press conferences and discovering them either to contain flimsy evidence or to be blank. Yet he and Connolly found common ground in charitable causes and Connolly threw lavish parties for him in Hollywood. Asked about the underpinnings of Connolly's views, Kupcinet said simply, "Hatred of Communists was typical of Irish Catholics."[12]

Back at the *Daily Illini*, Connolly's most potent weapon in the bawdy house battle had been the constant threat to print a list of prominent citizens who owned the red light district properties used for prostitution. But in Hollywood, there were no warnings. He regularly published the names of unrehabilitated Communists, the studios and other contractors employing them, and the films they were working on. His mentor in this technique was the *American Legion Magazine*, whose campaign to boycott and picket films not utterly free of Communist actors, directors, producers, or writers was at its height just as Connolly joined Wilkerson's team. An article in its December 1951 issue featured an exhaustive list of all contaminated films currently in release or production, and Connolly quoted it extensively.[13]

However, if a Communist repudiated the party and confessed his sins to HUAC, Connolly would use that fact to taunt those who were still sticking to their principles. "Richard Collins," he announced, "got his first scripting job since his friendly testimony. He's working at Republic." He reported that the Communist newspaper *People's World* was "screaming" because director Eddie Dmytryk, one of the Hollywood Ten who reversed course and named names before HUAC, had been hired by King Brothers Productions. "[This] move shatters the Party line that members might just as well stand on the Fifth Amendment since they'll never get another job in Hollywood anyway," he proclaimed.[14]

Although Connolly had had excellent training as a reporter and could ordinarily be counted on to check facts before rushing unverified information into print, his zeal in the pursuit of Communists often trumped his journalistic propriety. "[Director] John Huston's name came up in the Red hearings downtown Monday," he wrote, firing before aiming. "A typewriter repairman planted by the FBI in the local Commie party claimed that Huston, among others, participated in Red activities a few years back." The following day he had to carry a retraction: "Typewriter repairman planted by the FBI claims he was referring to John Houston, not Hollywood's Huston, at the downtown red hearings." During the blacklist years, Connolly libeled at least seven other film industry figures in the same reckless manner: director Lewis Milestone, screenwriter Garson Kanin, actor Marc Lawrence, composer Frank Loesser, writer-producer Frank Davis, screenwriter Michael Blankfort, and actor Bob Richards.[15]

Sometimes when names alone were not harmful enough, Connolly published addresses as well. "Charles Page, one of the three Screen Writers Guild secretaries who invoked the Fifth, is now teaching at U[niversity] of C[alifornia] in Riverside — a member of the Department of Humanities, Room 2234, Administration Building. No commies in our school system? Academic freedom?" If the "left-winging Unitarian Church" hosted a concert by civil rights activist Paul Robeson, or the Circle Theater sponsored a play produced by unfriendly witnesses who had taken the Fifth Amendment, Connolly would print the location of the event, presumably to incite picketing or worse.[16]

Occasionally Connolly would cross the line from mouthpiece to actual inquisitor. The blacklisted 1954 film *Salt of the Earth*, a story about miners on strike, was written, acted, and filmed by professionals who had been fired from various studios for Communist affiliations. When *Salt of the Earth* managed to open at a Hollywood Boulevard theater in spite of forceful industry opposition to its playing anywhere near Hollywood, Connolly spotted his chance to be a warrior for the cause. He phoned local radio stations who were airing advertisements for "this stomach-turning movie," and frightened them into ceasing and desisting on the spot. The movie's producers, Connolly gloated, "tried to sell KFAC a package of thirty-second commercials. Station's Cal Smith told us: "We turned them down flat ... Mort Hall of KLAC admitted a few plugs have been aired on his station but said: 'Come hell or high water, they won't go on again' ... Harry Maizish of KFWB said he got caught too, adding, "We've run three but we're throwing them off the air as of now' ... Bob Reynolds of KMPC told us he, too, is canceling the remaining seven plug-uglies they stuck him with."[17] There seemed to be no defense to such attacks. If Connolly smelled blood in the water, what could a few humble radio station managers and college professors do in the face of such overwhelming odds but roll over and play dead?

Philosophically, Connolly marched in lockstep with the anti–Communist movement's prophet, the Irish-Catholic Senator Joseph McCarthy, and he would alter his battle plan in reaction to McCarthy's dwindling fortunes. Shortly after the senator's famous self-destruction at the hands of army counsel Joseph Welch, on June 9, 1954, Connolly's vigilance began to shift from Hollywood to New York, and he sounded his trumpet to open the eastern front: "When are they going to start ridding Broadway of the rats that Hollywood flushed out?" Throughout the rest of the year, he kept predicting dire fates for "Broadway scummies on the lam from Hollywood" once HUAC — and *Confidential* magazine —caught up with them.[18]

Liz Smith, legendary gossip columnist for the *New York Post* and *Newsday*, recalled her minor role as one of Connolly's New York–based tipsters. "I met Mike at the height of his Commie-baiting career, where he was intent on ruining people's lives just because he could," Smith said. Their introduction was made by Lynn Bowers, a ghostwriter for Louella Parsons and publicist, while Smith was touring Hollywood as a *Modern Screen* reporter, circa 1952. "I was a total nobody at the time," Smith continued, "but Mike talked me into keeping my ears open and sending him items for his column. I soon discovered what a mean shit he could be. He had very little care for whether he was right or wrong, only whether he could get away with it or not. All the Hearst reporters at the time assumed there was a spy or traitor under every bed; Mike was much the same. I learned from knowing him that he was the kind of columnist I would never want to be like."[19]

The day before the Senate issued its grave censure of Joseph McCarthy, Connolly protested, "The commies have been fantastically successful in lambasting and defaming Senator McCarthy. In all the name-calling, let us NOT forget who our real enemies are!"[20] Eight days after the censure, Connolly condemned an off–Broadway production, *Sandhog*, at New York's Phoenix Theater, because its co-authors, Waldo Salt and Earl Robinson, were "identified commies" and both its directors, Howard da Silva and Howard Bay, had taken the Fifth Amendment. He also denounced *Sandhog's* producer (and founder of the Phoenix), Norris Houghton, as an "ex-employee of the Soviet Union's Intourist Bureau ... Houghton, as a matter of fact, once conducted a May Day tour to Moscow!"[21]

Norris Houghton, in his memoirs, observed, "When Joseph McCarthy was finally broken by the Senate's censure, we thought the nightmare was at last over. We were wrong." Houghton said he had hired Salt, Robinson, and the others because they were "the best possible talent.... We wanted them for their ability, not for their politics." Houghton *had* visited Moscow in the thirties—as a Guggenheim fellow, to study production methods in the Soviet theater. "It didn't fit into their scenario that I had also been there during my wartime naval service," he said. Connolly's attack "coincided with a good deal of unsavory reporting in the poison-pen publications *Red Channels* and *Counterattack*.... As usual, fact and fiction were skillfully confused in those days by gossip columnists." It cost the Phoenix Theater the sponsorship of some of its patrons, including Brooke Astor.[22]

Senator McCarthy's downfall did not initially put the brake on HUAC in its grand scheme to scorch every branch of show business. In April 1956, the Committee returned to Hollywood to hold a week of hearings on Communist influence in the local musicians' union. Because Connolly knew the music business so well, he took a heightened interest in the proceedings. Warner Bros. and Universal-International fired their contract musicians who refused to admit past Communist party membership. Connolly was peeved that MGM failed to do likewise; twice in one week he nagged MGM but its "unfriendly" musicians remained in place. The likely reason for MGM's steadfastness was the liberal politics of studio head Dore Schary.[23]

Finally, Connolly decided it was time for some hardball, as only he could play it. He wrote, "MGM still has two Fifth Amendment musicians on the payroll: Edgar Lustgarten and Sidney Greene ... The same Lustgarten worked, along with two other Fifth Amendment musicians, Eudice Shapiro and Victor Gottlieb, on Mario Lanza's RCA-Victor recording sessions May 14, 15, and 17. They were hired by MCA's music contractor, Robert Helfer."[24]

MGM did not give in to the bullying but remained silent on the issue. Connolly's next choice of target, however, would be anything but quiet. Two years earlier, Connolly had grumbled at a movie co-production agreement between Italy and the Soviet Union, perceiving it as a boon to Communist propaganda. Now, on May 6, 1956, the Soviet Ministry of Culture and the American impresario Mike Todd held a press conference in Moscow to announce a co-production venture comprising five films, using Todd's 65mm widescreen process, Todd-AO. Todd also revealed that his almost-completed picture, *Around the World in Eighty Days*, would premiere in Moscow in November.[25]

Connolly's initial reaction was to quip that Russia already had widescreen and stereophonic personalities (Khrushchev and Bulganin) but no wide screens. Then, arguing that the Soviets could not be trusted to fulfill any business agreement with Hollywood, he declared, "We'll guess right here that not Mike Todd nor yet any other Hollywood producer will ever enter into a co-production deal with the Russians."[26]

As the summer wore on, events appeared to be moving contrary to Connolly's prediction. On August 21, Russia's first vice-minister of culture, Vladimir Surin, was Todd's guest of honor at a Beverly Hills Hotel press luncheon. Surin said he was in town to finalize negotiations on *The Great Concert*, Todd's projected first motion picture production in the USSR. Todd, Surin averred, would have as much freedom producing Russian pictures as he enjoyed in America.[27]

While Todd was laboring during August to finalize his unprecedented deal with the Soviets, Connolly spent two madcap weeks covering politics instead of movie industry rumors. First he flew to Chicago for the Democratic National Convention, where he joined *Chicago Sun-Times* newsmen for their private luncheon with Harry Truman. He reported that the former president "blasted [me] for not sharing his political views (but BLASTED!)." Striking back from his own bully pulpit, Connolly regretted that Truman was one of those "who never know when the clock has struck and who get bundled up and shipped to the Limbo of Defeated Politicians."[28]

Much closer to Connolly's heart was his jaunt the following week to San Francisco, with Bunny Seidman on his arm, for the GOP convention. (Seidman, a Democrat, was under strict orders to "keep your mouth shut!") On one level, the convention bored him. "Did you ever hear so many gas bags, with so little to say, and taking hours to say it?" he asided in the column. He winked at Seidman and asked, "Do you want to cut out?" "We left early," Seidman reports, "and we hit all the gay bars, Gordon's and others. Then we went to a party and stayed up all night."[29]

But on another level, the GOP convention stirred up Connolly's deeply held feelings about America as defender of all things good and true. With the memories of the Democratic convention still fresh, the contrasts between the two parties could not be clearer to him, and he craved being part of the status quo that a Republican victory would vouchsafe. He wrote letters to both Eisenhower and Nixon expressing his delight at their renominations and predicting that he would surely be congratulating them again after the November election.[30]

Bursting with renewed enthusiasm and commitment to America as it was embodied by his idol, Nixon, Connolly felt strongly that he must not just sit there, but do something. His solution was to box Mike Todd's ears for consorting with the infidel Soviets. "In a recording session for *Around the World in Eighty Days*," Connolly charged, "music contractor Henry Hill is using some of the Fifth Amendment musicians, among them

Eudice Shapiro and Victor Gottlieb, both fired by Universal for taking the Fifth. Wasn't it *Eighty Days* producer Mike Todd who recently announced a production deal with the Soviets? Any connection?"[31]

Todd, who was nobody's patsy, wasted no time in fighting back, buying full-page ads the following day in both the *Hollywood Reporter* and *Daily Variety*. His response was forceful and blunt:

> "ANY CONNECTION?"
>
> My answer is "NO."
>
> And if Mr. Connolly or any other self-appointed defender of the nation's security or welfare, thinks or knows otherwise, let them have the guts to openly say so.
>
> The cute, vicious, destructive smear by innuendo is not only harmful to me and the picture — but is a reflection on our whole industry by stigmatizing innocent people, properties and motives. Innocent in the judgment of our country's highest authority on the subject.
>
> I will not be cute or subtle with you, Mr. Connolly — I will bluntly and flatly spell out for you, in a manner you do not have the courage to, that your vicious unsubstantiated smears are UN-AMERICAN.
>
> And to you or any other Mike Connollys who think they are heavy-weight enough, who want to slug it out with me on this subject, I promise you, you may find you are not playing with kids. Continue with these cracks if you have the courage.
>
> Normally I try to avoid fights — especially with little people — I am making an exception in this case as an example for other guiltless persons who can't hit back as hard as I think I can — Michael Todd.[32]

The Todd manifesto appeared on a Friday. On Monday morning, after the smoke had cleared somewhat, Connolly ran a few cryptic, out-of-context items in his column that only those who had followed the matter would understand. "Thank you, Louis B. Mayer, for your nice note ... Thanks, too, to you crackpots for your anonymous condemnations. We regard them tenderly, as love letters, just as we cherish blasts from the *Daily Worker* [a Communist newspaper]." Later in the week he printed notes from secretary of defense Charles E. Wilson, pointing out that "Communists are all corrupt (including those who make Soviet movies)"; and from former ambassador to the USSR William C. Bullitt, saying, "the men now attempting to prove themselves amiable souls are the same men who carried out murders, tortures, and mass starvations for Stalin."[33]

This decisive "Mike versus Mike" fracas was to Connolly what the more prominent "Joe versus Joe" (McCarthy and Welch) confrontation was to the senator: It marked the beginning of the end. Todd had in essence put to Connolly Joseph Welch's rhetorical question, "Have you no sense of decency, sir?" Based on Connolly's subsequent actions, the answer would seem to be an unrepentant no. The chain of events that would break the Hollywood blacklist had already been set in motion, but Connolly would soldier on until he was risibly out of step with the rest of Hollywood.

As if to demonstrate the hardening of his heart, Connolly lashed out once more against MGM within the week, writing, "Those two musicians who shrieked defiance at the HUAC are still working in the studios." At some point, the combination of Connolly's unflagging vendetta against the remaining ex–Communist musicians (Lustgarten and Greene) and the imminent sacking of the liberal Dore Schary as head of MGM resulted at last in the musicians' firing, according to Lustgarten's daughter.[34]

Concurrent with the harassment of musicians and Mike Todd, another highlight of 1956 in the "Rambling Reporter" was playwright Arthur Miller's refusal before HUAC to identify people he had seen at Communist party meetings years before. Already Connolly had criticized Miller for "wasting his time" writing *The Crucible*, a play about witch-burning, when "the horrors of Communism, today's most burning issue, are staring him in the face, begging to be dramatized." Now he took advantage of Miller's plight to vent accumulated resentment of Miller's wife, Marilyn Monroe. "That commie-loving Miller and Miss *Brothers Karamazov* Monroe deserve each other," Connolly wrote on the morning that the headlines blared the Miller-HUAC story. The mud was flung relentlessly, with Connolly demanding that Miller "come out from behind that lady's skirts" and referring to Monroe's earlier marriage to baseball great Joe DiMaggio with, "This is Your Life, Marilyn Monroe: From a four-base hitter to a Fifth Amendment hider." Connolly used every last insult he could think of, including the obvious "Mr. Marilyn Monroe." When Monroe's affair with Yves Montand became public information in August 1960, Connolly was deliberately cruel. Since Montand and his wife, actress Simone Signoret, both supported Communist causes, Connolly seemed to feel that both couples were getting what they deserved. "One consolation for Arthur Miller — it's all great material for a new play!" he gloated.[35]

Scholars differ on when the blacklist plague in Hollywood was genuinely "over," but there were significant milestones along the protracted way out of hell. The 1957 Best Screenplay Oscar, for *The Brave Ones*, went to the unknown "Robert Rich," a pseudonym for Hollywood Ten member Dalton Trumbo. In August 1958, 20th Century–Fox president Spyros

Skouras wrote a congratulatory letter to Arthur Miller on the overturn of Miller's contempt of Congress citation. Skouras had been among the most adamant industry proponents of the blacklist, so his letter was seen as evidence of HUAC's faltering influence in Hollywood. The presentation to Simone Signoret of the Best Actress Oscar in 1960 signified to Signoret Hollywood's wish to bury the memory of McCarthyism.[36]

The "Robert Rich" mishap, an embarrassment to the Motion Picture Academy, was bound to stir up virulent passions in the "Rambling Reporter." From the moment the orphan Oscar was announced, Connolly would spend the next two years trying to ferret out which vile blacklistee the phantom might be. When Dalton Trumbo unmasked himself as "Robert Rich" in January 1959, Connolly crowed lustily that he alone had been printing the rumors about the "vitriolic Fifth-Taker Trumbo." As with Arthur Miller, Connolly could not curb his unruly pen; he claimed the Internal Revenue Service would investigate which name Trumbo paid taxes under, if at all. He listed some of Trumbo's thirty claimed aliases and castigated "all you producers" for being duped. For his part, Dalton Trumbo is the only blacklist victim to have commented specifically on Connolly. Admiring Walter Winchell's tenacity with a scoop, Trumbo said Winchell "is not Mike Connelly [*sic*], whom everybody can and does ignore with perfect safety."[37]

"Robert Rich" was only the most extreme example of the widespread practice of blacklisted screenwriters' selling scripts pseudonymously. Connolly had a four-year running battle with producer Sam Spiegel over the true provenance of the *Bridge Over the River Kwai* screenplay; Connolly knew that blacklistee Carl Foreman was the author and so declared in his column. After his second jab at Spiegel, the producer phoned to deny any involvement by Foreman at all. But a year later Connolly was back at it like a horsefly, adding that Foreman not only scripted but owned a sizeable percentage of *Kwai*. This time Foreman himself rang up to say, "If Sam Spiegel states the final shooting script was prepared by [three others] I assume this statement is true and I have no intention or desire to challenge or dispute the credits." But Connolly insisted on having the last word two years later, taunting, "Remember Sam Spiegel's sputterings and stammerings when we reported Redskis writing *River Kwai*?"[38]

None of the signs of a declining blacklist fazed Connolly. The visit of the Soviet premier and Mrs. Khrushchev to 20th Century–Fox in September 1959, hosted as a gesture of hospitality and peace on Hollywood's part, set off unprecedented biliousness in the "Rambling Reporter," where they were dubbed "Fat Ol' Ma and Pa Kettle." He applauded Paris newspapers for refusing to print Simone Signoret's picture after she signed a declaration "supporting insubordination in the French army and advocating aid and comfort for the Reds ... But WE give aid and comfort to Mlle. S. by handing her an Oscar!" He would continue to hurl his thunderbolts even after publisher Wilkerson's death in September 1962. Indeed, with what were virtually his last breaths, he was castigating actress Vanessa Redgrave for her support of Cuba's Fidel Castro. In his view, Redgrave's interest in Cuban affairs was only a ploy for publicity. With unrestrained glee, he called attention to her upcoming role in *Camelot* for Warner Bros., the studio whose motto was "Combining Good Citizenship with Good Moviemaking."[39]

As the 1960s progressed, Connolly's head seemed to be telling him that the Communist threat in Hollywood had long since been discredited, but his heart was ruled by the reactionary passions that bubbled within him. It showed in his comments; without admitting that anything had changed, his attitude toward the blacklist metamorphosed to "Oh, *that* old thing!" He dismissed a group of screenwriters' "tired old lawsuit" against the studios for having a blacklist, despite their claim of proof of a conspiracy to withhold work from Communists: "How in blue blazes [do] they hope to win such a suit when there isn't a single studio in town that isn't hiring 'em?" He scoffed that Hollywood Ten member Ring Lardner, Jr., should "dry those no-work tears," as director Otto Preminger had just signed Lardner for a plum assignment. Underlying all this was a sense of revulsion and disgust that anyone could hire Communists.[40]

At other times he seemed to be letting bygones be bygones. Names of those he had skewered during the McCarthy reign might pop up in columns of the 1960s as mere gossip fodder. Writer Dorothy Parker, whom he had called a "sick soul," was wished happy birthday; Jules Dassin, fingered many times as a "fugitive from the HUAC," was reported to be mired in alimony hassles like any number of other film directors; and Signoret, formerly hissed as "France's top Commie thesp," was now "simply wonderful" in *Ship of Fools*.[41] The tacit message that his long, devastating campaign of harassment and injury had simply been all in a day's work, and thanks for the memories, must have seemed unbearable.

Decency, wrote H. L. Mencken,

> [is] the habit ... of viewing with tolerance and charity the acts and ideas of other individuals—the habit which makes a man a reliable friend, a generous opponent, and a good citizen. [The democrat's] eagerness to bring all his fellow citizens ... into accord with his own dull and docile way of thinking, and to force it upon them when they resist, leads him inevitably into acts of unfairness, oppression and dishonour....[42]

Connolly could be tolerant, charitable, even decent. He once wrote, "The point was not that Victor Hugo ran after young girls but that this runner after young girls wrote a masterpiece called *Les Misérables.*" Regrettably, Connolly never grasped the parallel point that Communists had given Hollywood many outstanding screenplays and performances.[43]

Chapter 9

Glutton for Punishment

"Dull week. Will somebody please slug somebody?"
— *Mike Connolly, Hollywood Reporter,*
Oct. 19, 1955

There are, in the annals of Hollywood vagaries, scores of landmark fracases and fisticuffs involving the Fourth Estate. "The Hollywood press," Ezra Goodman sighed, "does not merely chronicle the show. It is part of the show itself."[1]

Connolly was well aware of the risks. "Remember when Joe Cotten kicked Hedda Hopper in the derrière?" he asked. "And when Joan Fontaine threatened to sock Edith Gwynn in the kisser? Ah, for the good old days! Why is it they never call when you write nice things about them? But when you tell the TRUTH they snap and snarl like unlicked cubs."[2]

For many years, the reigning champion in columnist-star bouts was the Joseph Cotton–Hedda Hopper encounter Connolly cited with such reverence. Hopper, the hatted dowager columnist, was running items hinting (delicately, for it was 1943) that Cotten and singing actress Deanna Durbin, a juvenile at the time, were trysting while making *Hers to Hold* together. Cotten's wife, Lenore, the long-suffering type, was terribly upset, prompting Cotten to issue to Hopper a cease-and-desist warning. Hopper ignored the request. Soon after, at the Academy Awards, Cotten walked up to Hopper and kicked her posterior, sending her sprawling. The next day, a flood of telegrams and bouquets arrived at the Cotten home from individuals who had only dreamed of showing comparable courage in the face of Hopper's mischief. Cotten wallpapered his bathroom with the telegrams.[3]

Such were the hazards of navigating a fine line between giving the Hollywood bigwiggery the publicity it needed and vexing it with the publicity it did not want. In 1953, *People Today* noted, "Connolly's been threatened several times with murder, libel, and other court actions, and has been involved in several printers-ink feuds. So far he's unscathed." The reference to a murder threat surely referred to the Chicago underworld's warning to Connolly's parents when he was shutting down brothels in college. There was precedent in the Hollywood press for similar endangerment: Connolly's old boss Arthur Ungar had a police bodyguard and police protection of his home while *Daily Variety* was running a series on organized crime's grip on Hollywood unions. More often, though, Hollywood figures limited their revenge on columnists' jibes to insults or punches.[4]

Connolly's tone in the "Rambling Reporter" made it sound as if he thought the publicity game was all a big joke. Jayne Mansfield confessed to him in a restaurant that she herself had fed an item to Walter Winchell about her "breakup" with actor Robbie Robertson. On his way out of the restaurant, Connolly overheard Mansfield telling Robertson from a pay phone, "But Robbie, honey, don't believe all that stuff you read in the columns!" Stars *need* publicity, Connolly reasoned; how can they possibly have feelings about what in the long run is good for them? An up-and-coming actress, he reported, complained bitterly to him that a female columnist ("that witch") had been printing spiteful items about her for years—"and now, just when people are starting to take notice, she gets sore and refuses even to mention my name!"[5]

Another reason for Connolly's stance is that he believed the protested items were, regardless of the howls and wails they prompted, God's honest truth. On February 13, 1956, he predicted *Mister Roberts, Marty,* and *Love Me or Leave Me* would be the winners of the 1955 Screenwriters' Awards. The ink was hardly dry on that day's edition before the Awards Committee chairman, Frank Nugent, phoned Connolly and "waxed downright abusive and insulting" in demanding a retraction. Connolly's forecast, Nugent seethed, was "in error" and "caused confusion and embarrassment." One month later, those same three films were named the 1955 winners at the annual Screenwriters' banquet. "We have received no call, no telegram, no letter, no word at all, from word-slinger Nugent," Connolly noted in triumph.[6]

Irate readers such as Frank Nugent were an occupational hazard to which Connolly had developed a thick skin; listening to their grievances was part of his daily routine. After Connolly ran an item about one of Marion Davies's million-dollar gems, her husband, Horace Brown, phoned Connolly to grouse about having to double Davies' bodyguard detail.

Comedian Danny Thomas rang up, in response to the news that daughter Marlo was engaged, to rant that Marlo "has no intentions of marrying that boy this January or any January, as the would-be groom advised us." Shelley Winters, Connolly's all-time favorite target, once "pointed accusingly" at him and yelled, "I wasn't as good as I should have been on *Climax!* because I was upset over SOMEBODY printing that my guy was out with a brunette!"[7]

Producer Jerry Wald, although very friendly with Connolly, was in a class by himself as a prickly public figure. A former reporter himself, and a prolific generator of correspondence and memoranda, Wald bombarded Connolly incessantly with alternating gratitude and condemnation. The recurring gripe throughout Wald's notes was, how can you be telling me over and over how grateful you are for my input on the one hand and then turn around and embarrass the hell out of me on the other? Often the notes ended with a plea for Connolly to phone Wald before running an item on him. After Connolly mollified Wald with a rare correction, he quoted to Wald the classic line of a female columnist, "Goddammit, every time I check a story I lose it!"[8]

Perhaps the irate reader Connolly regretted offending the most was J. Edgar Hoover. Connolly allowed no attack on Hollywood to go unanswered, even if the foe was a fellow right-winger. He returned the fire even of such stalwarts as Billy Graham and Norman Vincent Peale. In the case of the director of the FBI, he wrote, "G-Man Hoover's continuing blasts at crime movies amuse us no end. Remember Hoover's own screen credit on the sizzlin'est shoot-'em-upper of them all, *G-Man*, way back in '35 when he needed the publicity?"[9]

Given publisher William R. Wilkerson's close friendship with Hoover, it is odd that such an item was allowed to go to press. Time and time again Hoover had supplied Wilkerson with confidential information to be used in the *Hollywood Reporter's* anti–Communist crusade. The means by which Hoover signaled he was not amused by Connolly's item are not known, but business manager George Kennedy drafted a letter of apology for Connolly to send, full of declarations of abject penitence. The letter blamed the movie industry's shrinking box office receipts for Connolly's temporary insanity. It confessed shame for having to apologize to the one man in America Connolly admired most.[10]

The fame of the two most highly visible Hollywood columnists, Hedda Hopper and Louella Parsons, was enhanced by their perennial rivalry (which may have been little more genuine than the so-called Jack Benny–Fred Allen feud). Interestingly, the Mike Connolly–Hedda Hopper wars were far more vitriolic than any defamations Hopper and Parsons might have slung at each other. The Connolly-Hopper feud's origins are much murkier than its manifestations. In print they referred to each other as "that dame" and "that busybody," but in private correspondence, Hopper called Connolly a "drunken faggot" and spread the word that she did not want her name appearing in the "Rambling Reporter."[11]

In the dawn of Connolly's career he seemed friendly enough with Hopper; he once reminded her of a day in 1946 when they had sat together in the Hollywood Derby, dishing the dirt. For several years, his mentions of her were complimentary and frequent. However, his obvious and fatuous favoritism of Louella Parsons, who was, after all, Catholic and an Illinois native to boot, must have rankled Hopper. Still, he and she were perfectly civil toward each other right up until December 1956, when they quarreled while flying to Alaska with Bob Hope. Connolly had been a guest at her June 24, 1956, garden party for Ernest Borgnine, and again at her Republican fundraising cocktail party in September, where she spied his "YCERSOYA" button picturing an elephant putting up his dukes (educated guess: "You Can't Elect Republicans Sitting On Your Ass") and stole it off his lapel.[12]

Both Connolly and Hopper, along with scores of other show business reporters, had signed on to Bob Hope's Alaska-bound troop-entertaining retinue. "The flight direct to Elmendorf Air Force Base at Anchorage took nine hours, during which the passengers changed seats as often as movie stars change husbands," wrote *San Francisco Chronicle* columnist Terrence O'Flaherty, one of many reporters on the junket. Singer Peggy King remembers, "I sat with Mike on the plane to Alaska. Everyone had been drinking a lot. It seems Hedda came across the aisle and accused him of something. Mike tried to avoid getting into anything, but she was tenacious and kept after him. I think she wanted to have a physical fight. They had an argument in the back of the plane, back by the bar. Bob Hope wasn't the type of man who would put up with a lot of that kind of thing, of course, but he just walked away from it."[13]

Frank Liberman, Hope's publicist, said he thought the trouble between these two titans of gossip began on the plane when Connolly, drunk, referred to Hopper's son, actor Bill Hopper, as a "faggot" in her presence. "They were out for blood," Liberman recalled. "They were yelling and screaming and I think he was going to hit her. I had to break them up." One year later, when Hope and his Christmas show were entertaining troops in Japan and Okinawa, Connolly and Hopper were once again part of the entourage. Liberman said, "Hope made Mike and Hedda kiss and make up for their fight the year before. But after they kissed, Hedda spat on the ground."[14]

After the two far-flung Hope junkets, the gloves were off. Hopper went after Connolly by attempting to debunk all of the high-profile divorce scoops he broke in his column. In each case, though, Connolly had the last laugh because he was not only a better writer but a better reporter than Hopper. "Cary Grant FIRST asked Betsy Drake for a divorce late in October 1957," he said sternly. "It was printed here FIRST. On November 2, 1957, another columnist [Hopper] corrected us: 'Grant doesn't mind that a columnist continues to write that he and Betsy will soon divorce. He said, 'I don't care what he says so long as he doesn't claim I murdered my grandmother. What's the difference? He has to write about somebody.' On October 18, 1958, the same columnist bylined this: 'Cary and Betsy last night announced their separation, which has been expected for some time.'"[15]

A few years later, the scenario was repeated almost detail-for-detail; only the names and dates changed. "That dame who keeps denying our scoops (and we don't mean Louella) has been at it again," Connolly gloated. "For the record—from this space, February 20, 1959: 'Sorry to hear Ann Miller and Bill Moss are having marital difficulties' ... From that other column, February 23, 1959: 'Ran into Ann Miller and her husband Bill Moss who put to shame that reporter [Hopper actually had said 'that busybody'] who swore they were having trouble' ... From Harrison Carroll, February 15, 1961: 'Now that the divorce suit against Bill Moss has been filed, Ann Miller tearfully admits that the marriage has been in trouble for a year and a half.' From Confucius, 477 B.C.: 'The early reporter catches the scoops.'"[16]

Hopper did not attend the Masquers Club's 1961 roasting of Connolly as "Irishman of the Year," a major snub as measured by any yardstick of Hollywood protocol. "After Mike's roast," said Frank Liberman, "Hedda asked me what they served, and I said corned beef and cabbage. She replied, sniffily, 'Corned beef and cabbage should only be served in the sanctity of one's home.'"[17]

One of Connolly's closer encounters with harm came in the wake of this December 22, 1959, item: "Lucille Ball's black-and-bruised eye, cheek, and elbow did NOT come from anything as unexciting as bumping into a glass doorknob imported from Venice by Desi—saying which Lucy lit out for Sun Valley solo." After Connolly's death, Jack Bradford wrote, "Not till now is it known the Venetian door knob item brought the rush of a gun and brass knuckles."[18]

Elaborating on his curious and still-cryptic item, Bradford said, "Desi Arnaz used to beat up Lucy and we knew about it—we knew her makeup man, Hal, who told Mike he had to cover Lucy's shiner with makeup. Desi and Lucy were just back from Venice. Desi knew Mike knew the story. He and George Murphy — the future senator from California! — showed up at the *Hollywood Reporter* office, looking for Mike. The receptionist called up to Mike to say Desi and George Murphy were armed and on their way up. Mike escaped by running down his private stairway."[19]

Perhaps it was fear of Arnaz's brass knuckles that impelled Connolly to issue the following correction: "We are glad to admit that the couple of lines here Monday regarding Lucille Ball and Desi Arnaz are wrong. We were fed this 'stiff' by one we thought knew what he was talking about. Sorry." Strangely, though, Connolly reversed course two months later and demanded credit for the original item he had repudiated. "We don't like to crow. Neither do we like to eat crow. Be that as it may, Lucy Ball's separation stirred up a storm of protest from parties concerned when this pillar tipped it off last December 22. So see today's headlines. Ho-hum."[20]

Connolly's next brush with assault and battery was averted by an even narrower margin. It was the culmination of a ten-year series of tongue-lashings of actress Lana Turner in the "Rambling Reporter" (and even in "Just for Variety" before that). The catalyst for the imbroglio was Turner's teenage daughter, Cheryl Crane, who had been in and out of detention homes since her tragic and widely sensationalized stabbing of her mother's mobster lover, Johnny Stompanato, on April 4, 1958. But apart from the issue of Cheryl's teenage angst, Connolly had played rough with Turner for over a decade, making snide comments whenever her weight exceeded what a major star ought to weigh or smirking in print at her succession of studly paramours. "Lana is certainly a zaftig-looking matron these days, so the cameraman on *Mr. Imperium* has really got his job cut out for him," he had written in 1950. True, if he thought she looked sensational in a movie or at an event, or was good in a particular role, he praised her, but the brickbats outnumbered the daisies roughly on a five-to-one basis.[21]

To be given such a hard time by the *Hollywood Reporter* was a source of chagrin to Turner, because her friendship with publisher William R. Wilkerson had been long and rewarding. Wilkerson was the one who made the famous discovery of Turner at a soda fountain across from Hollywood High, giving her career its start; she in turn asked him to be best man at her third wedding, to Bob Topping, and Wilkerson then insisted on hosting the wedding and reception at his Bel Air home.[22]

Cheryl Crane's name was appearing regularly in Connolly's column even before she turned ten. After the Stompanato stabbing, he tactfully refrained from mentioning her name for several months; however, he did write, "Town's sympathy is with Steve Crane and his daughter," making clear by omission who he thought was to blame in the mess.[23]

Events in Connolly's life leading up to a poisonous June 22, 1960, item implying Turner's unfitness as a mother followed a pattern similar to the events that precipitated his attack on Mike Todd four years earlier. While on a four-week trip to Europe, he became frustrated by the United States' humiliation over the shooting down of its U-2 spy plane by the Soviet Union and the consequent setbacks to America's credibility. He was in Paris when Khrushchev stalked out of the highly anticipated four-nation summit talks at the Elysée Palace and revoked Eisenhower's invitation to Moscow, and he had listened to Parisian commentators favor the Soviet Union and disparage the U.S. Then, just as he returned home, leftist riots erupted in Japan over that country's harboring of three more U-2 planes, forcing the cancellation of Eisenhower's planned state visit to Japan. In Connolly's view, the Communists had learned from American-style public relations and become better at the game than the inventors. "A handful [of Communists] succeeded where the 'Great Emperor' Hirohito and all his military might failed during World War II. They repulsed an American landing," he wrote in disgust. "What this country needs most is a GREAT publicity–public relations man, in the hottest Hollywood bally-hoo tradition! We must sell our great country abroad. The Voice of America can't because the Reds jam it. Power publicity by other means can ... and MUST!" If the alleged failure of American public relations had not riled Connolly enough, he raged further that during his absence from Hollywood, the screenplay business had been good enough for Hollywood Ten member Dalton Trumbo to afford two new cars.[24]

News awaiting Connolly at his office was not good, either. Before leaving for Europe, he had been monitoring carefully the ongoing Writers Guild of America strike, and in the usual *Hollywood Reporter* mode had fired a steady barrage of verbal barbs at what he considered the majority Communist element in the guild. "All you scripters unwittingly playing along with undercover commies in the WGA are due for a surprise when the facts behind the No-Work Curtain emerge! ... Shameless shenanigans by Reds within the writers' guild, as of RIGHT NOW, make the old days of [Hollywood Ten ringleader] John Howard Lawson look like a pink tea party." This was followed a day later by Connolly's declaration that the strike was the only walkout in history for less, not more, money, which he said could only make sense to "such extremists" as thirteen members of the guild whose names he printed.[25]

The strike was on the verge of being settled when Connolly returned to Hollywood from his Europe trip. While he was away, interested parties approached the *Hollywood Reporter* insisting on a retraction to Connolly's labeling as "extremists" the thirteen guild members so named. These parties' powers of persuasion must have been extraordinary, because the retraction Connolly was forced to print is unique in the fifteen-year run of his "Rambling Reporter" columns; never before had publisher Wilkerson bowed to potential litigants.

Robert Yale Libott, a script writer for *The Man from U.N.C.L.E.* and one of the thirteen "extremists" named in Connolly's item, said four decades later that he had forgotten about Connolly's libelous item. "This labeling of me as an extremist is kind of funny," Libott said, "because I was the token Republican on the Writers Guild's negotiating committee."

Libott eventually became an attorney and, ironically, an adviser to the *Hollywood Reporter* on libel actions, but that was after Connolly's death. He said he did not remember anyone in the Writers Guild threatening any libel action stemming from Connolly's "extremists" item. "But that retraction was surely made to avoid a lawsuit," Libott asserted. The strike, which Connolly thought boiled down to a demand for less money to satisfy some devious Communist agenda, was actually over whether a writer ought to give up all rights to a screenplay, said Libott. "The motion picture companies claimed that 'film rights' meant *all* rights in perpetuity to the work," he explained. "We didn't want to see that happen. We got this henceforth in the form of royalties."[26]

Connolly's retraction followed almost precisely the same format as the original offending item. "A man can be zealous without being an 'extremist' or a communist and this applies to names mentioned in this column," it began. The same thirteen names were then listed, in the same order (although some were spelled correctly this time). "[W]e believe [they] are neither communists nor communist sympathizers. Furthermore, it is certainly clear that the WGA of today is not run, nor has its policies determined, by communists or communist sympathizers."[27]

The retraction was the prelude to Connolly's diatribe on the Cheryl Crane situation. It is not hard to conceive how the retraction rankled an entrenched anti–Communist hardliner such as Connolly. The singular professional frustration of a very public career setback, combined with the personal frustration of Communist triumphs abroad, propelled Connolly to vent it all on something he felt was subject to his influence.

Cheryl had developed a habit of running away from her detention home, El Retiro. While she was confined to Los Angeles Juvenile Hall for a few days, a municipal judge wrestled with what was best for her.[28]

Describing Cheryl's case as a "kingsize King Solomon dilemma," Connolly said the teen preferred to return to El Retiro rather than be assigned to a foster home. His real target was the parents, Lana Turner and Steve Crane, whose absentee roles in their daughter's life he disdained. He quoted the judge as saying that most of the girls at El Retiro were "from underprivileged families" and sending Cheryl back there would be "like sending Tony Curtis or some such star to San Quentin. The cons would either clobber them or put them on a pedestal. It just wouldn't work out." Connolly was happy to offer his own free advice: with all Turner's money, "why not find a competent companion-tutor for Cheryl and set them up in a little hideaway home in the hills?"[29]

Another manifestation of Connolly's distress at that time was his bizarre ejection from a hopping Hollywood party the following Sunday. A number of friends, including the ubiquitous Hollywood private detective Fred Otash, banded together to host a farewell party at Plymouth House for attorney Arthur Crowley, famous for defending *Confidential* magazine during its 1957 trial, and another man who were going on an African safari. The party was far too crowded for anyone to have seen what really happened, but Otash accused Connolly of turning four hors d'oeuvres trays upside down "maliciously" and then leaning on them with his elbow. Escorted to the front door by a uniformed guard, Connolly said, "I don't know what I did." A number of guests left immediately to show solidarity with Connolly. Cara Williams, an actress who was often championed in the "Rambling Reporter," said, "He didn't touch the lousy hors d'oeuvres."[30]

Connolly got his comeuppance for the Cheryl Crane item two nights after the safari party at a glittering post-premiere celebration of Lana Turner's newest picture, *Portrait in Black*, at Romanoff's. Connolly approached Turner's table to congratulate her when her fiancé, Fred May, leaped up and seized Connolly by the lapel of his tuxedo. "I love this girl very much, and the things you're writing about her are unfair," May growled. With that, he started to throw a punch, but he was restrained by Turner and Army Archerd, Connolly's rival at *Daily Variety*. Turner began to sob. "I can't stand another headline," she wailed. Connolly left immediately.[31]

Although the incident was reported in many morning papers, the collective reaction to it was by and large subdued. From Chicago, Connolly's pal Irv Kupcinet told him, "Remember, standard equipment for a movie columnist includes a pair of boxing gloves as well as a typewriter." Connolly himself admitted the incident, peppering his account with references to the current and former world heavyweight champions: "Your Rambling Reporter lost a decision in the Romanoff arena. Looks like we'll have to adopt Floyd Patterson's seclusion training routine for a rematch with Hollywood's new Ingemar period paragraph." A month after the incident, Army Archerd referred cryptically to his intervention in the farrago when he wrote that the foul-mouthed comedian Lenny Bruce merited a punch in the nose — and Archerd "wouldn't have stopped this one."[32]

After the fuss died down, Connolly carried on with his duties as if nothing had happened. He did not shy away from subsequent news about Lana Turner or her daughter, even mentioning Cheryl's confinement to El Retiro once again a few months later. Neither mother nor daughter sought to exploit the Romanoff's incident for publicity.[33]

The most famous brawl of Connolly's career, on the other hand, was all about publicity. This time he had not been mouthing off while in a troubled state of mind. The offending item in this scenario was an eight-word lead-off item for his column of June 10, 1963, "Shirley MacLaine told Hal Wallis okay you win." As MacLaine would later write, producer Wallis, who had signed her to a personal services contract in 1954, had just offered to settle her lawsuit against him for nullification of the contract. She was unhappy with the poor quality of screenplays he typically chose for her. Confident that she would have won the case had it gone to trial, she interpreted Wallis's settlement offer as a victory for her. Connolly simply interpreted it the opposite way.[34]

MacLaine said she had suffered untold verbal abuse in Connolly's column over the years, from the allegation that a secret nose job had been botched to a suggestion of a suicide attempt over an unhappy affair to his implication that she had an abortion while out of the country. He had also criticized her views on capital punishment, opining that she must have "flipped her lid" to demonstrate with Marlon Brando and Steve Allen in Sacramento against executing one of the most heinous criminals in California history. These slurs MacLaine said she could handle, but when Connolly claimed she had capitulated to Hal Wallis, he had provoked her beyond what she could endure.[35]

In her memoirs, MacLaine said she called her attorney to ask if it was possible to hit someone in a manner that would not constitute assault and battery; he told her if she held her hand flat instead of making a fist, she would be innocent. Bringing along her secretary as a witness, she said, she entered the *Hollywood Reporter* offices and asked a receptionist to summon Connolly. He came downstairs and seemed delighted to see her. She asked if he was in the business of printing the truth. He said of course he was.

No two accounts of the ensuing melee agree. MacLaine said she slapped Connolly hard twice, turned and left. The Connolly camp has always claimed she actually swung her handbag at him and grazed his shoulder. "After Shirley hit his shoulder, she turned and ran out the front door, into a black limousine that was waiting for her," said Jack Bradford. "Mike ran right out to the limo and asked, 'What's the matter?' She was in tears. She said, 'Sorry, I shouldn't have done that,' and the limo sped off."

Later, Bradford would write that Connolly "rapped Shirley but

couldn't understand her slam-bang till he learned she was put up to it."
Bradford maintains that MacLaine's plan to hit Connolly was instigated
by Rogers and Cowan, her public relations firm. He said a photographer
from Rogers and Cowan had been in the *Hollywood Reporter's* lobby to
record the action.[36]

Many other press agents had been in the lobby when MacLaine struck
Connolly, and they lost no time in phoning the various city desks with the
news of the priceless encounter they had just witnessed. Contacted later in
the day by wire services, Connolly commented like the media pro he was.
"I'll never wash that shoulder again," he sighed. To another reporter, he
said MacLaine's blow was "just a love tap." In his own column the next day,
he kept a stiff upper lip. "Aside to gorgeous Shirley MacLaine: We're grateful you weren't wearing brass knuckles ... Another aside to Sexy Shirley:
Jim Bacon of the Associated Press called and told us to cheer up, things
could get worse. So we tried it, and, by George, things DID get worse!"[37]

Reporter James Bacon, a friend to both Connolly and MacLaine, was
trying to have it both ways in consoling Connolly; he had also warned
MacLaine in jest that she should watch her back, as Connolly could be lurk-
ing in the shadows to jump out and "hit you with his mesh bag."[38]

The Connolly scrape has generated a great deal of publicity for
MacLaine over the years, quite out of proportion to its significance. Even
as this book was nearing completion, word came from California that
MacLaine had repeated the story yet again, speaking at a dinner honoring
Warren Cowan. Five months after the pugilistic deed, a profile of MacLaine
appeared in the *Saturday Evening Post*, which gave the incident prominent
play. Connolly's reaction back in June had been to maintain good humor,
but by now he was peeved at what he said were MacLaine's exaggerations.[39]

In a rebuttal to the *Saturday Evening Post*, Connolly wrote, "A national
magazine, out today, tells the 'inside' on how an actress slugged a columnist ... Fiction: the columnist had been chronicling items about the actress
for months ... Fact: he chronicled three items, in a five-a-week column
that averages sixty to seventy items a day, from November 1962–June 1963
... Fiction: 'The columnist stepped from an elevator' ... Fact: There is no
elevator, just a flight of fifteen steps, from his office to the ground floor
... Fiction: 'I slugged him in the face' ... Fact: She connected with a glanc-
ing blow on the shoulder ... Fiction: 'I took his glasses off his nose' ... Fact:
He wasn't wearing glasses ... Fiction: 'I bashed him two more times' ...
Fact: She did not ... Final fact (and all could have been verified via a single
call to this office): the actress made an attempt to 'make up' with the columnist at Edie Adams' recent party for Leonard Bernstein — but failed."[40]

Jack Bradford says, "Of course, Mike didn't run Shirley's name for months after the incident! Later, at a sitdown dinner, he suspected that Shirley arranged beforehand to be seated in the chair behind him. She tried to rub elbows with him. But they didn't speak."[41]

MacLaine maintained Connolly "wasn't crazy about" her, but he was. The first time he printed her name, he said she was "nothing but sensational" in the rushes of her first movie, *The Trouble with Harry*, and was a "fascinating redhead," even a "female Brando." Later, he would gush, "Hey, we wanna be president of her fan club!" They often spoke on the phone and chatted at parties. Joseph Zappia's sister, Joyce, said she and Connolly "double-dated with Shirley and her escort before the 'incident!'"[42]

Regrettably, MacLaine and Connolly never did patch things up. Of all the scrapes Connolly got himself into, the most famous, the MacLaine incident, would be the one to confirm what Connolly maintained all along about stars: that it was all for publicity.

One of the biggest shocks of Connolly's later years must have come when Hedda Hopper broke the ice and phoned him. "Toward the end of her life, Hedda did call Mike and they spoke," relates Jack Bradford. "It was to get him to lend his name to some charity event. I took the call; I was very surprised. I gave the phone to Mike." This was quite a change of heart for Hopper, who had phoned Shirley MacLaine right after her slugging of Connolly to say MacLaine should be ashamed of herself—for not finishing the job and knocking Connolly out cold.[43]

At the very end of his life, Connolly was still at it, hammer-and-tongs. In a *Screen Stories* column published posthumously, he had written, "When I printed the original scoop that John Derek's marriage had broken up, John phoned and hollered that he was on his way over to my office to pound lumps on me. He was told to come on over, because I had had my lumps from experts, but he hadn't shown up by press-time."[44]

The outpouring of telegrams and tokens of appreciation that MacLaine says she received after throwing her punches revealed in the Hollywood community the same sentiments that had burst forth when Joseph Cotten kicked Hedda Hopper. Perhaps for Connolly to function from day to day and live with himself, it was necessary to harden his heart and gloss over hurt feelings by insisting that publicity was the greatest good. The Turner and MacLaine incidents should have made it clear to Connolly that even stars have feelings that can be hurt. MacLaine also turned the tables on Connolly in another significant way: When he complained that the *Saturday Evening Post* could have got its facts right with a simple telephone call to him, he was voicing inadvertently the same protest Jerry Wald was always making to him. There is little in Connolly's career to suggest that he was capable of taking what he dished out with such abandon.

Chapter 10

Coverage Coverage

"All members of [Sinatra's] X-15 cast and crew will
have to be okayed by the Government. And Frank
shouldn't have any trouble THERE!"
— *Mike Connolly, Hollywood Reporter,
Feb. 15, 1961*

The *Washington Post* and *Washington Times*. The *Chicago Tribune* and *Chicago Sun-Times*. The *Salt Lake Tribune* and the *Deseret News*. In any two-newspaper town, it is a law of nature that the papers will compete fiercely for scoops, circulation, and advertising while espousing viewpoints and politics that are often polar opposites. This rule obtains in Hollywood, a two-newspaper town served by the *Hollywood Reporter* and *Daily Variety* (the west coast outpost of New York's *Variety*). In Mike Connolly's heyday, these two papers had a rivalry no less intense than it is today.[1]

One of the unspoken protocols undergirding this rivalry was that the competition was not to be mentioned. Thus, in *Variety's* coverage of Bob Hope's Christmas 1956 junket to Alaska, Connolly's name was omitted from the otherwise complete roster of newspapermen in Hope's retinue. When *Hollywood Reporter* publisher William R. Wilkerson, a titanic figure in movie industry history by any standard, died in September 1962, *Variety* ran an obituary that was almost microscopic.[2]

On the rare occasion when this code of silence was breached, reprisal could be swift. Connolly's rival at *Daily Variety*, Army Archerd, once poked fun gingerly at publisher Wilkerson's notorious swinging door, noting obliquely that "a local rag" had gone through three editors in less than two weeks. Connolly returned fire immediately, deflecting attention from his paper's genuinely serious personnel problem by telling Archerd to cast the beam out of his own eye. "[As for] Army Archerd's remarks about the shift in editors here," Connolly wrote, "these shifts were made in order to clear the deck for Army's own editor, Al Scharper. Al will soon be sitting in the editor's chair here."[3]

A textbook example of the divergent political persuasions of Connolly's and Archerd's columns came in their coverage of an AFL-CIO banquet in honor of Bob Hope's eighteen years of entertaining troops overseas. Although Connolly's adoration of Hope bordered on unconditional love, the verbal contortions to which he resorted to avoid naming the AFL-CIO, the mother church of despised labor unions, were side-splitting; he could only bring himself to label the event "the Hope banquet." Down Sunset Boulevard at *Daily Variety*, Archerd had no such compunction; he not only identified the AFL-CIO as the hosting entity but quoted several of Hope's one-liners about unions. Connolly customarily devoted half a paragraph to Hope's jokes whenever he covered the comedian's performances, but in this case he sidestepped them as if they were leprous.[4]

The most protracted spectacle of Connolly's and Archerd's clashing politics was their coverage of the 1960 presidential race between Senator John F. Kennedy and Vice President Richard M. Nixon, and subsequently of President Kennedy's relations with the film industry. Exhibit Number One in the JFK-Hollywood nexus was the candidate's friendship (some considered it an unholy alliance) with Frank Sinatra and his "Clan," a sleeker, sixties version of the singer's erstwhile Rat Pack. Composing the Clan's nucleus with Sinatra were Kennedy's brother-in-law, the British-born actor Peter Lawford; vocalists Sammy Davis, Jr., and Dean Martin; and comedian Joey Bishop. While Archerd maintained friendly, even warm relations with Lawford and leaned Democratic in the news he chose to print, Connolly, a self-described "rabidly Republican [columnist]," did everything in his power to discredit the Kennedy campaign.[5]

In his heart, Connolly seemed to like Kennedy. In 1956, he may even have felt tempted to support the candidacy of this irresistibly handsome war hero who was, like himself, a product of Ireland's County Wexford. While covering the Democratic convention in Chicago that year, Connolly printed something confided to him by entertainer George Jessel, interesting mainly because Connolly chose to include it: "John F. Kennedy, a Roman Catholic, will have to be reckoned with by the American people in future elections. Maybe we'll have true Democracy in '60 or '64, and John will have a chance to be President.'" Connolly did meet Kennedy once, at a party honoring the steelworkers union leadership during the Democratic national convention in Los Angeles in July 1960. He was struck by Kennedy's "smiling Irish eyes that danced when he recognized the various movie stars who came to greet him" and his "firm, friendly handshake."[6]

But 1960 was the election year, and Connolly felt it expedient to keep those favorable impressions to himself. For years, he had chronicled Kennedy's comings and goings in Los Angeles, but as 1960 approached and it looked increasingly certain that Kennedy would be Nixon's opponent, his news items on the senator no longer appeared. Connolly was personally invested in Richard Nixon as the Waspish symbol of everything he aspired to be, and his wish to hitch his wagon to Nixon's star trumped any effects of Kennedy's seductive charisma. Publicizing the senator while he was locked in political combat with Connolly's beloved Nixon would be giving aid and comfort to the enemy.

Additionally, Connolly felt Kennedy was encumbered by unacceptable family baggage. Writing to Nixon in January 1960, Connolly said he was appalled at the very thought of Peter Lawford in the White House. Reminding Nixon of the influence of his "Rambling Reporter" column and the seventy-eight newspapers to which it was then syndicated, Connolly pledged his support and begged to be of help in the GOP campaign. He joined Nixon's "Celebrity Committee," formed to infuse the vice president's public image with extra glitter, and castigated Norman Vincent Peale for mailing cards advising that a vote for Nixon was a vote for Christ. "This is doing the GOP more harm than good," Connolly scolded.[7]

Over at *Daily Variety*, working in inverse proportion to Connolly's embargo, Army Archerd was cranking up the volume on Kennedy news. During 1959, only Archerd's column carried Kennedy sightings in southern California: the senator's appearance at a political cocktail party in May; a stopover on the way back from Hawaii in July; and house-guesting at Frank Sinatra's "winter White House" in Palm Springs in November. Archerd's favoring of Kennedy and the Democrats was obvious. He castigated Jerry Lewis for "downright disgusting" slurs against Kennedy's Catholic religion in his nightclub act. He congratulated Lawford in March 1960 for passing his U.S. citizenship exam, and pointed out the high ratings Lawford's television program, *The Thin Man*, had earned. But more subtly — and this was his real difference from Connolly — Archerd was never snide toward those in the opposite camp.[8]

Although Connolly's aim was to undermine the Kennedy campaign, he refrained from attacking or lampooning Kennedy himself. Instead, he disparaged those closely associated with the candidate, especially Kennedy's father, former ambassador to England Joseph P. Kennedy, and Frank Sinatra and Peter Lawford. Connolly suspected that dredging up Kennedy *père's* old affair with Gloria Swanson might cause some embarrassment; he alleged Swanson, who once called her tycoon paramour "the greatest actor in Hollywood," had "switched" her loyalties in the election at hand to Nixon. That tidbit was too good to let rest; after the election Connolly claimed Swanson had unearthed a 1925 fan letter from an eight-year-old John F. Kennedy.[9]

Sinatra needed no help from Connolly to be controversial, but that did not stop Connolly from getting all possible mileage out of the singer's foibles. Throughout his career he vented alternating feelings of admiration and revulsion for Sinatra. "No admirer of Sinatra personally," he had written, "we'll fight to the bitter end his right to entertain us whenever he's of the mind."[10]

Just as Kennedy was struggling to win primary elections in a number of crucial states, Sinatra hired Albert Maltz, an unreconstructed member of the Hollywood Ten, to write the screenplay for a planned World War II picture. Connolly, predictably, condemned Sinatra's hiring of "the biggest fink in town." The Maltz uproar may have influenced Kennedy's last-minute cancellation of an appearance by Sinatra and the Clan at a Milwaukee rally on the eve of the Wisconsin primary (although Connolly said it was "lest [Kennedy] be accused of 'going Hollywood'").[11]

Exploiting items of a more trivial nature, Connolly asserted that actress Juliet Prowse was getting film roles because Sinatra, whom she was dating, was pulling strings for her, and that Prowse wore her JFK button at Sinatra's behest. Right before the election, Connolly announced a bumper sticker in Beverly Hills that read, "Vote No On Kennedy, Lawford, and Sinatra."[12]

But the most bilious slurs were reserved for Peter Lawford. Just what Connolly knew or felt about Lawford to cause such enmity is unknown, although it may have been Irish resentment of the British. Even Sinatra's fondness for giving British names to his production ventures was a source of scorn; Connolly wondered in his column why Sinatra would "Blighty-title" his various companies with names like Essex and Dorchester.[13]

Connolly frequently reminded readers that Lawford's film career was long since washed up and Sinatra's clout was the only reason he was working in movies. The 1959 Sinatra vehicle *Never So Few* would be Lawford's first feature since 1952, observed Connolly, labeling the item the "Ever So Few Department." Twisting the knife further, he insinuated Lawford could not be cast even in a non–Sinatra picture, such as *Exodus*, without Sinatra's intervention. Later he would quote a Milton Berle line from a Hollywood dinner: "Jack Kennedy couldn't be here — he's going from door to door trying to get a picture for Pete Lawford!"[14]

The column reported with relish a tantrum Lawford had thrown in New York's TWA office over an insufficiently deferential seat assignment, and a rift between Lawford and his manager, Milt Ebbins, which Connolly alleged was over Ebbins's attention to "his other comedian," Mort Sahl. Even Lawford's children were fair game; just after the New Year, Connolly wrote, they were still receiving Christmas presents but bored by the whole thing, "yawning while the butler opens the gifts." It was certainly no compliment when Connolly wrote, during convention week, that Lawford patronized Puccini's, the restaurant he owned jointly with Sinatra, frequently "because he feels at least one star should be present at all times."[15]

Connolly's attacks on the Clan and anyone who might wrest victory from Nixon cleared the field for Army Archerd to be the conduit for Clan and Kennedy administration gossip. Lawford had Archerd's ear and fed news to him with alacrity. For the historian of the Kennedy presidency's Hollywood connections, Archerd's columns from that time are the best single source. However, in many instances Connolly printed news that Archerd would not carry for fear of offending such a prized source as Lawford. Connolly was also the exclusive source for Joseph P. Kennedy's pre–1960 summers spent at Lake Tahoe, brokering deals designed to put his son in the White House. The elder Kennedy, wrote Connolly, "borrowed a T-bird from a barrister buddy in Reno to promote son Jack for President through Nevada."[16]

Nineteen-sixty was the banner year for Clan news. The Sinatra crew kicked off the year with tidal waves of publicity from Las Vegas, where they filmed *Ocean's Eleven* by day and regaled gaggles of gamblers at the Sands by night with their self-styled "Summit Meeting" show (a bow to the other Summit Meeting of Eisenhower, Khrushchev, and other world leaders announced for May 1960 in Paris). The most luminous member of the Summit Meeting's audience was candidate Kennedy. Although the first weekend in February is notorious in Kennedy lore as the occasion for his introduction to Mafia mistress Judith Campbell, Archerd's column carried the unheralded fact that Kennedy had also cavorted in Las Vegas the previous weekend (January 30), information completely overlooked by historians. On this weekend, Archerd wrote, Kennedy attended double-header Summit Meeting shows where he was introduced to the audience by Sinatra and applauded. Other noteworthy Clan follies of 1960 reported by Archerd and ignored by Connolly were the August *Ocean's Eleven* premiere in Las Vegas; the election night party Sinatra attended at the Tony Curtis home; and the group's stag dinner at the Villa Capri in honor of Sammy Davis, Jr.'s impending marriage to Mai Britt.[17]

As the Democratic convention unfolded in Los Angeles during the week of July 10, Archerd faithfully reported news from the proceedings and festivities. Along with Sinatra, Lawford, Tony Curtis, and other celebrities, Archerd stood on the platform behind the speakers' podium, which afforded a superb vantage point from which to watch Kennedy seize the Democratic nomination for president. He virtually endorsed Kennedy in his column, opining that the film industry would receive unprecedented attention from such a presidency.[18]

But the convention presented Connolly with a conundrum. While he had seen fit in 1956 to travel two thousand miles to cover the Democratic convention in Chicago, his fierce loyalty to Nixon now impelled him to ignore the same gathering in his own back yard. To fill the hole in his column where convention news should have been appearing, Connolly went on an absurd police ride-along, tooling around Los Angeles in the prowl car of the city's chief of detectives with director Delbert Mann and producer Sy Bartlett in tow. It was a "dull" night with "no crimes, just conventions." According to Connolly, the chief bragged, "What city other than Los Angeles could handle three conventions in one swoop — Democrats, Alcoholics Anonymous and Jehovah's Witnesses?" Even on a slow night, Connolly could find ways to dilute news of the convention.[19]

When he was not bedeviling the Clan, Connolly utilized other techniques to deflate Hollywood's collective preference for Kennedy. He injected Republican angles into Democratic stories, reporting that the first RSVP to a Democratic convention soirée came from California's GOP governor, Goody Knight, or that Arlene Dahl, Ann Miller, and Cobina Wright, Republicans all, sat through the convention to the bitter end. He wrote that Helen Hayes and director Mervyn LeRoy, co-chairs of Nixon's "Celebrity Committee," would "help derail Jack Kennedy's Rat Pack." With glee, he bruited about the news that liberal television moderator David Susskind "would be coming out for Nixon."[20]

Another strategy was to exacerbate class differences by harping on the great wealth of Kennedy's family and supporters. Jealousy of the rich was a perennial subtext in Connolly's column, and in the Kennedys he had a splendid target. Joseph P. Kennedy had "forked over five hundred thousand dollars for a private plane," so the "Senator's campaign will be airborne," he revealed. Another tale he spun was that the senator told his mother, Rose, that he felt "like a million" after receiving the nomination. "Why so despondent?" retorted Rose in Connolly's version. Sinatra's bulging coffers provoked the same treatment. Connolly noted disdainfully how Capitol Records chauffeured Sinatra (and Lawford) from Palm Springs to Los Angeles for a three-hour recording session and back again in the same day. While Sinatra toured Europe in June 1960, Connolly circulated a rejoinder the singer made when a reporter asked what brought him to Germany. "I came over to buy East Berlin," Sinatra is supposed to have said.[21]

Yet another ploy was to debunk claims of support or front-runner status that the Kennedy camp might make. Bookies, Connolly said early in 1960, were giving three-to-one odds that Senator Stuart Symington of Missouri would emerge as the Democrats' "compromise candidate." Also in Missouri, crowed Connolly, former president Harry Truman walked out of a Kennedy banquet to listen in on a popular trio performing in an adjacent ballroom. In an aside to the Clan, Connolly wrote, "Don't count on Jerry Lewis being for JFK!" after Lewis reported that a crowd greeting him in Hawaii had spelled out "Nixon."[22]

Unlike Connolly, Archerd never manifested any interest in labeling the subjects of his "Just for Variety" column according to their political beliefs, and he never mocked Rosalind Russell, Ginger Rogers, Roy Rogers, or other stars who supported the Republican ticket. He did make a few cracks about Nixon's beard, after the vice president's four o'clock shadow was said to repulse viewers during his debates with Kennedy, but these were not mean-spirited, and everyone was talking about it — even Connolly, who observed that Jerry Lewis declined to make Nixon's makeup artist the subject of any jokes.[23]

On October 17, 1960, the *Los Angeles Times* ran a short item claiming that odds in Las Vegas had shifted two days earlier from Nixon to Kennedy as the probable winner of the 1960 election. Nixon had been a nine-to-five favorite in the immediate wake of the Republican convention, but Kennedy had caught up and the odds were now six-to-five in the Democrat's favor. (One enterprising casino was offering seven-to-five odds for Kennedy.) Connolly took umbrage at the *Times*' assertion. "Those highly-touted six-to-five Las Vegas odds favoring Kennedy are Demmy propaganda," he scoffed. "Proof: Dick Blackwell [the designer later notorious as "Mr. Blackwell"] tried to bet on Nixon at those odds all over Vegas last night but couldn't get crackers for tuppence."[24]

If the *Times* had provoked Connolly, he had now provoked Frank Sinatra. In a telegram, Sinatra asked Connolly to tell Blackwell ("whoever he is") that not only were both of them wrong about the six-to-five odds in Las Vegas being mere Democrat propaganda but it would be Sinatra's pleasure to lay six-to-five for whatever Blackwell could afford. Sinatra cautioned Blackwell to make it easy on himself. So Connolly relayed the details to Blackwell's office, where an assistant called Sinatra right away to make the bet. Itching for the contest, Sinatra replied he would trust Blackwell and it was not necessary for anyone to hold the money. He assured the assistant that he would be calling for the loot the day after the election, and he would be glad to cover whatever money Blackwell's friends could put up, too. Connolly related all this in his column and ended with, "Dear Frank: We're holding Blackwell's one hundred bucks." Obviously, Sinatra won the bet, but Connolly was not about to print anything further about the incident.[25]

After Kennedy's victory, Lawford quotes and news began taking up more and more space in "Just for Variety," reflecting Hollywood's appetite for an insider's news of the exciting Kennedy regime. Archerd's first lengthy chat with the president-elect's brother-in-law appeared a month after the election. Lawford talked comfortably and in excellent humor about the upcoming inaugural gala, which he and Sinatra were co-chairing, and predicted it would eliminate the Democrats' combined deficits from both the 1956 and 1960 campaigns. He also predicted "more cultural exchange" under the new administration.[26]

The Inaugural did not bring a more mellow tone to Connolly's column; his potshots at the Clan continued apace. "Practice calling Peter Lawford 'Your Excellency,'" he wrote peevishly, two days after the election. He implied that Sinatra had given Juliet Prowse "bad advice" in urging her to back out of her commitment to film *Blue Hawaii* with Elvis Presley. Often he let others do the needling for him. One comedian was quoted as saying Sinatra had it made: "he's got his own President now." Another jokester, warming up an audience in Washington, D.C., said, "Mr. Sinatra asked me to thank all of you for coming here tonight." These taunts were not lost on Sinatra. As with his response to Connolly on the item about Las Vegas odds, Sinatra sent a surly telegram after Connolly's referral in several columns to the clan's planned remake of *Gunga Din* (the eventual *Sergeants Three*). "Once and for all," the singer responded testily, "we are not remaking *Gunga Din* but a comedy-western."[27]

The most notable Clan news to be avoided by Archerd but pounced on by Connolly stemmed from Kennedy's snub of Sinatra in connection with a March 1962 weekend visit to Palm Springs, during which the president opted to bunk not at Sinatra's estate but at rival singer (and Republican, at that) Bing Crosby's. Sinatra channeled his rage over the freeze-out at Lawford and refused to have anything further to do with him. Connolly's first bulletin on the meltdown came only three days after the unfortunate weekend, claiming that Sinatra was excising two songs composed by Jimmy Van Heusen from his next record album, "reportedly because of the JFK-Crosby-Van Heusen-Lawford axis." (Van Heusen's Palm Springs digs had been headquarters for the president's security detail.) A second item followed two days later: "That Sinatra-Lawford spat stems from the big boodle requested by Frank's agents for his starring stint in Pete's *Great Train Robbery.*" Both items had the details wrong, but the rift was a fact.[28]

The partial dissolution of the Clan delighted Connolly. When he wrote in mid–April that "Clansmen Sinatra, Martin, Davis, and Bishop are pitching for remake rights" to an old movie, there was no ambiguity about what he was really saying.[29]

Archerd, meanwhile, kept any hint of either Sinatra's fall from grace or Lawford's excommunication out of "Just for Variety" until late May, when he quoted singer Eddie Fisher's gag about a "JFK Almost Slept Here" plaque in Sinatra's Palm Springs home. He seemed, in fact, to be asking, "What rift?" in subsequent items, such as Lawford's alleged wish for Sinatra to star in his production company's *Johnny Cool*, or Sinatra's supposed hope that the audience at the Washington, D.C., premiere of his *Manchurian Candidate* would include Kennedy. At least where the status of Kennedy family friendships was concerned, Connolly was the one to be printing the facts. In late August, he noted soberly that Lawford had failed to "deliver" Sinatra as part of a package he had promised to United Artists.[30]

When Kennedy was assassinated on November 22, 1963, Connolly, despite the political distance he had kept, seemed as shaken and saddened as everyone else. Here, his abundance of what Alice McDermott labels as the "Irish penchant for pursuing any mention of death" had its finest hour. A fellow columnist at the *Hollywood Reporter*, Hank Grant, recalled that it took Connolly more time to write three-line eulogies than a whole column and that he was tense and nervous while writing them. "The most difficult words to write are those in praise of a friend who won't be able to read them," Connolly told Grant.[31]

He characterized Hollywood's reaction to the assassination as "stunned horror" and "mournful as an Irish wake." Most of the stars importuned for comments by national magazines did not "want that kind of 'space," preferring to remain silent, he noted, and many were unable to work. "Ironically," he added, "Frank Sinatra, Sammy Davis, Jr., and Barbara Rush, staunch Democrats all and hard workers in the Kennedy campaign, were locationing *Robin and the Seven Hoods* in a cemetery when the news hit them. They couldn't finish the day's shooting."[32]

Most of his Monday column and much additional space throughout the week was devoted to eulogizing the fallen president. He lamented that "a great man is gone, tall as the truth, who wore his life like the sky." Playing up the mutual love between Kennedy and show business, he said the president's doors had always been open to his entertainer friends; he pointed out that Lena Horne and Carol Lawrence had visited Kennedy just two days before his death about an upcoming inaugural anniversary celebration, and that a December White House luncheon with Hollywood's hierarchy had been planned to outline a worldwide cultural campaign for the film industry. The loss, he said, was a mystery too deep for words— "the silence of the dead, the empty room, the unreturning traveler."[33]

Connolly also showered lavish praise on television and radio networks for their dignified and memorable broadcasts of Kennedy's funeral. Macmillan Publishers, he wrote, was recalling all copies of Victor Lasky's hatchet job, *JFK, The Man and the Myth*, from the country's bookstores. But he could not resist another dig at Peter Lawford, whose own way of dealing with the tragedy was to return to work. He wrote that the private plane of Harrah's Lake Tahoe Casino picked Lawford up to bring him back to his "saloon stand" with Jimmy Durante.[34]

By the time the next campaign season rolled around in 1964, Connolly had lost his appetite for presidential politics. He had supported Nixon's 1962 bid for the California governorship, but his florid one-sided correspondence with the former vice president had slowed to a trickle even then. Nixon's absence from the 1964 Republican ticket was a blow to Connolly; the nominee, Senator Barry Goldwater of Arizona, failed to evoke his enthusiasm. Goldwater was mentioned only perfunctorily in the column, and in comparison with Connolly's all-out barrages for Nixon in 1960, the silence was deafening. He would not live to see Nixon elected president in 1968.[35]

Chapter 11

Tasks for Tomorrow

"While pictures don't rock the world like politicians
do, they do help to keep tomorrow from being more
dreadful than today."
        — *Mike Connolly, Hollywood Reporter,*
            Dec. 31, 1964

Mike Connolly's longevity in the pitiless, dog-eat-dog world of Hollywood journalism can be interpreted either as a triumph or as career stag-
nation. It was no mean feat to survive for a dozen years as court jester to
a hard-to-please publisher who had not hesitated to fire other longtime
columnists, such as Irving Hoffman ("Tales of Hoffman") and Radie Harris
("Broadway Ballyhoo"), when they no longer suited the trade paper's aims.

But Connolly had stayed so busy with the "Rambling Reporter," syndicated columns, *Modern Screen* pieces, and *Screen Stories* work for so long
that he had written only one book, *I'll Cry Tomorrow,* and even that had
to be largely reworked by another author. Although he had confessed to
"every reporter's dream of retiring to do some serious writing," and told
Hedda Hopper that he wished he could get off his "single-item write-it-
and-run kick," he was not getting any closer to doing any of the great
things he daydreamed about: writing for the *New Yorker,* writing a great
novel à la James Joyce, or even writing a biography of Joyce.[1]

One of Connolly's longtime dreams was to be a mover and shaker
behind a film adaptation of Joyce's *Ulysses.* He felt a strong kinship with
Joyce, not only because he considered himself one of the select few who
could understand the great Irishman's meaning but because Joyce had
worked from 1906 to 1909 as a press agent for Dublin's first movie house.

Ulysses, to Connolly, was the "literary lodestone of the twentieth century." The opportunity knocked in mid–1960, when Jerry Wald added *Ulysses* to his list of productions for 20th Century–Fox. Wald harbored a certain pride in bringing complicated adaptations to the screen, remarking smugly to Connolly that the powers-that-be had all laughed at Wald's earlier schemes to make *Sons and Lovers* and *Peyton Place*.[2]

While Wald worked at the logistics of the movie, Connolly drummed up enthusiasm through frequent mentions of both the project and the novel. "Knock it off, ye cynics who've been sneering" at Wald's plans, he blasted. Claiming that Joyce had lived "one of the most exciting lives of the century," he gave an excellent thumbnail sketch of the plot of *Ulysses* and the real-life models for the characters. Joyce was not the "King of the Cult of the Unintelligible," claimed Connolly, but a "fifty-years-ahead-of-his-time hipster" in the judgment of such geniuses as Woolf, Faulkner, and Pound. Nor was *Ulysses* any longer a banned book in Ireland, he stressed, because the Jesuits were now treating Joyce as a prodigal son to be welcomed back.[3]

To generate a high level of buzz for Wald's project, Connolly spread the word that top writers such as Sean O'Casey (the world's greatest living playwright, in Connolly's opinion), Clifford Odets, and S. N. Behrman were vying for the job of scripting *Ulysses*, while directors like John Huston and Richard Brooks were throwing their prestigious hats in the ring. On the acting side, he beat the drum for Sir Alec Guinness to star as Leopold Bloom, the father; Lawrence Harvey, Warren Beatty, or Gardner McKay to play Stephen Dedalus, the son; and James Mason for the boisterous villain, Buck Mulligan. For the "richest role of the season," Molly Bloom, he said Wald was wooing Geraldine Page. According to Connolly, the synergy from Wald's project had inspired a Santa Fe hotel magnate to form a syndicate to bring to the screen Joyce's *Finnegans Wake*, "which has the same plot as *Ulysses*."[4]

Jerry Wald kicked off Phase Two of the project by flying to Shannon, Ireland, on June 15, 1961, to scout locations. Wald thanked Connolly for a "capital" description of his Irish itinerary in the "Rambling Reporter" and said he counted on Connolly to brief him on Dun Laoghaire, Chapelizod, Number Seven Eccles Street, and other key *Ulysses* landmarks. Connolly replied, "If you encounter any IRA resistance, Jerry, call us." Several months later he announced that Wald had reserved all of Dublin's Ardmore Studios for *Ulysses* shooting during June and July 1962, and that the movie would roll on Bloomsday itself (June 16, 1962). In appreciation for Connolly's faithful promotions, Wald sent him a copy of *Finnegans Wake*.[5]

Unfortunately, Wald's workaholic ways had taken a significant toll on his health, and he died of a heart attack at age forty-nine on July 13, 1962. The shooting of *Ulysses* had already been postponed until the following March, and it was only one of many projects pending when Wald's untimely death occurred. Of all those projects, said his *Variety* obituary, *Ulysses* "was the plum of his eye." Connolly's tribute to Wald centered around the *Ulysses* project, which he said would be "a shame" if not completed. Certifying that Wald's passion for it was "no gag," he said Wald would read his favorite chapter of *Ulysses*, "The Cave of the Winds," set in a Dublin newspaper plant, and "roar at Leopold Bloom's attempts to plant an item and an ad." Sadly for all the principals, the loss of Wald doomed the film version of *Ulysses*.[6]

Connolly never had the desire to rise through the ranks of journalism to an editor or publisher post. Instead, he found great satisfaction in facilitating things from behind the scenes, using his vast network of connections to make introductions, arrange interviews, and promote friends he deemed worthy of a boost; he fancied himself as "the man to see." His backing of a film project, as in the case of *Ulysses*, could add considerably to its viability. At a more elemental level, he was proud of being sufficiently important to make a difference to a newcomer in show business. "Fond of giving the neophyte a break," wrote Jack Bradford, "he was the first to print the names of Marilyn Monroe, Tony Curtis, Connie Stevens, and many others." However, Larry Quirk's observation of Connolly's fascination with heterosexual young men is particularly apt here, because the preponderance of Connolly's aid went to more straight boys than can be counted. Aside from Connolly's major protegé, James DeCloss, another beneficiary of note was George Bon Salle, who was not an actor but a promising basketball player at the University of Illinois. They met in November 1956, when Connolly made his first visit to his alma mater since going on the lam from the Champaign police in 1938. "Went to Champaign-Urbana for a late-late-LATE homecoming with the boys at the Phi Kappa house, including a surefire All-American for '57 named George Bon Salle," he reported.[7]

Connolly was given a hero's welcome at Phi Kappa. "Mike was terrific," recalled Bon Salle. "He whittled the group down to about five of those he wanted to talk to the most — our president and treasurer and some other athletes. We had pizza and beer in the basement, which he paid for. We stayed up talking until three a.m. He told us he'd been arrested more than once on campus for drunkenness." Bon Salle was a kid on his own; his father was dead and his mother was in a nursing home, and Connolly sensed he was amenable to having a mentor. The talented young athlete did achieve All-American status, but instead of opting for professional basketball in the United States, he chose to play in Italy for fifteen months. "NBA players didn't make all that much in those days; there was more to be made in Europe, and tax free," Bon Salle explained. "I was really in the first wave of American athletes in Europe."

At six-feet-eight, Bon Salle found himself a media sensation in Europe, and he sent Connolly news clippings about his feats. The next thing he knew, Connolly arranged for him to escort Jayne Mansfield throughout Europe as part of her global publicity tour for her latest film, *Oh for a Man*. The escort 20th Century–Fox had hired for her, Lord Kilbracken of Northern Ireland, had been unable to keep up with Mansfield and her jam-packed schedule. Bon Salle met Mansfield's plane in Italy and squired her for the next three weeks. After he returned to the U.S., he met Connolly for dinner in Los Angeles and kept in regular contact afterwards. "I admired the hell out of Mike," Bon Salle recalls. "He always impacted my life. The thing was, he always made time for me, busy as he was."[8]

As Connolly grew older, he turned avidly to Catholic organizations as an additional outlet for his public-spiritedness. He joined the Catholic Press Council of Los Angeles, chaired and acted as master of ceremonies at the annual Blessed Sacrament Communion Breakfast (the major event for Catholics in the industry), and co-founded the Associates of St. Mary's College of Moraga, California, which gave an annual St. Genesius Award to exemplars of Catholic values in show business. The choice of actress Rosalind Russell as the 1967 recipient "was one of Mike's final good deeds as chairman of that committee," noted Jack Bradford.[9]

The column never failed to glitter and dazzle, but by the sixties it was showing obvious signs of age, precisely because counterculture and concern over the Vietnam War were making glitter and dazzle passé. The Mocambo, Ciro's, and other vestiges of postwar Sunset Strip elegance and glamor had all closed. Connolly still acted well his part of "best plant in town" and continued to work as hard as ever, but he began to refer to himself as a "tired old voyeur." He made his rounds gamely of Whiskey-a-Go-Go and other new haunts where the Twist and Watusi were *de rigueur*. But the new look and attitude were not his style, and it showed.[10]

The sophisticated pop music and nightclub scenes he loved were being displaced rapidly by a number of cultural forces, including television; the emerging youth culture and its chief symptom, rock-and-roll; and changes in tastes brought about by post–World War II affluence and boredom. As early as 1951, Connolly wrote that Chicagoans were no longer going to the theater or niteries but staying home and watching Dean Martin and Jerry Lewis on television. Beginning in 1956, a palpably snide attitude toward the new phenomena crept into his column. "Rock-and-rollers can all drop dead as far as we're concerned," he lamented. A televised jazz performance by Les Brown's Band of Renown of the music of Gershwin and Rodgers and Hart caused Connolly to exclaim, "This could bring back Music!" He began to harp on the influence of "the teen set" on studios' movie-making decisions, criticizing director Joshua Logan for choosing too-young leads for *South Pacific* simply to appeal to the "younger set."[11]

The frustration of the displaced person gradually became one of the major themes of the "Rambling Reporter," with Connolly issuing primal cries such as "What's become of the 'family entertainment' that built this business?" in response to foreign films about call girls and beatniks. *Sleeping Beauty*, he held, was a welcome respite from the "boy-rapes-girl stuff." He was ready with advice for movie studios, but they seemed not to pay attention. "If we were a major studio head facing today's market of so many stories totally unfit for filming," he declaimed, "we would dig out those hits of other years that haven't been sold to TV, order new treatments, and rush 'em into production."[12]

The slow leak in the column's reserves of *joie de vivre* coincided with a national political shift away from Connolly's beloved Republican party, starting in California with the Democrats' capture of the governorship and U.S. Senate seat in 1958 and continuing through John F. Kennedy's narrow 1960 victory over Connolly's Great American Hope, Richard Nixon. Politically, Connolly was a forerunner of the gay Log Cabin Republicans, so it is not surprising that his column's greatest efflorescence occurred during Eisenhower's first term in the White House (1953–1957). Southern California was his Promised Land, and during those golden years he sounded like the "It's Morning Again in America" ads made famous in Ronald Reagan's 1984 presidential campaign. "And didn't it do your heart good over the weekend," Connolly gushed, "to see those lines out in front of *A Star Is Born, Dragnet, Brigadoon, Seven Brides for Seven Brothers, Sabrina, Magnificent Obsession, The Egyptian,* and *Caine Mutiny*? And aren't you glad you live in this great town of Hollywood?"[13]

Another possible reason for the "Rambling Reporter" losing its edge is that, after years of back-breaking work, Mike Connolly had transformed from a Young Turk into an institution, and the awards appropriate to a community's pillar began to pour in. There were the Masquers Club's "Irishman of the Year" award on St. Patrick's Day, 1961, and the Hollywood Foreign Press Association's Distinguished Reporting citation during the Golden Globe ceremonies in 1962. The City of Hope had given him its journalism award in 1957.

As his personal highlight of the sixties, Connolly may well have cited his trip to Ireland in 1964. It was not his first visit to the country of his forebears, but John F. Kennedy's well-publicized ancestral pilgrimage to Ireland the previous year heightened Connolly's sense of destiny there. Now that he was the age of a grandfather, his heart had turned toward the familial. He visited the birthplaces of his mother and father and looked up previously unknown cousins. He sought out the old stomping grounds of James Joyce and Oscar Wilde. It had always been a source of delight to him that Catholic Dublin had elected a Jewish mayor, and hence he was thrilled to be received by Lord Mayor James Briscoe.

The Ireland trip was most likely the catalyst for Connolly's famous "Do It Yourself Peace on Earth Kit" that he published during the 1964 holiday season, which was reprinted with his permission in many American newspapers for years thereafter. Connolly had improvised a conflation of Christmas and Hannukah traditions and recitations, beginning with placing a Hanukkah menorah in the middle of one's Christmas wreath. Priests, ministers, and rabbis would read the column aloud during their services.[14]

The illness that finally did Connolly in began in August 1966, during what was to have been a happy and relaxing vacation in Honolulu. Instead of venturing out into the Hawaiian capital city's luxurious environs and enjoying the hijinks of Jimmy Donahue, who was also on the island, Connolly spent most of his time cooped up in his hotel room, coughing and feeling weak. He even allowed his torpor to creep into his dispatches from the fiftieth state. Describing his malaise as "Polynesian paralysis," he said it was "a vacation-time tiredness-type ailment which prevents you from lifting the phone to so much as call Room Service." At first, he thought his problem was an allergic reaction to jasmine that he discovered was growing just outside his hotel window, but the weakness was far out of proportion to an attack of allergies. Finally, Joseph Zappia became so worried about Connolly that he flew to Hawaii to bring him home.[15]

With the exception of medical bills from August to November of 1966 that were appended to his probate file, there is only anecdotal evidence to flesh out Connolly's adult medical history. He wrote with obvious joy in November 1956 that his long-time physician, Dr. Sidney Leo, had just given him a "clean bill of health," clearing him to rush with the relief of a pardoned criminal to Henry Willson's first-anniversary "blowout" for Rock and Phyllis Hudson and the overindulgence awaiting all the lucky invitees. The indications are that his heavy smoking and drinking continued unflaggingly throughout the following ten years. Upon his August 1966 return from Honolulu he consulted Dr. Leo immediately, the first of

In July 1964 Connolly was welcomed to the New York World's Fair, accompanied by his Irish cousins Kathleen and Dick Cotter. After visiting the fair, Connolly and the Cotters toured Ireland together. (Photofest)

nine visits in the next two months, during which he underwent a seemingly endless battery of tests including two EKGs, four circulation time examinations, and two chest fluoroscopies. Dr. Leo concluded that Connolly needed to have open heart surgery as soon as possible.[16]

Friends say Connolly arranged to have his surgery at the renowned Mayo Clinic in Rochester, Minnesota, thanks to the intervention of Jack Benny and Princess Grace of Monaco. The operation was scheduled for November 9, 1966, to be done by Dr. Dwight McGoon. Connolly's last column appeared on October 21, concluding with a cheerful-sounding announcement: "In this business you gotta have heart and mine has been giving me fits of late, so I'm off to the Mayo Clinic to have it fixed. Nothing serious. Back in a couple of weeks." However, in September Connolly had written his will and purchased a crypt at Holy Cross Cemetery and Mausoleum in Los Angeles, so he had been advised that he might not survive the operation.[17]

Perhaps the clearest indication of Connolly's state of mind after receiving his grim prognosis was his adieu to his good friend actor Clifton Webb. Webb's death came just a week before Connolly's final column. Good Irishman that he was, Connolly was well known as a skilled eulogist who penned respectful tributes when anyone of note in Hollywood died. However, his farewells often included a bit of humor and usually ended on a positive note. This was not the case with his requiem for Webb, which sounded utterly pathetic, hammering home the finality of the grave. "Clifton left no instructions, except that he be laid to rest in the crypt he purchased for himself and [his mother] in Hollywood Park Cemetery's Abbey of the Psalms, a whisper away from the resting places of pals Marion Davies and Tyrone Power," Connolly droned. "[His secretary] tells it best: 'I just don't think Clifton could face the thought of another anniversary of his mother's death.'"[18]

Before checking into the Mayo Clinic, Connolly spent a week in Chicago at the Ambassador East Hotel, hard at work as if nothing were wrong, cranking out upcoming columns for *Screen Stories* through the February 1967 issue. In an item about himself, he wrote that sedation for his upcoming surgery had addled him to the point that he had retracted by mistake a scoop about newscaster David Brinkley's divorce even though it was accurate. When he could spare the time from writing, he visited family and friends, including Irv Kupcinet, who later revealed that Connolly "repeatedly expressed his concern to us that he 'wouldn't make it.'" Studying a Picasso statue one afternoon at the Art Institute of Chicago, he bumped into a dear colleague he had worked with on the *Daily Illini*, Ines Caudera. "We spent the rest of the afternoon together, reminiscing about our college days," Caudera said. "He said that he often had to stand on his head to get more air to breathe. He escorted me to my train back to Champaign. We embraced in a sad goodbye."[19]

Although the newspapers initially reported that his open heart surgery had been a success, Connolly died of kidney malfunction on November 18, 1966, nine days after the operation. The only redeeming aspect of those last days is that Joseph Zappia was at his bedside. Connolly's death was, naturally, hardest of all on Zappia. At a reception at their home after the funeral, Zappia asked Willie Wilkerson, who was then fifteen, to take a look at Connolly's bedroom, which was just as Connolly had left it. There were piles of books everywhere, the same mixture of classics and best sellers that Connolly had advocated as a high school boy. "It was clear that this person had insomnia," said Wilkerson. "He'd had a dozen books going at a time, and several half-smoked packages of cigarettes as well. Joe wanted to show me that Mike loved to read. It's as if Joe were trying to say, 'Don't give up your education; see what you can learn.'"[20]

Connolly rarely commented publicly on the impact his career had in Hollywood. Frank Liberman said, "Mike made reading the *Hollywood Reporter* fun; you wanted to read it first, to learn who was doing what to whom." A reporter who interviewed him in 1953 for *People Today* asserted, "He believes his column does more good than harm. He points to his persistent anti-communist fight and to 'the kids whose careers have been helped, like Tony Curtis and Marilyn Monroe.'" To the bitter end, Connolly believed he had been right in the anti–Communist struggle, once reminding Richard Nixon, "You know my anti–Communist stand and that of the *Hollywood Reporter*." Those who agreed with Connolly held that he lived according to "an almost medieval code of ethics."[21]

Hollywood had been good to Connolly, but it became a gaping blind spot in his world view. Rather than recognize that the movie industry's only mission was to make money, he saw it as America's secret weapon in vanquishing evil. "Ours is the industry that single-handedly, above and beyond anything accomplished by the State Department or the Marshall Plan, has sold the American way of life to the world," he boasted. Notwithstanding his keen intelligence, he seemed to believe there was no Iron Curtain that a good movie could not break down, nor any world crisis that a public relations expert could not solve. The State Department, he announced, had talked the Soviet Union into broadcasting an American newsreel once a week. "Now why can't we get Walt Disney on?" he persisted. "One night a week of Mickey Mouse Club and they'll ALL be on our side!" Occasionally, rave reviews and religious cant would fuse in his column: "Show-biz action was in the beginning, is now and ever shall be, movie-making without end, amen." Hollywood had supplanted Catholicism as his religion.[22]

Mike Connolly lived a writing life, an American life, and a gay life, inextricably bound together. His opinions—imperialistic, puritanical, and materialistic—were shaped by external forces: Depression-era deprivation and uncontrollable social changes set in motion by World War II. On the other hand, his talent and creativity, as well as his homosexuality, were inherent. All these elements jockeyed for supremacy within the whole of the man, and Mike Connolly was the end product.

Everything one writes betrays who one is, and in an era when Connolly could not say who he was, he could and did write who he was. This speaks to the question of whether there is actually a "gay sensibility" in the arts and show business as we know them. There certainly was such a sensibility with Connolly; despite all his talk of breasts and "gams" and bikinis and having a "girl on our arm" in public, his gayness leapt out of the pages of his column and hit the reader between the eyes.

Hollywood, for all its flaws and excesses, is an unequalled forum for nurturing and rewarding a broad spectrum of talent. Connolly and his column could not have existed without it. By the same token, the societal role of a columnist is to create and hold together a community of readers. This Connolly did superbly, and Hollywood was justly repaid.

Notes

Key to Abbreviations in Notes

MC = Mike Connolly
RR = "Rambling Reporter," the *Hollywood Reporter's* gossip column
JV = "Just for Variety," *Daily Variety's* gossip column
TT = "Talk of the Town," Connolly's column in the *Daily Illini*

Introduction

1. James H. Jones, *Alfred C. Kinsey: A Public/Private Life*, New York: Norton (1997), 387.

2. "Hollywood's Press: Why the Stars Are in Your Eyes," *Newsweek*, Feb. 2, 1954. Much of *Newsweek's* commentary on Connolly had been lifted verbatim from "The Lowdown on Hollywood's Connolly," *People Today*, Mar. 11, 1953.

3. RR, Aug. 18, 1955; Nov. 8, 1954.

4. RR, July 26, 1954; Aug. 30, 1955.

5. RR, Dec. 1, 1958; July 29, 1954.

6. Ezra Goodman, *The Fifty-Year Decline and Fall of Hollywood*, New York: Simon & Schuster (1961), 21, 58.

7. RR, Aug. 11, 1966; Aug. 5, 1959; July 29, 1959; Jan. 28, 1960; DV, Jan. 29, 1960.

8. Jack Bradford to author, Nov. 1997; RR, June 4, 1963; Nov. 30, 1964; May 31, 1961; June 10, 1963.

9. Jack Bradford interview, Sept. 6, 1997; RR, Mar. 9, 1959.

10. RR, Nov. 14, 1958.

11. Barbara Leaming, *Marilyn Monroe*,

New York: Crown (1998), 41; Donald Spoto, *Marilyn Monroe: The Biography*, New York: Harper-Collins (1992), 212; RR, Feb. 22, 1952. In RR, July 11, 1952, MC wrote, "Earl Wilson picked our Marilyn Monroe calendar story as one of '52's hottest scoops. Thanks, Earl." Wilson, in "The Laugh Roundup," *N.Y. Post*, July 6, 1952, had included Monroe's calendar in "The Best Laughs for the first half of '52" but said nothing about MC. Jack Egan's profile of Connolly in "Daily Illini's Ex-Crusader Now Hollywood Gossip Ace," *Champaign-Urbana Courier*, late 1956, says, "The scoop that skyrocketed him to the top was unearthing a calendar for which a young contractee named Marilyn Monroe had posed."

12. RR, Mar. 19, 1952; Elia Kazan, *Elia Kazan: A Life*, New York: Knopf (1988), 455; Leaming, *Marilyn Monroe*, 44–45; Patrick Goldstein, "A Fateful Decision, Damaging Fallout," *L.A. Times*, Mar. 16, 1999.

13. Mary-jane Ryan Snyder interview, Feb. 11, 2000; RR, May 27, 1960; Carl Pelleck interview, Dec. 9, 1998.

14. Robert Wayne Tysl, *Continuity and*

Evolution in a Public Symbol: An Investigation into the Creation and Communication of the James Dean Image in Mid-Century America. Ann Arbor: University Microfilms, Inc., 1965, 12–13.

15. MC to Jerry Wald, Oct. 8, 1958, Jerry Wald Collection, Cinema-Television Library, Univ. of So. Calif; RR, Jan. 27, 1953; Feb. 23, 1956.

16. RR, Sept. 29, 1952; Dec. 2, 1952; Aug. 19, 1963; MC, liner notes to *Trini Lopez at PJ's* , Reprise 6093, released Apr. 1963.

Chapter 1

1. For a discussion of queer work, see William J. Mann, *Behind the Screen: How Gays and Lesbians Shaped Hollywood, 1910–1969,* New York: Viking (2001), 197–201.

2. Robert Hofler interview, Feb. 1, 2002; James DeCloss interview, May 12, 2000; RR, Mar. 27, 1959; Nov. 25, 1957.

3. RR, Oct. 5, 1955; Nov. 12, 1956.

4. RR, Mar. 31, 1955; Feb. 6, 1956; Aug. 15, 1956.

5. Arthur Laurents, *Original Story By,* New York: Knopf (2000), 84; RR, Aug. 13, 1946.

6. Parsons-Farney: RR, Mar. 20, 1961; Mapes-Hunter: RR, Apr. 13, 1960; Hatcher-Laurents: RR, Aug. 26, 1960; McCarthy-Allan: RR, Feb. 6, 1956 and Apr. 6, 1960; Leisen-Daniels: JV, Feb. 26, 1951 and RR, Oct. 6, 1952; Haines-Shields: RR, July 21, 1952; Dec. 14, 1953; Aug. 28, 1956; Jan. 4, 1957; Shields' facelift: RR, May 25 and Aug. 18, 1953; Hanna-Wilson: RR, Apr. 6, 1955; Beebe-Clegg: RR, Apr. 6 and 9, 1954.

7. RR, Nov. 25, 1963. Jim Henaghan, MC's predecessor, was denying that he had called Danny Kaye's comic material "lavender-hued," RR, Aug. 3, 1951.

8. RR, Mar. 30, 1956; July 17, 1956.

9. RR, Dec. 20, 1954.

10. RR, Nov. 25, 1952; Mar. 2, 1955; July 23, 1953.

11. Joseph Zappia obituary, *The Desert Sun,* Jan. 20, 2002; Zappia to author, Aug. 19, 1998.

12. RR, Apr. 13, 1953; July 20, 1953; July 23, 1953; June 17, 1954; July 8, 1954; Aug. 19–29, 1957; Oct. 25, 1957.

13. Goodman, *Fifty-Year Decline,* 21.

14. Dave Peck interview, Nov. 25, 1998; William McBrien, *Cole Porter: A Biography,* New York: Knopf (1998), 331.

15. Wally Seawell interview, June 30, 2000.

16. RR, Sept. 2, 1952; June 24, 1953; Aug. 13, 1964.

17. Walter Winchell, *New York Mirror,* Sept. 5, 1957.

18. Dave Peck interview, May 10, 2000.

19. "Bunny Seidman" is a pseudonym. "Dexamyls were diet pills," said Seidman, "but they gave you lots of energy. They were great for hangovers, but they made you smoke more."

20. Irv Kupcinet, "Kup's Column," *Chicago Sun-Times,* Sept. 1, 1957; RR, Mar. 21, 1956; Jan. 20, 1958.

21. Dave Peck interview, May 10, 2000; Jack Bradford interview, May 12, 2000; RR, Mar. 26, 1953; Apr. 4, 1956.

22. Dousings with cocktails as a form of revenge were chronicled in MC's column, e.g., during a spat between Errol Flynn's girlfriend and ex-wife, RR, Sept. 17, 1959.

23. RR, Mar. 4, 1953. The Bankhead party was described in RR, Feb. 1, 1954; Harrison Carroll, *Los Angeles Herald-Express,* Feb. 2, 1954; Hedda Hopper, *L.A. Times,* Feb. 3, 1954; Sidney Skolsky, *N.Y. Post,* Feb. 4 and 5, 1954; MC to Thomas Connolly, Feb. 16, 1954.

24. Lawrence J. Quirk interview, Dec. 23, 1999.

25. Quirk interview, Nov. 14, 1998. Quirk's quotation of MC's adage is possibly verbatim; Cf. RR, Jan. 15, 1960: "Eleanor Roosevelt is whistling in the dark with her remarks about this country's swastika-scum-bums being 'just kids' who don't know any better. Tall sick oaks from tiny sick acorns grow, Eleanor."

26. Quirk interview, Dec. 23, 1999.

27. Quirk interview, May 27, 2000.

28. Quirk interview, May 19, 1999.

29. RR, June 20, 1956; Aug. 31, 1964; Oct. 15, 1952; Aug. 27, 1954; Feb. 17, 1956.

30. Quirk interview, May 27, 2000.

31. Quirk interview, Mar. 27, 1999. The pink ribbon story resonates in two RR items. "Georgie de Witt met a starlet who played hard to get — rid of." (Feb. 15, 1957.) "Aline Mosby tied up Jayne Mansfield with a big bow and 'gave' her to Leonard Slater as a going-away present." (Oct. 22, 1956.) Asher was good for an occasional zinger

in RR: "When Joan Collins slunk up to accept her Most Promising Actress Award," MC wrote, "Jerry Asher cracked, 'That's what you call the contract walk.'" (Feb. 13, 1956.)

32. Ed Hutshing interview, June 5, 2000.

33. RR, Jan. 24, 1957; Apr. 5, 1957; Sept. 20, 1957.

34. James DeCloss interviews, Mar. 31 and May 12, 2000; James Hill interview, Nov. 20, 2002.

35. RR, Apr. 12, 1956; July 11, 1958; Jan. 20, 1961.

36. Larry Quirk interview, May 19, 1999.

37. Lester Strong, "L.A. and 'Lily Law': A Talk with David Hanna," 4 *Journal of Gay, Lesbian, and Bisexual Identity* 182 (1999).

Chapter 2

1. Theo Wilson, *Headline Justice: Inside the Courtroom: The Country's Most Controversial Trials*, New York: Thunder's Mouth Press (1996), 53–68; Jeannette Walls, *Dish: The Inside Story on the World of Gossip*, New York: Spike Books (2000), 11–28.

2. Walter Winchell, *New York Mirror*, Sept. 12, 1957.

3. J. Howard Rutledge, "Gossipy Private Peeks at Celebrities' Lives Start Magazine Bonanza: Confidential's Racy Exposes Crack Newstand Records," *Wall St. Journal*, July 5, 1955.

4. RR, May 11, 1955.

5. Goodman, *Fifty-Year Decline*, 51.

6. James Bacon interview, Apr. 10, 2002; Frank Liberman interview, Mar. 29, 1999 (Liberman said Mosby "needed the money for analysis"); "Putting the Papers to Bed," *Time*, Aug. 26, 1957. Florabel Muir of the *New York Daily News* was, like Mosby, unmasked by Rushmore while covering the trial in the press gallery.

7. RR, Nov. 4, 1960; Mar. 8, 1965; Ezra Goodman, "Low Budget Movies with POW!", *New York Times Magazine*, Feb. 28, 1965. MC also refrained from mentioning Aline Mosby in his column between Oct. 22, 1956, and Apr. 1, 1959. There was no such embargo at *Daily Variety*, where Army Archerd continued to mention Mosby throughout the period of her disgrace and rehabilitation.

8. William J. Mann, *Behind the Screen: How Gays and Lesbians Shaped Hollywood 1910–1969*. New York: Viking (2001), 157.

9. RR, Sept. 23, 1954; Oct. 14, 1954; May 6, 1955; Aug. 30, 1955; Dec. 15, 1954; May 3, 1955; Aug. 10, 1955.

10. RR, May 13, 1955; Sept. 6, 1955; Dec. 23, 1955; Mar. 18, 1955 (emphasis added).

11. MC to Thomas Connolly, Feb. 16, 1954.

12. MC to Fred H. Turner, Apr. 16, 1956.

13. RR, Feb. 11, 1953.

14. RR, Feb. 29, 1952; July 3, 1952. Yet another antecedent item in RR to a *Confidential* story came from Jim Henaghan, pinch-hitting during MC's vacation, on May 5, 1954: "Fan mag says it has a piece coming out titled, 'Why Liberace Has Never Married!' They wouldn't dare!"

15. For example, RR, Sept. 21, 1954: "*Confidential* publisher Bob Harrison checks into the Bevhills Friday." RR, Feb. 21, 1955.

16. See also James R. Petersen, "Playboy's History of the Sexual Revolution: Something Cool, Part VI: 1950–59," *Playboy*, Feb. 1998; "Counsel Appears for Confidential," *N.Y. Times*, Aug. 20, 1957.

17. Thomas K. Wolfe, "Public Lives: Confidential Magazine; Reflections in Tranquility by the Former Owner, Robert Harrison, Who Managed to Get Away with It," *Esquire*, Apr. 1964; Jeannette Walls, *Dish*, 25.

18. RR, Jan. 25, 1954; Aug. 16, 1954; Aug. 19, 1955.

19. RR, Oct. 22, 1956; Mar. 11, 1957.

20. RR, Aug. 5, 1957.

21. "Actor Must Testify at Magazine Trial," *N.Y. Times*, Aug. 1, 1957; RR, Nov. 23, 1955; Dec. 20, 1955; Hedda Hopper, "Shift to TV Explained by Calhoun," *L.A. Times*, Jan. 27, 1957.

22. Jerry Oppenheimer and Jack Vitek, *Idol: Rock Hudson, the True Story of an American Film Hero*, New York: Villard (1986), 55; Rock Hudson and Sara Davidson, *Rock Hudson: His Story*, New York: Morrow (1986), 74; Emily J. McMurray and Owen O'Donnell, eds., *Contemporary Theatre, Film, and Television*, Vol. 9, Detroit: Gale Research, Inc. (1992), 72; Budget Documents for Calhoun's films, U-I Collection, Cinema-Television Library, Univ. of So. Calif.

23. Gladwin Hill, "Film Colony Fidgets in Confidential Case," *N.Y. Times*, Aug. 18, 1957.

24. RR, Aug. 2 and 23, 1957.

25. JV, Sept. 4, 1957; Harold Conrad, *Dear Muffo: Thirty-Five Years in the Fast Lane*, New York: Stein & Day (1982).

26. James Hill interview, Dec. 9, 2002; Steve Govoni, "Now It Can Be Told," *American Film*, Feb. 1990, 31.

27. Irv Kupcinet, "Kup's Column," *Chicago Sun-Times*, Mar. 19, 1961; Neal Graham, "Mike Connolly on the Receiving End at Masquer's 'Irishman's' Testimonial," *Hollywood Reporter*, Mar. 20, 1961; RR, May 14, 1957.

28. Quirk interview, Nov. 14, 1998.

29. Quirk interview, Mar. 27, 1999.

30. JV, Sept. 7, 1951; RR, May 11, 1954; Jan. 19, 1953; Apr. 10, 1953; Apr. 3, 1953; Lester Strong, "L.A. and 'Lily Law.'"

31. JV, Feb. 19, 1951; RR, May 14 and 16, 1957.

32. Joseph Wechsberg, "The Loves of Hoffman," *Esquire*, Aug. 1953; RR, Mar. 7, 1960.

Chapter 3

1. MC, "Boston Can't Afford Lillian Roth Any More," *Chicago Sun-Times*, Sept. 6, 1956; Certificate of Baptism, Saint Monica's Church, Santa Monica, Calif., Aug. 14, 1948, in possession of Julie Sanges.

2. Assignment of One-Third Interest in *I'll Cry Tomorrow* to Burt McGuire, Mar. 27, 1950, in possession of Julie Sanges; Jack Egan, "Daily Illini's Ex-Crusader Now Hollywood Gossip Ace," *Champaign-Urbana-Courier*, late 1956; RR, Aug. 2, 1957; Julie Sanges to author, July 19, 2000.

3. Alma Connolly interview, May 4, 2002; MC to Thomas Connolly, Mar. 13 and June 30, 1951; JV, July 24 and 25, 1950. MC: "Stanley Rose's was THE Hollywood story: All the glitter and the shambles, the glory and the shame, from repping Scott Fitzgerald at Fitzgerald's peak to agenting for Lillian Roth at her nadir ... [he] ran the Pickwick Bookshop and this was a more exciting town for his having been here." (RR, Oct. 19, 1954.)

4. RR, Mar. 10, 1952; Hedda Hopper column, *L.A. Times*, Mar. 26, 1952; Louella Parsons column, *L.A. Herald-Examiner*, Mar. 25, 1952; RR, Mar. 25, 27, 1952; Apr. 4, 1952; Apr. 18, 1952.

5. Lillian Roth to Julie Sanges, Jan. 22, 1959; RR, Feb. 6, 1953; Alma Connolly interview, May 4, 2002. The only surviving kinescope of Roth's *This Is Your Life* segment is of a rebroadcast, from which, unfortunately, MC's tail-end appearance was excised.

6. Roth to Sanges, Jan. 22, 1959; Robert Hamner to Lillian Roth, Sept. 7, 1954; Julie Sanges to author, Oct. 16, 2000.

7. Paul O'Neil, "Great Tell-It-All Ghost," *Life*, June 29, 1959; RR, May 24, 1954.

8. RR, May 24, 1954; "1950s Bestsellers," Cader Books, <www.caderbooks.com/best50.html> (visited June 25, 2002); "Christopher Awards Announced," *N.Y. Times*, Aug. 26, 1954, 23; Parsons, Mar. 25, 1953.

9. Production Budget for *I'll Cry Tomorrow*, MGM, Reid Weingarten Collection, Cinema-Television Library, Univ. of So. Calif.; RR, June 25, 1959.

10. MC to Roth, Sept. 7, 1954.

11. Gerold Frank to Roth, Oct. 16, 1954; Gilbert Millstein, "A Redeemed Captive," *N.Y. Times*, July 11, 1954.

12. RR, Aug. 11, 1954; Nov. 29, 1954; Jan. 23, 1957.

13. RR, Mar. 27, 1957; Sept. 17, 1959; Art Buchwald, "Gerold Frank, Renowned Ghost," *L.A. Times*, Aug. 16, 1960; RR, Aug. 17, 1960.

14. O'Neil, "Great Tell-It-All Ghost."

15. RR, Mar. 9, 1956; Aug. 1 and 2, 1957. Underscoring the *Hollywood Reporter's* reputation as a family newspaper, the vulgarity of the rejected title provoked a rash of complaints to MC.

16. Gerold Frank to author, Mar. 7, 1993.

17. RR, May 4, 1956; Sept. 19, 1957.

18. Dave Peck interview, May 12, 2000; RR, Dec. 23, 1955.

19. RR, Oct. 16, 1957; Apr. 1, 1958.

20. RR, Dec. 19, 1957; MC to Thomas Connolly, Mar. 13, 1951.

21. RR, Sept. 10, 1952; June 5, 1953; July 10, 1953; July 15, 1954; Oct. 28, 1954; June 5, 1956; Aug. 2, 1954; Jan. 24, 1956.

22. MC to Roth, Sept. 7, 1954; RR, June 16, 1954; Nov. 16, 1954.

23. Gore Vidal to author, Dec. 15, 1997; Willie Wilkerson interview, June 30, 2002.

24. MC, "Hollywood," *Chicago Sun-Times*, Sept. 6, 1956; RR, Sept. 4, 1956.

25. RR, May 21, 1957; Jan. 15, 1957.

26. Herb Caen, "Baghdad-by-the-Bay," *San Francisco Examiner*, Feb. 13, 1957; Art Ryon, "Ham on Ryon," *L.A. Times*, Feb. 20, 1957; RR, Feb. 21, 1957. Caen to author, July 24, 1995: "I read and admired [Mike's] stuff, and he seemed to like mine, but we met only once and were quite drunk." RR, Feb. 25, 1953: "We'll drink champagne out of [Rosemary] Clooney's clodhoppers any time."

27. Irv Kupcinet with Paul Neimark, *Kup: a Man, an Era, a City*, Chicago: Bonus Books (1988), 61–64; Kup's Column ("Kup Encounters An Occupational Hazard"), *Chicago Sun-Times*, Aug. 28, 1958; RR, Sept. 26, 1958; Dec. 15, 1958. Ever the gentleman, Kupcinet said he had been the "chauffeur" of Mrs. Dodge's car when the L.A. police pulled them over. Not until his 1988 autobiography did he admit that Mrs. Dodge had been at the wheel.

28. TT, Dec. 1, 1937; RR, January 28, 1952; Sept. 2, 1952; Sept. 5, 1952; Nov. 27, 1956; May 14, 1952; Sept. 23, 1955; Feb. 9, 1956.

29. RR, Sept. 10, 1954; Dec. 11, 1951; Apr. 1, 1954; Sept. 30, 1957; Oct. 26, 1955; May 10, 1956.

30. RR, Aug. 13, 1952; Jan. 31, 1952.

31. RR, Feb. 16, 1955; Apr. 5, 1955.

32. RR, Apr. 11, 1956; July 28, 1953; Dec. 7, 1954.

33. RR, May 5, 1953; Oct. 31, 1955; Sept. 14, 1956; Dec. 3, 1957.

34. RR, Dec. 26, 1956; Jan. 14, 1957; Sept. 13, 1957. George Nader would actually play the alcholic newsman.

35. RR, Dec. 31, 1953; Dec. 5, 1957.

36. Richard Foster interview, Jan. 27, 2002.

37. Julie Sanges to author, July 3, 2002; Alan Eichler interview, Mar. 22, 2000; Lillian Roth obituary, *Variety*, May 14, 1980; RR, July 27, 1960; Dec. 27, 1961; Oct. 17, 1961.

Chapter 4

1. MC to Dr. A. Walton Litz, Sept. 24, 1961; Thomas Connolly interview, May 4, 2002; RR, Aug. 12, 1964; May 21, 1953.

2. Thomas Connolly interview, Dec. 15, 1998.

3. MC to Richard Nixon, Jan. 8, 1960; RR, Sept. 16, 1952; May 20, 1957.

4. MC, *The Victory*, May 7, 1931; Apr. 25, 1930.

5. Files from MC's WWII Transportation Corps file, Natl. Personnel Records Center, St. Louis, Mo.; Alice McDermott, *Charming Billy*, 132.

6. *The Victory*, Apr. 25, 1930; RR, May 9, 1952; JV, May 11, 1951; RR, Mar. 17, 1954.

7. Thomas Connolly interview, Dec. 15, 1998; Alma Connolly interview, May 4, 2002. Connolly adored Fazenda for the rest of her life. When he was honored in 1961 by the Masquers Club as Irishman of the Year, Fazenda was on the dais to pay tribute to him. When she died, Connolly wrote a long, sincere tribute: "Louise was THE Great Lady of Hollywood ... She quit acting after her last picture, *The Old Maid*, in 1938, to spend her time (ALL her time) helping Protestant, Catholic and Jewish charities, the Motion Picture Relief Fund, unwed mothers, alcoholics, hop-heads — anyone who needed her help, any kind of help — a buck, a Gee, or just a kind word ... She went out of her way looking for people to help. She loved to put on an old shirt and dungarees and go scouting for them in Skid Row ... She had three phones in her bedroom-office that rang night and day with calls for help. The help was always there ... Goodbye, Aunt Kate. May God be as good to you as you were to His other poor creatures." (RR, Apr. 18, 1962.)

8. RR, June 8, 1956; JV, June 4, 1951; RR, Feb. 7, 1955; Aug. 10, 1955.

9. Richard Cohen and Elizabeth Taylor, *American Pharaoh: Mayor Richard J. Daley: His Battle for Chicago and the Nation*, Boston: Little, Brown & Co. (2000) 25–26; MC, De La Salle Alumni Banquet invitation, 1954. Half a century after the two mayors MC referred to, De La Salle can also claim both Mayors Daley as alumni.

10. Brother Kevin Griffin, director of alumni relations, to author, June 10 and 25, 1998; RR, Mar. 13, 1953; MC to Thomas Connolly, June 23, 1956.

11. TT, undated clipping, circa Mar. 1938.

12. Carl Bode, *Mencken*, Carbondale: So. Illinois Univ. Press (1969) 21–22; Jack Egan, "Daily Illini's Ex-Crusader Now Hollywood Gossip Ace," *Champaign-Urbana Courier*, undated clipping, late 1956; RR, Mar. 25, 1960; *The Victory*, May 7, 1931.

13. *The Victory*, Jan. 16, 1931.

14. *The Victory*, Dec. 13, 1929; RR, Sept. 23, 1964.

15. *The Victory*, May 28, 1931.

16. MC, *The Victory*, May 28, 1931; RR, Jan. 7, 1955.

17. RR, Feb. 17, 1955.

18. *The Victory*, May 28, 1931.

19. Ibid.

20. *The Victory*, May 7, 1931; Bro. Kevin Griffin to author, June 10, 1998.

21. MC's file, Natl. Personnel Records Center; Bro Kevin Griffin to author, June 10, 1998.

22. MC's file, Natl. Personnel Records Center; MC, Alumni Banquet invitation; Cohen & Taylor, *American Pharaoh*, 26–27.

23. RR, Dec. 31, 1951; Jan. 15, 1953.

24. JV, Nov. 30, 1949.

25. James DeCloss interview, May 12, 2000.

26. MC to Litz; RR, Jan. 16, 1957; Apr. 1, 1957.

27. RR, Feb. 7, 1956; Aug. 15, 1952.

28. MC to Litz; A Walton Litz, *The Art of James Joyce: Method and Design in* Ulysses *and* Finnegans Wake, London: Oxford Univ. Press (1961), 60–61.

29. RR, Jan. 17, 1957.

30. RR, Aug. 18, 1955.

31. MC to Richard Nixon, Aug. 27, 1956; Sept. 6, 1956; Sept. 21, 1956; Nov. 7, 1956. MC's comments on son-father themes include RR, Dec. 13, 1954: "There's a 'father-and-son' scene in *East of Eden* that will be the talk of this town and any place where it's seen," and RR, June 22, 1960: "Stephen in *Ulysses*, see, is [James] Joyce himself, the self-exiled one in search of the father-image." Cf. MC's critique of *Who's Afraid of Virginia Woolf?*, RR, June 22, 1966: "Little Orphan Albee's crystal-clear switch on the classic son-in-search-of-a-father message."

32. MC to Richard Nixon, Aug. 12, 1959.

33. MC to Richard Nixon, Jan. 8, 1960.

34. MC to Richard Nixon, Jan. 15, 1961.

Chapter 5

1. Application for Employment, MC's file, Natl. Personnel Records Center; Univ. of Illinois student directories, 1934–37; John A. O'Brien, *Where Dwellest Thou?: Intimate Personal Stories of Twelve Converts to the Catholic Faith*, New York: Gilbert Press, 1956, 40.

2. Mary-jane Ryan Snyder to author, Feb. 24, 2000; Hallie Rives Amiel interview, Feb. 15, 2000; Winton Solberg, "The Catholic Presence at the University of Illinois," 76 *Catholic Historical Review* 790 (1990).

3. Mary-jane Ryan Snyder interview, Feb. 11, 2000.

4. Solberg, "The Catholic Presence," 795–796.

5. Winton Solberg to author, Apr. 4, 2002. MC's subsequent close friendships among the Catholic clergy would include James Francis Cardinal McIntyre in Los Angeles; Bro. Matthew Benney of St. Mary's College; and Rev. Willis Egan, brother of actor Richard Egan, who would deliver the eulogy at MC's funeral.

6. Mary-jane Ryan Snyder interview, May 4, 2002.

7. Mary-jane Ryan Snyder interview, Feb. 11, 2000; TT, Sept. 23, 1937.

8. Hallie Rives Amiel interviews, Feb. 15 and Mar. 17, 2000.

9. Jack Egan, "Daily Illini's Ex-Crusader Now Hollywood Gossip Ace," *Champaign-Urbana Courier*, undated clipping, late 1956; Sam Abarbanel to author, May 6, 2002; RR, Oct. 15, 1951.

10. Mary-jane Ryan Snyder interview, Feb. 11, 2000.

11. Hallie Rives Amiel interviews, Feb. 15 and Mar. 17, 2000.

12. Ibid.

13. TT, Oct. 2, 1937; Nov. 23, 1937; Jan. 18, 1938.

14. Mary-jane Ryan Snyder interview, May 4, 2002; Angus Thuermer interview, Feb. 10, 2000.

15. TT, Oct. 28, 1937.

16. Jack Mabley interview, July 10, 1998; TT, Nov. 10, 1937.

17. Mabley interview, July 10, 1998.

18. TT, May 1, 1936.

19. Mabley interview, July 10, 1998.

20. TT, Oct. 2 and 3, 1937.

21. Mary-jane Ryan Snyder interview, May 4, 2002; Jack Mabley, "The Exclamation Point," *Daily Illini*, Oct. 16, 1937.

22. Mabley, "The Exclamation Point," Oct. 16, 1937.

23. TT, Oct. 16, 1937.

24. TT, Oct, 21, 1937.

25. Mabley, "The Exclamation Point," Oct. 24, 1937.

26. MC, "Willard Seeks Twin Cities' Backing," *Daily Illini*, Oct. 23, 1937.

27. "U. of Illinois Joins Student Paper's Anti-Syphilis Fight," *Chicago Tribune*, Oct. 23, 1937.

28. *Daily Illini*, Oct. 24, 26, and 27, 1937; Mabley interview, July 10, 1998.

29. "Five Fraternities Join Crusade on Disease," *Daily Illini*, Oct. 27, 1937.

30. Mabley, "The Exclamation Point," Oct. 27, 1937; TT, Oct. 28, 1937.

31. TT, Nov. 4 and 24, 1937. Mabley's Halloween ultimatum, ironically, would have allowed the brothels one last night of lucrative business, since it was the day after homecoming.

32. Mabley, "The Exclamation Point," Nov. 17, 1937.

33. Mabley to author, June 8, 1998; TT, Dec. 1, 1937; Jan. 14, 1938.

34. Mabley to author, May 22, 2002. The *Champaign-Urbana Courier's* obituary for MC (Nov. 19, 1966) stated, "One of Connolly's *Daily Illini* girl reporters called a north end 'madam' and got a job over the telephone. She then wrote a word-for-word account of the incident in the *Daily Illini*." MC's TT of Mar. 3, 1938, which listed the top stories of his senior year, included, "Coed gets job in bawdy house." Neither the author nor various researchers in the Connolly family has ever discovered the story in *Daily Illini* archives.

35. RR, Aug. 11, 1954.

36. Thomas and Alma Connolly interview, May 4, 2002.

37. Hallie Rives Amiel interview, Feb. 15, 2000.

38. TT, Oct. 28, 1937.

39. Mabley interview, July 10, 1998.

40. Egan, "Daily Illini's Ex-Crusader," 1956; MC to Jim Colvin, Oct. 3, 1956.

41. Thuermer to Mabley, quoted in "Mabley's Report," *Chicago Today*, Mar. 14, 1974.

42. Ibid.

43. In RR, Apr. 2, 1957, MC wrote that while he listened to a Gerald L. K. Smith diatribe against "the Zionist conspirators," he "smelled Munich in the air." He must not have noticed parallels in the methods he and Smith used to achieve their ends.

44. TT, Apr. 2, 1938; Oct. 29, 1937; Oct. 28, 1937.

45. TT, Oct, 15, 16, and 28, 1937; Mabley, "The Exclamation Point," Oct. 20, 1937.

46. TT, Oct. 28, 1937 (capitals in original).

47. TT, Oct. 26, 28, and 16, 1937.

48. It is interesting that, despite the plethora of memories of Champaign and Chicago dredged up by MC in two decades' worth of Hollywood columns, he never alluded to his anti-vice crusade, probably because he feared his audience would regard it as unsophisticated. Prostitution became a source of provocative one-liners in his Hollywood columns, as in JV, Apr. 27, 1951: "Password at a new bordello is causing a lotta guffaws." As well, during his first trip to Europe, he would write about the prostitutes of Paris, Zurich, and Amsterdam in great detail without an iota of moral outrage (RR, May 7, 15 and 19, 1953).

Chapter 6

1. Egan, "Daily Illini's Ex-Crusader," 1956; MC's Application for Senior Clerkship, file at Natl. Personnel Records Center, St. Louis, Mo.; RR, Feb. 27, 1961; "Chi Travel Bureaus See N.Y. Niteries Back to Normal, Bids for Tour Biz," *Variety*, Apr. 17, 1946, 43.

2. RR, Sept. 17, 1956; Sept. 27, 1957; Oct. 18, 1956; July 22, 1953.

3. Jack Mabley, "Subpoenas a Way of Life for Reporter," *Chicago Today*, Apr. 9, 1970; Mabley to author, Apr. 15, 1999.

4. MC's registration card and classification record, Selective Service System Archives.

5. Egan, "Daily Illini's Ex-Crusader," 1956; *Variety* obituary, Nov. 23, 1966; *Hollywood Reporter* obituary, Nov. 21, 1966; Larry Quirk interview, Nov. 4, 1998. The United States was divided into Service Commands during the War, and the Sixth

Service Command was headquartered in Chicago.

6. MC's file, Natl. Personnel Records Center; RR, Sept. 26, 1956.

7. "Check Slip" in MC's Personnel File. The Army paid him forty dollars per week; Powers had paid forty-five.

8. Personnel File; *Logistics in World War II: Final Report of the Army Service Forces.* Washington, D.C.: Center of Military History, U.S. Army, 1993, 149; Thomas Connolly interview, May 4, 2002.

9. JV, Dec. 8, 1949; RR, Aug. 7, 1953; Dec. 7, 1954; Sept. 28, 1960; May 17, 1966.

10. Resignation letter in Personnel Files; RR, July 6, 1956. The Santa Fe Railroad occupied a handsome building on the west side of Michigan Avenue. When Lee Lyles died, MC wrote, "With newsmen who know their flacks, it's Jim Merrick ten-to-one to succeed the late Lee Lyles as Santa Fe public relations chief" (JV, July 24, 1950).

11. "Shoe-Leather School," *Newsweek*, Jan. 4, 1965; Dave Peck interview, Nov. 13, 1998.

12. "Shoe-Leather Newsmen," *Newsweek*, Jan. 23, 1961; RR, Dec. 31, 1964.

13. Morry Rotman interview, Dec. 2, 1998; Rotman to author, Dec. 20, 1998; RR, Feb. 17, 1953. The statement in MC's *Variety* obituary that he had worked for CNB before World War II is erroneous.

14. RR, Jan. 12, 1953.

15. Bigelow v. RKO Radio Pictures, 150 F. 2d 877, 327 U.S. 251; Egan, "Daily Illini's Ex-Crusader," 1956; RR, Nov. 28, 1951; *N.Y. Times*, Mar. 11, 1944, 11.

16. Thomas and Alma Connolly interviews, May 4, 2002.

17. See obituary of Jack Lait, former *Variety* bureau chief in Chicago, *Variety*, Apr. 7, 1954. MC's bylined *Variety* articles appeared on Apr. 25, 1945; Aug. 8, 1945; Aug. 29, 1945; Dec. 26, 1945; May 22, 1946.

18. RR, Oct. 17, 1956; Sept. 19, 1957. As city editor of *The Daily Illini*, MC had written that Helen Morgan was one of his "dislikes." His tastes must have matured. (TT, Sept. 23, 1937.)

19. Thomas Connolly interview, May 4, 2002; Trini Lopez to author, Apr. 15, 2002; RR, Feb. 17, 1958; MC, "The Lennon Sisters' Plea: 'Stop Telling Those Lies About Us!'," *Screen Stories*, Jan. 1967.

20. *Variety*, May 22, 1946; July 3, 1946.

21. Irv Kupcinet interviews, July 25, 1995; Nov. 25, 1998.

22. RR, Apr. 13, 1960.

23. JV, July 13 and August 29, 1951; RR, Apr. 5, 1957.

24. Allan Berube, *Coming Out Under Fire*, New York: The Free Press (1990), 107; Kup's Column, *Chicago Times*, Nov. 5, 1943. For further information on the mammoth influx of servicemen into Chicago during the War, the oral history of General Henry S. Aurand, at the Dwight D. Eisenhower Presidential Library, is enlightening. It can be accessed at <http:// carlisle-www.army. mil/cgi-bin/usamhi/DL/showdoc.pl?doc num=90> (visited June 23, 2000).

25. James H. Jones, *Alfred C. Kinsey: A Public/Private Life*, New York: Norton (1997), 369–387. The Kinsey Institute's archivist reports that neither MC nor Joseph Zappia was among the multitude of Kinsey's Chicago correspondents during this period.

26. David K. Johnson, "The Kids of Fairytown," in *Creating a Place for Ourselves*, ed. Brett Beemyn (New York: Routledge, 1997), 97–118.

27. Ibid.

28. Neil Steinberg, "A Century of Gay Life on Exhibit at U. of C.," *Chicago Sun-Times*, Sept. 17, 2000; Jones, *Alfred C. Kinsey*, 371; Johnson, "The Kids of Fairytown," 102; "Pansy Parlors: Tough Chicago Has Epidemic of Male Butterflies," *Variety*, Dec. 10, 1930, 1.

29. TT, Sept. 23, 1937; RR, Dec. 11, 1958; Mary-jane Ryan Snyder interview, May 4, 2002; RR, Feb. 10, 1954 (although MC did not say so, Bodenheim had just been killed).

30. James H. Hill interviews, Sept. 14 and Nov. 20, 2002; "Personal Security Questionnaire," MC's file, Natl. Personnel Records Center; Zappia's registration card, Selective Service System Archives.

31. James Hill interviews, Sept. 14 and Nov. 20, 2002; MC's registration card, Selective Service System Archives.

32. James Hill interview, Dec. 3, 2002.

33. James Hill interview, Nov. 20, 2002.

34. James Hill interview, Nov. 20, 2002; Joseph Zappia interview, May 11, 1999. Thomas and Alma Connolly say they were never aware of Zappia until their January 1949 honeymoon in Los Angeles.

35. "Loyalty and Character Report for War Department," Dec. 16, 1942, Personnel Files.

36. Berube, *Coming Out Under Fire*, 115.

37. *Variety*, July 4, 1945; Feb. 27, 1946.

38. *Variety*, Feb. 20, 1946; Mar. 28, 1945.

39. *Variety*, Mar. 14, 1945.

40. *Variety*, Nov. 23, 1966.

Chapter 7

1. MC to Thomas Connolly, Mar. 13, 1951; RR, Dec. 20, 1954.

2. TT, Sept. 23, 1937.

3. Ed Hutshing interview, June 5, 2000; MC's *Daily Variety* obituary, Nov. 21, 1966.

4. David Hanna, *Mafia Over Hollywood*, New York: Manor Books (1980), 76–77.

5. Hutshing interview, June 5, 2000.

6. JV, Nov. 28, 1949; Goodman, *Fifty-Year Decline*, 17; "The Lowdown on Hollywood's Connolly," *People Today*, Mar. 11, 1953; MC's *Daily Variety* obituary, Nov. 21, 1966; Hutshing interview, June 14, 2000; Hanna, *Mafia Over Hollywood*, 77.

7. Sheilah Graham, *The Rest of the Story*, New York: Coward-McCann (1964), 167, 175.

8. JV, Apr. 6, 1950; June 28, 1950.

9. RR, Feb. 26, 1954; Dec. 8, 1954.

10. MC to Thomas Connolly, Feb. 26, 1950. The first MC byline came on July 31, 1950.

11. Goodman, *Fifty-Year Decline*, 60–61.

12. Graham, *Rest of the Story*, 168–176.

13. James Henaghan, Jr., interview, May 12, 2000; Frances Henaghan Ehrlich interview, Mar. 5, 2001; Graham, *Rest of the Story*, 175. When Herb Stein died, MC's Oct. 18, 1965, column said, "The death of our beloved Herb Stein, a staggering blow, leaves all of us here equally desolate."

14. Goodman, *Fifty-Year Decline*, 58; Edith Gwynn, RR, Aug. 15, 1946; "House Detective," *Time*, Nov. 10, 1947.

15. JV, Mar. 7, 1951.

16. Willie Wilkerson interviews, May 11 and July 6, 2000.

17. William R. ("Willie") Wilkerson III, *The Man Who Invented Las Vegas*, Los Angeles: Ciro's Books, 9–10.

18. Hanna, *Mafia Over Hollywood*, 157.

19. William R. Wilkerson, "Trade Views," Aug. 13, 1946.

20. Willie Wilkerson to author, Jan. 10, 2002.

21. David Hanna, *Ava: Portrait of a Star*, New York: Putnam (1960), 15; David Hanna, *"Come Up and See Me Sometime,"* New York: Belmont Tower Books (1976), 134; Hanna, *Mafia Over Hollywood*, 158.

22. Wilkerson, *The Man Who Invented Las Vegas*, 51; RR, Oct. 3, 1958.

23. MC to Hedda Hopper, Oct. 1, 1951, Margaret Herrick Library Special Collections; Hutshing interview, June 5, 2000.

24. "The Lowdown on Hollywood's Connolly," *People Today*, Mar. 11, 1953; Egan, "Daily Illini's Ex-Crusader"; Dan Jenkins, "On the Air," *Hollywood Reporter*, June 26, 1953; Dan Jenkins interview, Dec. 3, 1998.

25. Sidney Carroll, "A Tale of Hoffman," *Esquire*, Nov. 1946; Joseph Wechsberg, "The Loves of Hoffman," *Esquire*, Aug. 1953.

26. Willie Wilkerson interview, June 20, 2000; Hanna, *Mafia Over Hollywood*, 158.

27. Jack L. Warner to Wilkerson, Oct. 30 and Nov. 5, 1959, Jack L. Warner Collection, Cinema-Television Library, University of Southern California.

28. Joseph Zappia to author, Aug. 8, 1998.

29. Jack Bradford, RR, Nov. 21 and 22, 1966; Thomas M. Pryor, "No. 2 Open End News-Front Winds Up a Wide-Open Rhubarb," *Variety*, Sept. 7, 1960; RR, Mar. 19, 1952; Bradford interview, May 12, 2000.

30. "The Lowdown on Hollywood's Connolly"; RR, Jan. 6, 1961.

31. Willie Wilkerson interview, May 11, 2000; Bradford interview, May 12, 2000.

32. Jack Bradford to author, Nov. 2, 1997.

33. Jack Bradford interview, Sept. 6, 1997.

34. Jack Bradford interview, May 12, 2000.

35. Joseph Zappia to author, July 8, 1998; Joseph Zappia interview, July 13, 1998; RR, Aug. 14, 1959; MC to Richard Nixon, Aug. 12, 1959, Natl. Archives, Laguna Niguel Office.

36. "The Lowdown on Hollywood's Connolly"; A. C. Lyles interview, Dec. 15, 1998; RR, Oct. 19, 1964.

37. Frank Liberman interviews, July 2, 1998; Mar. 29, 1999; May 10, 2000. The Florsheims item appeared in both JV, July 19, 1951; and RR, Aug. 9, 1955.

38. Bill Diehl, "Christmas, Hanukkah Joys Join," *St. Paul Pioneer Press*, Dec. 18, 1992.

39. Bill Diehl to author, June 9, 1993; Will Jones interview, July 18, 2001; RR, July 29, 1957.

40. Jack Bradford interview, May 12, 2000; RR, Nov. 23, 1966.

41. Jack Bradford to author, Nov. 2, 1997; Robert LaGuardia and Gene Arceri, *Red: The Tempestuous Life of Susan Hayward*, New York: Macmillan (1985), 113–118. MC probably thought he would never be caught in the act of recycling his items, which he did incessantly. While digging up the Mar. 20, 1953, item on Jane Powell, he spotted another squib in the same old column, that bids for the Duchess of Windsor's memoirs had hit $150,000. He reprinted this one, too, on Feb. 17, 1956, except now he claimed the amount was $200,000.

42. RR, Nov. 21, 1966; Nov. 30, 1964; Suzanne Finstad, *Natasha*, New York: Three Rivers Books (2001), 298; RR, June 23 and 24, 1960.

43. "The Lowdown on Hollywood's Connolly"; RR, Jan. 13, 1953; Oct. 13, 1952.

44. RR, Apr. 30, 1956; Aug. 23, 1956; JV, Aug. 8, 1951; RR, June 12, 1953.

45. RR, Aug. 25, 1960; June 4, 1953; Gerald Clarke to author, Aug. 6, 2001.

46. RR, Apr. 3, 1953; Jan. 22, 1957; Jan. 18, 1957.

47. RR, Feb. 23, 1959.

48. RR, Nov. 3, 1959. In RR, Jan. 4, 1960, MC noted "Merle Oberon & Zsa Zsa snubbing each other en route to L'Escoffier." Like Garland, Gabor was not immune to MC's constant jabs. In eulogizing MC, Jack Bradford wrote, "his enemies turned into loving friends like the actress thrusting money to have him fired only to become the guest of honor in his home some years later." MC's friends say Gabor was the actress.

49. RR, Apr. 7 and 8, May 12, July 17 and 29, Aug. 5, Sept. 10 and 16, 1959. *Daily Variety's* Army Archerd had already speculated correctly that Taylor would play Cleopatra (JV, July 28 and 29, Aug. 7, 1959).

Chapter 8

1. Dore Schary, *Heyday: An Autobiography*, Boston: Little, Brown (1979), 164–

167; Larry Ceplair and Steven Englund, *The Inquisition in Hollywood: Politics in the Film Community 1930–1960*, New York: Anchor Press (1980), 254–261.

2. David Ehrenstein, *Open Secret: Gay Hollywood 1928–1998*, New York: Morrow (1998), 114–115.

3. Arthur Laurents, *Original Story By*, New York: Knopf (2000), 84.

4. RR, Mar. 25, 1953.

5. RR, July 6, 1956; RR, Mar. 26, 1952.

6. RR, July 29, and 30, 1954; Aug. 30, 1956. The brickbat to Diana Dors illuminates MC's comment, noted in Chapter One, that although no one pushed Dors into a swimming pool, "several would have liked to."

Charlie Chaplin was an anti–Christ to MC, even though he was a British citizen and was never a Communist. MC's attacks on Chaplin were probably louder, more frequent, and more sustained than for any other target. Visiting Chaplin's *Limelight* set, MC found him "insufferable simply because we wouldn't kowtow." MC claimed that Chaplin had stolen his "Little Tramp" identity from Italian movie clowns of the early 1900s and was no genius but a mere mimic. (RR, Aug. 14, 1956.) Typical was this blast from RR, Feb. 17, 1954: "Wonderful to wash our hands of those dreary Chaplins, even though he did make a lousy twenty million forture here. It's almost worth it to be rid of such crumbums."

7. JV, Nov. 29, 1949; Lauren Barack, "Accused Felt Press Pressure," *Daily Variety*, Sept. 11, 1996.

8. Dalton Trumbo, "Blacklist = Black Market," *The Nation*, May 4, 1957; Roy Hoopes, *[James M.] Cain*, New York: Holt, Rinehard & Winston (1982), 397; Lester Cole, *Hollywood Red*, Palo Alto: Ramparts Press (1981), 162; Goodman, *Fifty-Year Decline*, 62–63.

9. RR, Oct. 3 and 4, 1951. Wilkerson had used the term "scummie" twice in his Trade Views column of Sept. 26, 1951, the week before MC started working for him.

10. Elia Kazan, *Elia Kazan: A Life*, New York: Knopf (1988), 455.

11. RR, Aug. 17 and 19, 1955.

12. Kupcinet, *Kup: A Man, a City, an Era*, 166–167, 246–247; Irv Kupcinet interview, July 25, 1995.

13. J.B. Matthews, "Did the Movies Really Clean House?", *American Legion Magazine*, Dec. 1951, 12.

14. RR, Feb. 14, 1952; JV, May 18, 1951.

15. The libels and retractions were as follows: Huston, RR, Mar. 26 and 27, 1952; Milestone, JV, Aug. 28 and 29, 1951; Kanin, RR, Apr. 8 and 10, 1952; Lawrence, RR, May 7 and 8, 1953; Loesser, RR, May 19 and 24, 1954; Davis, RR, Feb. 1 and 14, 1956; Blankfort, RR, Feb. 26 and 27, 1957; Richards, RR, Jan. 28 and 29, 1959. Cf. MC's JV of Apr. 24, 1951: "Scripter Andrew Solt is steaming about being confused with 'unfriendly' Waldo Salt."

16. RR, June 2, 1954. Addresses were also published in RR on May 27, 1952; Mar. 16, 1955; May 24, 1955; Nov. 22, 1955. See also Jan. 18, 1952; Apr. 9, 1954; May 24, 1954.

17. RR, Aug. 2, 1954; June 18, 1954.

18. RR, June 21, 1954; Aug. 20, 1954; Nov. 9, 1954; Nov. 12, 1954.

19. Liz Smith to author, Apr. 5, 2002.

20. RR, Dec. 1, 1954.

21. RR, Dec. 10, 1954.

22. Norris Houghton, *Entrances and Exits: A Life in and Out of the Theatre*, New York: Limelight Editions (1991), 255–258; Houghton to author, June 22, 1995.

23. *Investigation of Communist Activities in the Los Angeles, Calif., Area — Pt. 9*, Hearing before the Committee on Un-American Activities, Apr. 19, 1956; RR, May 1 and 7, 1956.

24. RR, May 25, 1956.

25. RR, Apr. 9, 1954; Jack Raymond, "Russians and Todd Are Planning to Produce 5 Films in Soviet," *N.Y. Times*, May 6, 1956.

26. RR, May 9, 1956; June 1, 1956.

27. *Hollywood Reporter*, Aug. 22, 1956.

28. RR, Aug. 16 and 17, 1956.

29. RR, Aug. 23, 1956.

30. MC to Eisenhower, Aug. 27, 1956, Eisenhower Presidential Library, Abilene, KS; MC to Nixon, Aug. 27, 1956, Natl. Archives, Laguna Niguel Office.

31. RR, Aug. 23, 1956; the column that day even printed a joke that included the phrase, "Don't Just Sit There."

32. Mike Todd, signed full-page ad, *Hollywood Reporter* and *Daily Variety*, Aug. 24, 1956.

33. RR, Aug. 27 and 30, Sept. 4, 1956.

34. RR, Aug. 31, 1956; Monica Lustgarten Moore interview, Mar. 8, 2001. Another instance of specific harm done by MC's column is claimed by screenwriter Allen Boretz, who said he was fired after MC wrote, "What's Allen Boretz the red, named by Martin Berkeley, doing working for Twentieth-Century Fox?" (Patrick McGilligan and Paul Buhle, eds., *Tender Comrades: A Backstory of the Hollywood Blacklist*, New York: St. Martin's Press (1997), 125.) However, what MC actually wrote seemed too after-the-fact to be responsible: "Allen Boretz, fingered as Red by Martin Berkeley at the last HUAC hearings here, finished his writing chore on 20th's *Music in the Air* and checked off the lot." (RR, Feb. 14, 1952.)

35. RR, Jan. 28, 1953; June 22, 1956; July 5 and 9, 1956; Jan. 27, 1958; Aug. 31, 1960. The *Brothers Karamazov* comment was intended to mock Monroe's wish to play serious roles.

36. Leaming, *Marilyn Monroe*, 312, 352.

37. RR, Jan. 27, 1959; Feb. 4, 1959; Apr. 21, 1960; Helen Manfull, ed., *Additional Dialogue: Letters of Dalton Trumbo, 1942–1962*, New York: M. Evans & Co (1970), 534.

38. RR, Dec. 10, 1956; Jan. 17 and 21, 1957; Jan. 3 1958; Mar. 3, 1958; Apr. 21, 1960.

39. RR, Sept. 23, 1959; Nov. 7, 1960; MC, "Exclusive Report from Hollywood, *Screen Stories*, Dec. 1966.

40. RR, Nov. 3, 1960; Mar. 4, 1963.

41. Parker: RR, Oct. 10, 1956, and Aug. 21, 1964; Dassin: RR, May 13, 1955, and June 2, 1961; Signoret: RR, June 3, 1957, and Sept. 4, 1964.

42. H. L. Mencken, *Notes on Democracy*, New York: Knopf (1926), 173.

43. RR, July 12, 1957.

Chapter 9

1. Goodman, *Fifty-Year Decline*, 17.

2. RR, Oct. 31, 1951.

3. George Eells, *Hedda and Louella*, New York: Putnam (1972), 204; RR, Oct. 31, 1951; Amy Fine Collins, "Idol Gossips," *Vanity Fair*, Apr. 1997.

4. "The Lowdown on Hollywood's Connolly," *People Today*, Mar. 11, 1953; Goodman, *Fifty-Year Decline*, 59.

5. RR, Apr. 30, 1956; Nov. 12, 1954.

6. RR, Mar. 12, 1956.

7. RR, Oct. 6, 1952; Nov. 2, 1960; Apr. 11, 1957.

8. Jerry Wald to MC, Mar. 28, 1952; Mar. 28, 1960; MC to Wald, Mar. 29, 1960, Jerry Wald Collection, Cinema-Television Library, Univ. of So. Calif.

9. RR, July 9, 1958; Sept. 16, 1960; May 2, 1958.

10. Wilkerson, *The Man Who Invented Las Vegas*, 91; undated draft found among George H. Kennedy's papers, courtesy of Willie Wilkerson.

11. Anthony Slide, "Hedda Hopper," *Stallion*, June 1986. (The author is grateful to William J. Mann for sharing this item.)

12. MC to Hedda Hopper, Oct. 1, 1951; Hedda Hopper Collection, Margaret Herrick Library, AMPAS; RR, June 26, 1956; MC to Richard Nixon, Sept. 21, 1956, Natl. Archives, Laguna Niguel, Calif., Office.

13. Terrence O'Flaherty, "Baked Alaska," *San Francisco Chronicle*, Dec. 27, 1956; Peggy King Rudofker interview, Dec. 21, 1998.

14. Frank Liberman interviews, Aug. 11, 1998; Jan. 13, 1999; May 10, 2000.

15. RR, Oct. 20, 1958.

16. RR, Feb. 16, 1961.

17. Frank Liberman interview, May 10, 2000.

18. RR, Dec. 22, 1959; Nov. 21, 1966.

19. Jack Bradford interview, July 25, 1995. Oddly, MC's relations with Murphy had been cordial in the previous few years: Murphy was a true-blue Republican and had virtually run the entire show at the 1956 GOP Convention in San Francisco, for which he was praised fulsomely by MC; see RR, Aug. 21 and 22, 1956.

20. RR, Dec. 24, 1959; Mar. 4, 1960.

21. JV, July 24, 1950.

22. Willie Wilkerson, "Writing the End to a True-to-Life Cinderella Story," *L.A. Times*, July 1, 1995; Lana Turner, *Lana: The Lady, the Legened, the Truth*, New York: Dutton (1984), 26–27, 133–134.

23. RR, Apr. 7, 1958.

24. RR, June 17, 1960.

25. RR, May 5 and 6, 1960.

26. Robert Yale Libott interviews, Mar. 26 and Apr. 9, 2002.

27. RR, June 21, 1960.

28. Cheryl Crane, *Detour: A Hollywood Story*, New York: Arbor House (1988), 235, 290–292.

29. RR, June 22, 1960. Earlier, MC had written, "When she springs her sprout from the local moppet pokey, look for Lana Turner to shlep Cheryl and herself to Europe ... Meaning a new start and 'better education' for Cheryl plus 'tax stay' for Lana" (RR, May 10, 1960).

30. Lee Belser, "Columnist Connolly Ousted from Party," *L.A. Mirror-News*, June 27, 1960. MC's own comment was that the incident had been "a tempest in an hors d'oeuvres tray" (RR, June 28, 1960).

31. James Bacon, "Escort Defends Lana's Honor by Taking Poke at Columnist," *L.A. Mirror News*, June 29, 1960; "Columnist in Wrangle Over Lana," uncredited clipping in Herrick Library files, June 29, 1960; "Lana Sobs as Escort Flings Fist at Writer," uncredited clipping in Herrick Library files, June 30, 1960.

32. "Kup's Column," *Chicago Sun-Times*, June 30, 1960; RR, June 30, 1960; JV, July 25, 1960.

33. RR, Oct. 5, 1960.

34. RR, June 10, 1963; Shirley MacLaine, *Don't Fall Off the Mountain*, New York: Norton (1970), 107–110.

35. MacLaine, *Don't Fall Off the Mountain*. MC's capital punishment item (his actual words were, "This MacLaine gal should tend to her P's & Q's and Pretty Quick, she's that flip-topped") was RR, May 5, 1960; the other items MacLaine cited could not be located. He did mock her when he heard she claimed to have talked for hours to India's Nehru on an international flight about "how to clean up this whole mess." "Atta girl, Shirl," he snickered. (RR, Sept. 30, 1960.)

36. Jack Bradford interviews, Sept. 7, 1997; May 12, 2000; RR, Nov. 21, 1966.

37. "Columnist Is Belted by Shirley MacLaine," *N.Y. Daily News*, June 11, 1963; "Shirley Slugs Male Scribe," *Newark (N.J.) Evening News*, June 11, 1963; RR, June 11, 1963.

38. MacLaine, *Don't Fall Off the Mountain*, 110.

39. James Bacon interview, Apr. 10, 2002.

40. RR, Nov. 26, 1963.

41. Jack Bradford interview, Sept. 7, 1997.

42. RR, Oct. 11, 1954; Sept. 23, 1957; Joyce Zappia Leiske interview, Oct. 2, 1998.

43. Jack Bradford interview, May 12,

2000; MacLaine, *Don't Fall Off the Mountain*, 109–110.

44. MC, "Exclusive Report from Hollywood," *Screen Stories*, Dec. 1966.

Chapter 10

1. Hollywood's trade papers remain at each other's throats today. In 1999, the publisher of the *Hollywood Reporter* said, "They [*Variety*] are the number two paper in town." *Variety's* editor-in-chief retorted, "Our competition is not the *Hollywood Reporter* but the *Wall Street Journal*, the *New York Times*, and the *Los Angeles Times*. The *Reporter* hasn't been competition for years." (Bernard Weinraub, "Papers Battle to Control Hollywood's Buzz," *N.Y. Times*, May 3, 1999.)

2. Al Scharper, "Hope Grins and Bears It," *Variety*, Dec. 26, 1956; William R. Wilkerson obituary, *Variety*, Sept. 5, 1962.

3. JV, Jan. 20, 1958; RR, Jan. 22, 1958.

4. RR, Nov. 18, 1958; JV, Nov. 18, 1958.

5. RR, July 13, 1960.

6. RR, Aug. 15, 1956; Nov. 25, 1963. When actress Shelley Winters spotted Connolly at the steelworkers event, she protested, "I thought this party was for Democrats."

7. MC to Richard Nixon, Jan. 8, 1960; RR, Aug. 17, Sept. 16, 1960.

8. MC had written in 1958, for instance, of JFK's houseguesting with the Lawfords. (RR, Feb. 25, 1958.) JV, May 1, May 5, July 9, Nov. 4, 1959; Apr. 19, Mar. 14, Mar. 17, July 29, 1960. Jerry Lewis apologized for his anti–Kennedy slurs in JV, Apr. 20, 1960.

9 . RR, Sept. 20, Dec. 7, 1960.

10. RR, Nov. 30, 1955.

11. RR, Mar. 25, Apr. 1, 1960. After Joseph P. Kennedy pressured Sinatra into cancelling his hiring of Maltz, MC exulted, "Congratulations, Pal Frankie!" (RR, Apr. 11, 1960.) Sinatra biographer Derek Jewell averred that MC's attacks on Maltz and Sinatra "scarcely indicate the strength of his poison." (Derek Jewell, *Frank Sinatra*, Boston: Little, Brown (1985), 99.) Writer Gore Vidal, who ran for Congress from New York as a Democrat in 1960, said MC "was a natural fascist and regarded me, naturally, as a Communist." (Vidal to author, Dec. 15, 1997.)

12. RR, May 4, July 12, Oct. 27, 1960.

13. MC sparred regularly with British actors, e.g., John Gielgud and Alec Guinness, who criticized Hollywood, saying, "Love those British. You feed 'em, they needle you!" (RR, Dec. 1, 1952.) In response to Peter Sellers's calling Hollywood "swine," MC wrote, "Gosh, and we were so nice to them when King Edward VIII abdicated!" (RR, Dec. 11, 1964.) In the same vein, he wrote, "We ribbed the first-generation Irish Mayor of Chicago, new prexy of the U.S. Conference of Mayors, for hosting England's Queen so elegantly. Dick Daley, His Hibernian Honor, replied, 'Everything's okay — I tipped my Irish constituents that we were saluting a lovely lady, not the Crown!'" (RR, July 15, 1959.)

14. RR, Jan. 15, 1959; July 18, 1960, Aug. 28, 1962. Otto Preminger, the director of *Exodus*, told MC the following week that he chose Lawford for the picture on merit alone and was "happy to pay his price." (RR, July 26, 1960.)

15. RR, July 1, 14, 15; Jan. 4; July 12, 1960.

16. RR, Sept. 25, 1959. MC had also written a year earlier that Joseph P. Kennedy was "summering at Cal-Neva" (RR, June 25, 1958). No biography of the elder Kennedy mentions these summers at Tahoe. Cf. Gus Russo, *The Outfit: The Role of Chicago's Underworld in the Shaping of Modern America*, New York: Bloomsbury (2001), 376–377, which says Joseph P. Kennedy was the shadow owner of the Cal-Neva Lodge in Tahoe from 1955–1960.

17. JV, Feb. 2, Aug. 5, Nov. 10 and 14, 1960.

18. JV, July 13 and 15, 1960. In JV, July 19, 1999, Archerd recounted with pride his day on that platform as part of his eulogy to John F. Kennedy, Jr.

19. RR, July 11, 1960.

20. RR, July 1 and 14, Aug. 15, Aug. 1, 1960.

21. RR, July 15, 1959; July 27, Apr. 15, June 16, 1960. MC's columns are rife with examples of money envy. "Irene Dunne, who has nothing but money" (RR, Jan. 18, 1952); "New prez of the You-Can't-Take-It-With-You Club: Tex Feldman. Has homes in Beverly Hills, Dallas, New York, Paris, and Cannes and chases the sun and the fun twelve months a year" (RR, Oct. 6, 1955). Even after the elder Kennedy's incapacitating stroke, MC joked that his motto was,

"Another Day, Another $42,625" (RR, Apr. 3, 1962) and observed, "If Joe Kennedy put his four hundred million into tax-free four percent municipal bonds, his annual net income would be 16 million or forty-four thousand per day. So Sinatra thinks HE'S a tycoon!" (RR, June 15, 1962.)

22. RR, Apr. 26, Oct. 6, and Aug. 8, 1960.

23. JV, Oct. 7, 10, 12, 13, and 24, 1960; RR, Oct. 10, 1960.

24. "Las Vegas Odds Shift to Kennedy to Win Election," *Los Angeles Times*, Oct. 17, 1960; RR, Oct. 20, 1960.

25. RR, Oct. 24, 1960. Archerd had reported seven-to-five odds for Nixon in Las Vegas two months earlier and said Sinatra had rushed to bet on Kennedy when he heard about it. (JV, Aug. 5, 1960)

26. JV, Dec. 7, 1960.

27. RR, Nov. 11, 1960; Mar. 17, Feb. 28, Mar. 3, Jan. 3, 5, and 9, 1961.

28. RR, Mar. 28 and 30, 1962. Jonathan Schwartz's notes to *Frank Sinatra: The Reprise Collection* (1990) explain that a Van Heusen tune, *Come Waltz With Me*, "resisted Sinatra's best efforts to the point of eventual exclusion" from the *All Alone* album, recorded Jan. 15–17, 1962. MC was not the first to break the news of the Kennedy-Sinatra-Lawford imbroglio; the earliest may have been Dave Sheehan of the *Santa Monica Evening Outlook*, who wrote on Mar. 26 that "strong rumors" were circulating among Palm Springs intelligentsia that Sinatra was "thoroughly miffed" that Kennedy chose to stay at Crosby's.

29. RR, Apr. 18, 1962.

30. JV, May 28, July 31, Aug. 15, 1962; RR, Aug. 29, 1962.

31. Alice McDermott, *Charming Billy*, 26; Hank Grant, "On the Air," *Hollywood Reporter*, Nov. 21, 1966.

32. RR, Nov. 25, 1963.

33. Ibid.

34. RR, Nov. 26 and 27, 1963.

35. MC to Richard Nixon, Nov. 12, 1961, and June 7, 1962; RR, July 10 and Oct. 8, 1964.

Chapter 11

1. JV, June 19, 1951; MC to Hedda Hopper, Oct. 1, 1951, Hedda Hopper Collection,

Margaret Herrick Library; Egan, "Daily Illini's Ex-Crusader," 1956; Zappia to author, Aug. 8, 1998.

2. RR, Apr. 21 and 17, 1958; Wald to MC, Sept. 22, 1960.

3. RR, June 22, 1960; Sept. 21, 1960.

4. RR, Sept. 26 and 29, 1960; Oct. 10, 1960; Nov. 22, 1961; June 12, 1962; June 11, 1962; June 6, 1961; Jan. 19, 1961.

5. RR, May 31, 1961; Wald to MC, May 31, 1961; RR, Feb. 26, 1962; Nov. 22, 1961; Wald to MC, Oct. 17, 1961.

6. Wald obituary, *Variety*, July 18, 1962; RR, July 16, 1962. *Ulysses* was first filmed in 1967 by Joseph Strick, but banned in Ireland for the next thirty years.

7. RR, Nov. 21, 1966; Nov. 5, 1956.

8. George Bon Salle interview, Dec. 16, 1998; "Peer Escort Loses Miss Mansfield, *London Daily Telegraph*, Sept. 26, 1957; Dick Richards, "20th Hires Lord Kilbracken," *Variety*, Oct. 2, 1957.

9. RR, Nov. 22, 1966.

10. RR, Dec. 10, 1964.

11. JV, Aug. 7, 1951; RR, June 21, 1956; July 10, 1956; Aug. 13, 1957; Aug. 26, 1957.

12. RR, Nov. 13, 1958; Jan. 16, 1959; Oct. 7, 1960.

13. RR, Oct. 4, 1954.

14. Bill Diehl, "Christmas, Hannukah Joys Join," *St. Paul Pioneer Press*, Dec. 18, 1992.

15. RR, Aug. 8, 1966; Jack Bradford interview, Sept. 6, 1997.

16. RR, Nov. 12, 1956; Creditor's Claim by Dr. Sidney Leo, MC Probate File, No. P-516214, Los Angeles County Superior Court Archives.

17. RR, Nov. 1, 1966; Oct. 21, 1966.

18. RR, Oct. 17, 1966.

19. RR, Oct. 19, 1966; "Mike Connolly's Exclusive Report from Hollywood," *Screen Stories*, Jan. 1967; Kup's Column, *Chicago Sun-Times*, Nov. 20, 1966; Ines Caudera Keller to author, Feb. 24, 2000.

20. Willie Wilkerson interview, May 11, 2000.

21. Frank Liberman interview; May 10, 2000; "The Lowdown on Hollywood's Connolly"; MC to Richard Nixon, Aug. 12, 1959; RR, Nov. 21, 1966.

22. RR, Mar.7, 1960; Feb. 3, 1956; Dec. 31, 1964.

Bibliography

Books

Berube, Allan. *Coming Out Under Fire: The History of Gay Men and Women in World War Two.* New York: The Free Press, 1990.

Brown, Peter Harry, and Pat H. Broeske. *Howard Hughes: The Untold Story.* New York: E. P. Dutton, 1996.

Brown, Ricardo J. *The Evening Crowd at Kirmser's.* Minneapolis: University of Minnesota Press, 2001.

Cahill, Thomas. *How the Irish Saved Civilization.* New York: Doubleday, 1995.

Ceplair, Larry, and Steven Englund. *The Inquisition in Hollywood: Politics in the Film Community 1930–1960.* Garden City, N.Y.: Anchor Press/Doubleday, 1980.

Cohen, Adam, and Elizabeth Taylor. *American Pharaoh: Mayor Richard J. Daley: His Battle for Chicago and the Nation.* Boston: Little, Brown, 2000.

Cole, Lester. *Hollywood Red.* Palo Alto: Ramparts, 1981.

Conrad, Harold. *Dear Muffo: Thirty-Five Years in the Fast Lane.* New York: Stein and Day, 1982.

Crane, Cheryl, with Cliff Jahr. *Detour: A Hollywood Story.* New York: Arbor House/William Morrow, 1988.

D[aily] I[llini] Covers the Century: Front Pages from the Twentieth Century. Champaign: Illini Media Company, 1999.

Ebert, Roger, ed. *An Illini Century: One Hundred Years of Campus Life.* Urbana: Univ. of Illinois Press, 1967.

Eells, George. *Hedda and Louella.* New York: Putnam, 1972.

Ehrenstein, David. *Open Secret (Gay Hollywood 1928–1998).* New York: William Morrow, 1998.

Farrell, James T. *Studs Lonigan, a Trilogy.* New York: Vanguard, 1935.

Finstad, Suzanne. *Natasha.* New York: Three Rivers, 2001.

Fisher, Eddie. *Been There, Done That.* New York: St. Martin's, 1999.

Fisher, James T. *Dr. America: The Lives of Thomas A. Dooley, 1927–1961.* Amherst: Univ. of Massachusetts Press, 1997.

163

Gabler, Neal. *Winchell: Gossip, Power, and the Culture of Celebrity*. New York: Knopf, 1994.

Gavin, James. *Intimate Nights: The Golden Age of New York Cabaret*. New York: Grove Weidenfeld, 1991.

Gilmore, John. *Laid Bare: A Memoir of Wrecked Lives and the Hollywood Death Trip*. Los Angeles: Amok, 1997.

Goodman, Ezra. *The Fifty-Year Decline and Fall of Hollywood*. New York: Simon and Schuster, 1961.

Graham, Sheilah. *Confessions of a Hollywood Reporter*. New York: Morrow, 1969.

_____. *The Rest of the Story*. New York: Coward-McCann, 1964.

Guild, Leo. *Hollywood Screwballs*. Los Angeles: Holloway House, 1962.

Hanna, David. *Ava: Portrait of a Star*. New York: Putnam, 1960.

_____. *"Come Up and See Me Sometime!" Mae West: A Confidential Biography*. New York: Belmont Tower, 1976.

_____. *Mafia Over Hollywood: The Untold Story of Hollywood and the Mob*. New York: Manor, 1980.

Hanson, Peter. *Dalton Trumbo, Hollywood Rebel*. Jefferson, N.C.: McFarland, 2001.

Harris, Daniel. *The Rise and Fall of Gay Culture*. New York: Hyperion, 1997.

Harris, Radie. *Radie's World*. New York: Putnam, 1975.

Hirsch, Phil, ed. *Hollywood Uncensored: The Stars, Their Secrets and Their Scandals*. New York: Pyramid, 1965.

Holley, Val. *James Dean: The Biography*. New York: St. Martin's, 1995.

Hoopes, Roy. *Cain*. New York: Holt, Rinehart, and Winston, 1982.

Hope, Bob. *I Owe Russia $1200*. Garden City, N.Y.: Doubleday, 1963.

Hopper, Hedda. *From Under My Hat*. Garden City, N.Y.: Doubleday, 1952.

_____, and James Brough. *The Whole Truth and Nothing But*. New York: Pyramid, 1963.

Houghton, Norris. *Entrances and Exits: A Life In and Out of the Theatre*. New York: Limelight, 1991.

Hudson, Rock, and Sara Davidson. *Rock Hudson: His Story*. New York: William Morrow, 1986.

Investigation of Communist Activities in the Los Angeles, Calif., Area, Part 9. Hearing before the Committee on Un-American Activities, Apr. 19, 1956. Washington, D.C.: U.S. Government Printing Office, 1956.

Israel, Lee. *Kilgallen*. New York: Delacorte, 1979.

Jewell, Derek. *Frank Sinatra*. Boston: Little, Brown, 1985.

Johnson, David K. "The Kids of Fairytown," in *Creating a Place for Ourselves*, ed. Brett Beemyn (New York: Routledge, 1997), 97–118.

Jones, James. *Alfred C. Kinsey: A Public/Private Life*. New York: Norton, 1997.

Kaiser, Charles. *The Gay Metropolis 1940–1996*. New York: Houghton Mifflin, 1997.

Kazan, Elia. *Elia Kazan: A Life*. New York: Knopf, 1988.

Kilpatrick, Sidney D. *A Cast of Killers*. New York: Dutton, 1986.

Kitt, Eartha. *I'm Still Here: Confessions of a Sex Kitten*. New York: Barricade, 1989.

Kupcinet, Irv, with Paul Neimark. *Kup: A Man, an Era, a City*. Chicago: Bonus, 1988.

LaGuardia, Robert, and Gene Arceri. *Red: The Tempestuous Life of Susan Hayward*. New York: Macmillan, 1985.

Lait, Jack, and Lee Mortimer. *Chicago Confidential*. New York: Crown, 1950.

Lardner, Ring, Jr. *I'd Hate Myself in the Morning*. New York: Thunder's Mouth/ Nation, 2000.

Laurents, Arthur. *Original Story By: A Memoir of Broadway and Hollywood*. New York: Knopf, 2000.

Leaming, Barbara. *Marilyn Monroe*. New York: Crown, 1998.

Lewis, Jon. *Hollywood v. Hard Core: How the Struggle Over Censorship Saved the Modern Film Industry*. New York: New York University Press, 2000.

Linet, Beverly. *Susan Hayward, Portrait of a Survivor*. New York: Atheneum, 1980.

Litz, A. Walton. *The Art of James Joyce: Method and Design in* Ulysses *and* Finnegans Wake. London: Oxford University Press, 1961.

Loughery, John. *The Other Side of Silence, Men's Lives and Gay Identities: A Twentieth-Century History*. New York: Holt, 1998.

McBrien, William. *Cole Porter: A Biography*. New York: Knopf, 1998.

McDermott, Alice. *Charming Billy*. New York: Farrar, Straus and Giroux, 1998.

McGilligan, Patrick. *George Cukor: A Double Life*. New York: St. Martin's, 1991.

_____, and Paul Buhle, eds. *Tender Comrades: A Backstory of the Hollywood Blacklist*. New York: St. Martin's Press, 1997.

MacLaine, Shirley. *Don't Fall Off the Mountain*. New York: Dutton, 1970.

Manfull, Helen, ed. *Additional Dialogue: Letters of Dalton Trumbo, 1942–1962*. New York: M. Evans, 1970.

Mann, William J. *Behind the Screen: How Gays and Lesbians Shaped Hollywood, 1910–1969*. New York: Viking, 2001.

_____. *Wisecracker: The Life and Times of William Haines, Hollywood's First Openly Gay Star*. New York: Viking, 1998.

Mencken, H. L. *Notes on Democracy*. New York: Knopf, 1926.

Muir, Florabel. *Headline Happy*. New York: Holt, 1950.

Navasky, Victor S. *Naming Names*. New York: Viking, 1980.

O'Brien, John A. *Catching Up with the Church*. New York: Herder and Herder, 1967.

_____. *The Faith of Millions*. Huntington, Ind.: Our Sunday Visitor, 1938.

_____. *Where Dwellest Thou? Intimate Personal Stories of Twelve Converts to the Catholic Faith*. New York: Gilbert, 1956.

_____. *Why Priests Leave*. New York: Hawthorn, 1969.

O'Connor, Edwin. *The Last Hurrah*. Boston: Little, Brown, 1956.

Oppenheimer, Jerry, and Jack Vitek. *Idol: Rock Hudson, the True Story of an American Film Hero*. New York: Villard, 1986.

Parsons, Louella. *The Gay Illiterate*. Garden City, N.Y.: Doubleday, 1944.

_____. *Tell It to Louella*. New York: Putnam, 1961.

Payn, Graham, and Sheridan Morley, eds. *The Noel Coward Diaries*. Boston: Little, Brown, 1982.

Previn, Andre. *No Minor Chords: My Days in Hollywood*. New York: Doubleday, 1991.

Quirk, Lawrence J. *Bob Hope: The Road Well-Traveled*. New York: Applause, 1998.

_____. *Fasten Your Seat Belts: The Passionate Life of Bette Davis*. New York: Morrow, 1990.

Reynolds, Debbie, with David Patrick Columbia. *Debbie: My Life*. New York: Morrow, 1988.

Rogers, Henry C. *Walking the Tightrope: The Private Confessions of a Public Relations Man*. New York: Morrow, 1980.

Roth, Lillian. *Beyond My Worth*. New York: Fell, 1958.

_____, with Mike Connolly and Gerold Frank. *I'll Cry Tomorrow*. New York: Fell, 1954.

Russell, Ina. *Jeb and Dash: A Diary of Gay Life, 1918–1945*. Boston: Faber and Faber, 1994.

Russo, Gus. *The Outfit: The Role of Chicago's Underworld in the Shaping of Modern America*. New York: Bloomsbury, 2001.

Russo, Vito. *The Celluloid Closet*. New York: Harper and Row, 1981.

St. Johns, Adela Rogers. *The Honeycomb*. Garden City, N.Y.: Doubleday, 1969.

Schary, Dore. *Heyday: An Autobiography*. Boston: Little, Brown, 1979.

Schwartz, Nancy Lynn, completed by Sheila Schwartz. *The Hollywood Writers' Wars*. New York: Knopf, 1982.

Skolsky, Sidney. *Don't Get Me Wrong, I Love Hollywood*. New York: Putnam, 1975.

Smith, Liz. *Natural Blonde: A Memoir*. New York: Hyperion, 2000.

Spada, James. *Peter Lawford: The Man Who Kept the Secrets*. New York: Bantam, 1991.

Spoto, Donald. *Marilyn Monroe: The Biography*. New York: HarperCollins, 1993.

Stoddart, Dayton. *Lord Broadway: Variety's Sime*. New York: Funk, 1941.

Stricklyn, Ray. *Angels and Demons: One Actor's Hollywood Journey, an Autobiography*. Los Angeles: Belle, 1999.

Turner, Lana. *Lana: The Lady, the Legend, the Truth*. New York: Dutton, 1982.

Tysl, Robert Wayne. *Continuity and Evolution in a Public Symbol: An Investigation into the Creation and Communication of the James Dean Image in Mid-Century America*. Ann Arbor: University Microfilms, 1965.

United States Army Service Forces. *Logistics in World War II*. Washington, D.C.: Center of Military History, 1993.

Vidal, Gore. *Palimpsest: A Memoir*. New York: Penguin, 1995.

Walker, Danton. *Danton's Inferno: The Story of a Columnist and How He Grew*. New York: Hastings House, 1955.

Walls, Jeannette. *Dish: The Inside Story on the World of Gossip*. New York: Spike, 2000.

Weber, Francis J. *His Eminence of Los Angeles: James Francis Cardinal McIntyre*. Mission Hills, Calif.: St. Francis Historical Society, 1997.

Wilkerson, Tichi, and Marcia Borie. *The Hollywood Reporter: The Golden Years*. New York: Coward-McCann, Inc., 1984.

Wilkerson, W. R. III. *The Man Who Invented Las Vegas*. Los Angeles: Ciro's Books, 2000.

Wilson, Christopher. *Dancing with the Devil: The Windsors and Jimmy Donahue*. New York: St. Martin's, 2000.

Wilson, Theo. *Headline Justice: Inside the Courtroom: The Country's Most Controversial Trials*. New York: Thunder's Mouth Press, 1997.

Wright, Cobina. *I Never Grew Up*. New York: Prentice Hall, 1952.

Articles

"Actor Must Testify at Magazine Trial," *N.Y. Times*, Aug. 1, 1957.

"Agreement Set on Confidential; Under Plan Awaiting Court Approval Magazine Will Alter Editorial Policy," *N.Y. Times*, Nov. 8, 1957.

Alford, Henry. "'Oh My God, It's Taylor Dayne!'" *New York Times Magazine*, Oct. 19, 1997.

Andersen, Kurt. "Only Gossip," *N.Y. Times Magazine*, Mar. 3, 2002.

Anderson, A. Donald. "Hollywood's Version of Trade Wars," *N.Y. Times*, Aug. 7, 1988.

Bachardy, Don. "Life with (and without) Isherwood," *Harvard Gay and Lesbian Review*, Mar. 31, 1999.

Bacon, James. "Escort Defends Lana's Honor by Taking Poke at Columnist," *L.A. Mirror News*, June 29, 1960.

Barack, Lauren. "Accused Felt Press Pressure," *Daily Variety*, Sept. 11, 1996.

Belser, Lee. "Columnist Connolly Ousted from Party," *Los Angeles Mirror-News*, June 27, 1960.

Bernstein, Sharon. "Bugsy I: So Vegas Wasn't His Idea and He Was a Bigot to Boot," *Los Angeles Times*, Mar. 29, 1992.

Blumenthal, Ralph. "John Berry, 82, Stage and Film Director Who Exiled Himself During Blacklisting of 1950's," *N.Y. Times*, Dec. 1, 1999.

"Board of Supervisors in Tribute to Connolly," *Hollywood Reporter*, Dec. 5, 1966.

"Bob Hope, Entertainers Back from Alaska Trip," *Los Angeles Times*, Dec. 25, 1956.

Borman, Ed. "Vice Investigation Nears Half-Way Mark as Jury Indicts Mrs. Strothers; Ex-Sheriff Roth, Wife Questioned in Busy Session; John Mabley, Former Illini Editor, Tells of Campaign," *Daily Illini*, Mar. 4, 1939.

Brady, Thomas F. "Hollywood's Shifting Sands: Rumblings Against Projected Film on the Life of Rommel — the Gossips Are Put on the Carpet and Other Matters," *N.Y. Times*, Feb. 25, 1951.

Buchwald, Art. "Gerold Frank, Renowned Ghost," *Los Angeles Times*, Aug. 16, 1960.

"Bull Fights Start in Mexico City," *Chicago Tribune*, Oct. 5, 1941.

Caen, Herb. "Let's Have a Party," *San Francisco Chronicle*, Aug. 16, 1992.

_____. "The Memories Linger On," *San Francisco Examiner*, Aug. 26, 1956.

_____. "Pocketful of Notes," *San Francisco Examiner*, Aug. 22, 1956.

_____. "Repubbernecking Around," *San Francisco Examiner*, Aug. 23, 1956.

Calhoun, Rory, as told to Maurice Zolotow. "My Dark Past: The Famous Movie Star's Own Story of His Prison Ordeal and How He Overcame His Past," Parts One and Two, *American Weekly*, Aug. 21 and 28, 1955.

"A Caller Every Two Minutes at Truman's Political Court," *Chicago Sun-Times*, Aug. 14, 1956.

Carlson, Peter. "The 100–Proof Fifth: Enron Execs' Watered-Down Pleas Are No Match for the Punch of McCarthy Era," *Washington Post*, Feb. 13, 2002.

Carroll, Sidney. "A Tale of Hoffman," *Esquire*, Nov. 1946.

"Chi Exhibs-Distribs Seething, Open Flareups Due After Jan. 1," *Variety*, Nov. 15, 1944.

"Chi Niteries Beef to Local WMC; That U.S. Body Wonders If Curfew Can Stick," *Variety*, Mar. 14, 1945.

"Chi Reversal Important in Govt.'s Suit; WB's Setback by Goldman in Philly," *Variety*, Aug. 8, 1945.

"Chi Times Slaps Back at Walker," *Variety*, Apr. 17, 1946.

"Chi Travel Bureaus See N.Y. Niteries Back to Normal, Bids for Tour Biz," *Variety*, Apr. 17, 1946.

"Clean — and Otherwise," *Newsweek*, Aug. 26, 1957.

Collins, Amy Fine. "Idol Gossips," *Vanity Fair*, Apr. 1997.

"Columnist in Wrangle Over Lana," *Los Angeles Mirror-News*, June 29, 1960.

"Columnist Is Belted by Shirley MacLaine," *N.Y. Daily News*, June 11, 1963.

"Commie Hearings Fizzle Out: Strange Developments Mark Final Day; Sidney Buchman, Geo. Beck Among Witnesses," *Hollywood Reporter*, Sept. 26, 1951.

Connolly, Mike. "Boston Can't Afford Lillian Roth Any More," *Chicago Sun-Times*, Sept. 6, 1956.

_____. "Chicago American 'Front Pages' Local Gambling Cleanup, Prasies Students," *Daily Illini*, June 4, 1937.

_____. "Chi's Drama School Racket: Put Annual Gyp at $5,000,000," *Variety*, Apr. 25, 1945.

_____. "Elizabeth Montgomery: 'The Risks I Take with My Marriage!'" *Screen Stories*, Feb. 1967.

_____. "Faculty Praise Pays Tribute to Memory of Professor Zeitlin," *Daily Illini*, Dec. 9, 1937.

_____. "How Susan Got Her Man (and How He Got Her to Leave Hollywood)," *Modern Screen*, July 1957.

_____. "Johnny on the Spot!" *Modern Screen*, Dec. 1958.

_____. "The Lennon Sisters' Plea: 'Stop Telling Those Lies About Us!'" *Screen Stories*, Jan. 1967.

_____. "The Mistletoe Comes Down: It's at the Request of University Officials," *Daily Illini*, Dec. 18, 1937.

_____. "Music Shows Seen Coming to Fore Now That Gabbing Decline Looms," *Variety*, Aug. 29, 1945.

_____. "Negro Choristers Sing Spirituals; 5 Twin City Choirs Participate in Program," *Daily Illini*, Apr. 22, 1938.

_____. "'One-Arm Bandits' Seek 'Pardon' on Basis of War Contributions," *Variety*, Dec. 26, 1945.

_____. "Raquel Welch: 'What a Star Is Made of!'" *Screen Stories*, Dec. 1966.

_____. "She Ran the Other Way Until He Caught Her," *Modern Screen*, Aug. 1956.

_____. "Spot Talent Rides Gravy Train with Jingle Biz Radio's Widest Open Field," *Variety*, Aug. 8, 1945.

_____. "State Health Department Ratifies Champaign Plan of Social Disease Control; County Med Society Will Aid in Work of Health District," *Daily Illini*, Dec. 2, 1937.

_____. "State-Wide Illinois Fears New Rap Upping Amus. Tax as High as 40 Percent," *Variety*, May 22, 1946.

_____. "This Was My Friend, Jimmy Dean." *Modern Screen*, Dec. 1955.

Crivello, Kirk. "Mary McCarty, A Story of Shattered Dreams," *Hollywood Studio Magazine*, Aug. 1980.

"The Curious Craze for 'Confidential' Magazines ... Editor Says: 'Contrive,' Suggest," *Newsweek*, July 11, 1955.

Cusolito, Karen. "Reporter Enters New Era with Move to Wilshire Blvd.," *Hollywood Reporter*, Sept. 15, 1992.

Daku, "Bob Hope Chevy Show," *Variety*, Dec. 31, 1956.

Daley, David. "Hello! The Dish on Gossip," *Hartford Courant*, Mar. 7, 2000.

Dallek, Robert. "The Medical Ordeals of JFK," *The Atlantic*, Dec. 2002.

Davidson, Muriel. "Shirley MacLaine Sounds Off," *Sat. Evening Post*, Nov. 30, 1963.

Day, Brenda. "Murder, All Three of Them Wrote," *Los Angeles Times*, June 1, 1986.

"Despite M.D.'s Nix, Sexer Does Big B.O.," *Variety*, June 27, 1945.

Diehl, Bill. "Christmas, Hanukkah Joys Join," *St. Paul Pioneer Press*, Dec. 18, 1992.

Egan, Jack. "Daily Illini's Ex-Crusader Now Hollywood Gossip Ace," *Champaign-Urbana Courier*, circa 1956.

"Esther Deutch and Dave Hoff Are Married in Shreveport, La.," *Daily Illini*, June 13, 1937.

"Father O'Brien Finds Address Was Misconstrued," *N.Y. Times*, Feb. 9, 1941.

"Film 'Trust' Found by Chicago Jury," *N.Y. Times*, Mar. 11, 1944.

"Five Fraternities Join Crusade on Disease," *Daily Illini*, Oct. 27, 1937.

"Florabel Bounced by L.A. Mirror," *Variety*, Oct. 14, 1953.

Fox, David J. "Q&A with Army Archerd, 40 Years as Hollywood's Must-Read," *Los Angeles Times*, Jan. 28, 1993.

Gardetta, Dave. "The Strip: Something's Happening, What It Is Ain't Exactly Clear," *Los Angeles Times Magazine*, Dec. 15, 1996.

Goldstein, Patrick. "A Fateful Decision, Damaging Fallout," *Los Angeles Times*, Mar. 16, 1999.

Goodman, Ezra. "Low Budget Movies with POW!" *N.Y. Times Magazine*, Feb. 28, 1965.

Gottlieb, Robert. "Blue Period: Two Books Look at Hollywood Cinema Before the Code Came Along and Took Out the Naughty Bits," *New York Times Book Review*, Nov. 28, 1999.

Govoni, Steve. "Now It Can Be Told," *American Film*, Feb. 1990.

Graham, Neal. "Mike Connolly on the Receiving End at Masquer's 'Irishman's' Testimonial," *Hollywood Reporter*, Mar. 20, 1961.

Grant, Hank. "The Bob Hope Show," *Hollywood Reporter*, Jan. 20, 1958.

_____. "On the Air [Requiem for a Reporter]," *Hollywood Reporter*, Nov. 21, 1966.

Grimes, William. "Jean Muir, Actress Penalized by 50's Blacklist, Dies at 85," *N.Y. Times*, July 25, 1996.

Gross, Nate. "Illini Students Crush Gambling," *Chicago American*, June 3, 1937.

Harris, Kathryn. "Writers at Variety Ask: Will Sale End Freewheeling Era?" *Los Angeles Times*, July 15, 1987.

Hayner, Don, and Tom McNamee. "Start the Presses: Sun-Times Reported and Made History," *Chicago Sun-Times*, Aug. 9, 1998.

Hawkins, William. "'Miss Liberty' Star Came Up Hard Way," *N.Y. World-Telegram*, Aug. 8, 1949.

Henry, William A. III "Trades Blow No Ill Winds: Hollywood's Variety and Reporter Serve a Company Town," *Time*, Sept. 27, 1982.

Hertzberg, Hendrik. "Changing Times," *New Yorker*, Apr. 23, 2001.

Hill, Gladwin. "Accord Approved for Confidential; Magazine Agrees It Will Run No More Exposes and State Drops Major Charges," *N.Y. Times*, Nov. 13, 1957.

_____. "Coast Trial Airs Scandal Stories," *N.Y. Times*, Aug. 10, 1957.

_____. "Counsel Appears for Confidential; Attorney Says Magazine's Material Was Deemed Safe in Legal Scrutiny," *N.Y. Times*, Aug. 20, 1957.

_____. "Film Colony Fidgets in Confidential Case; But Industry, Seeing It as Serious Threat, Has Taken No Action," *N.Y. Times*, Aug. 18, 1957.

_____. "Jury Told Family Ran Confidential; Prosecutor Displays Chart on the Relationships of Magazine Principals," *N.Y. Times*, Sept. 11, 1957.

_____. "Magazine Denies California Link; Confidential Attacks State's Charge It Has Hollywood Branch to Spy on Stars," *N.Y. Times*, Aug. 22, 1957.

_____. "Magazine Linked to Coast Agency; Defense Admits Hollywood Office Got $150,000 from Confidential for Data," *N.Y. Times*, Aug. 24, 1957.

_____. "Magazine Policy Cited by Witness; Admitted Ex-Prostitute Says Publisher of Confidential Wanted Lewd Stories," *N.Y. Times*, Aug. 14, 1957.

_____. "Magazine Raises Obscenity Issue; Confidential Cites Writings by O'Hara and Steinbeck — Quotes Newspapers," *N.Y. Times*, Aug. 21, 1957.

_____. "Magazine Rests Defense in Trial; Confidential Discards Plans to Call Stars— Manager of Theatre Testifies," *N.Y. Times*, Aug. 31, 1957.

_____. "Magazine Stories Are Read to Jury; Purported Escapades of Film asnd Theatre Personalities Quoted from Confidential," *N.Y. Times*, Aug. 15, 1957.

_____. "Magazine Trial Put Off on Coast; California's Libel Action Against Publications Runs into Series of Snags," *N.Y. Times*, July 30, 1957.

_____. "Police Here Cited at Scandal Trial; Ex-Editor Says Confidential Also Obtained Data from a New York Law Aide," *N.Y. Times*, Aug. 13, 1957.

_____. "Scandal Magazine's Trial Threatens More Scandal; Defense in Libel Suit Theatens to Call Scores of Hollywood Witnesses," *N.Y. Times*, Aug. 4, 1957.

"Hollywood's Press: Why the Stars Are in Your Eyes," *Newsweek*, Feb. 22, 1954.

Hopper, Hedda. "Bob Hope Entourage Returns from Alaska," *Los Angeles Times*, Dec. 28, 1956.

_____. "Shift to TV Explained by Calhoun," *Los Angeles Times*, Jan. 27, 1957.

"House Detective," *Time*, Nov. 10, 1947.

Hutshing, Ed. "A Hollywood Murder Unreels," *San Diego Union-Tribune*, June 15, 1986.

"Indictments Name Eleven in Confidential Quiz," *Los Angeles Times*, May 16, 1957.

"Jackson Park (Chicago) 360G Award, Confirmed by U.S. Supreme Court, Seen Having Wide Trust Significance," *Variety*, Feb. 27, 1946.

"Jackson Park's 2d Suit for $600,000 Asks Chi Release System Be Voided," *Variety*, Apr. 10, 1946.

Jacobson, Mark. "What Makes Budd Run?" *New York*, Aug. 19, 2002.

Johnson, David K. "Homosexual Citizens," 6 *Washington History* 44–63 (1994–1995).

"Jose." "Bob Hope Show," *Variety*, Jan. 22, 1958.

"Judge and a Witness," *Newsweek*, Aug. 19, 1957.

Kehr, Dave. "New Translation for 'Rififi,'" *N.Y. Times*, July 28, 2000.

Kuczynski, Alex. "Hollywood Vitriol Meets Tech Suave: Variety Braces as Competitors Enter Hallowed Precincts," *N.Y. Times*, Dec. 4, 2000.

Kupcinet, Irv. "And Then I Wrote ... and Wrote ... and Wrote," *Chicago Sun-Times*, Jan. 18, 1998.

_____. "Be It Ever So Humble," *Chicago Sun-Times*, Sept. 1, 1957.

_____. "Kup Encounters an Occupational Hazard," *Chicago Sun-Times*, Aug. 28, 1958.

"'Kup's Column' Ballyhoo," *Variety*, Apr. 10, 1946.

Kurtz, Howard. "The Dirt on Matt Drudge," *Washington Post*, May 19, 1997.

"'Lady of Business' Is Indignant; Can't Imagine Why City Police, University Don't Protect Her," *Daily Illini*, May 1, 1936.

Lahr, John. "Bottom Feeders," *New Yorker*, Mar. 25, 2002.

_____. "The C.E.O. of Comedy," *New Yorker*, Dec. 21, 1998.

"Lana Sobs as Escort Flings Fist at Writer," *Los Angeles Mirror-News*, June 30, 1960.

Landman-Keil, Beth. "The Scoop on Neal Travis," *New York*, Aug. 12, 2002.

"Laxity of Studios Charged in Trial; Magazine Says Hollywood Would Not Be Target If It Cleaned House," *N.Y. Times*, Aug. 27, 1957.

Levey, Bob. "Saying Goodbye to the Two Who Blazed the Columnizing Trail," *Washington Post*, Feb. 7, 1997.

"Lillian Roth [obituary]," *Variety*, May 14, 1980.

"Lillian Roth Paged for 'Average' Musical," *Daily Variety*, June 8, 1948.

"Lillian Roth Ropes Tahoe Biltmore Date," *Daily Variety*, Aug. 25, 1948.

Love, Dennis. "Veteran Scribes Follow the Stars," *Daily News of Los Angeles*, Mar. 24, 1997.

"The Lowdown on Hollywood's Connolly," *People Today*, Mar. 11, 1953.

Lowe, Herman A. "Dmytryk Says Reds Aimed to Get Control of Pic Biz; Fingers Over 25 Comrades," *Daily Variety*, Apr. 26, 1951.

_____. "Parks Admits Commie Past: Red in '41–'45, But Chary of Naming His Comrades; Da Silva Defies Committee," *Daily Variety*, Mar. 22, 1951.

_____. "Red Probers May Arrest 'Reluctant 9'; Revere, Moore, Buchman Duck $64 Question," *Daily Variety*, Apr. 18, 1951.

Lowe, Walter. "TV Trade Publishers in the Good Ol' Days," *Video Age International*, Apr. 1992.

Mabley, John. "One Reaction to Subpoena Dispute," *Chicago Today*, Mar. 14, 1973.

_____. "Subpoenas a Way of Life for Reporter," *Chicago Today*, Apr. 6, 1970.

_____. "Truman Rival's Quote Carries Familiar Ring," *Chicago Today*, Mar. 14, 1974.

Marks, Peter. "A Portrait of the Artist as a Young Man in Jail," *N.Y. Times*, Feb. 24, 2002.

Matthews, J. B. "Did the Movies Really Clean House?" *American Legion Magazine*, Dec. 1951.

"Maureen O'Hara, Liberace Hit 'Lies,'" *Los Angeles Times*, May 15, 1957.

Mendelsohn, Daniel. "Emerald Bile," *New York*, Mar. 12, 2001.

Mendez, Carlos. "'I Began Reading the Diaries on the Day He Died': A Conversation with Don Bachardy," *Harvard Gay and Lesbian Review*, Apr. 30, 1997.

Millstein, Gilbert. "A Redeemed Captive," *N.Y. Times Book Review*, July 11, 1954.

"Mike." "Balaban and Katz Television," *Variety*, Mar. 21, 1945.

_____. "Bob Hope's Hollywood Show," *Variety*, July 3, 1946.

_____. "Gypsy Rose Lee, Comedienne," *Variety*, Mar. 14, 1945.

_____. "Mayor Kelly's Report," *Variety*, Jan. 30, 1946.

"Mike Connolly [obituary]," *Variety*, Nov. 23, 1966.

"Mike Connolly, 52 [*sic*], Screen Columnist," *N.Y. Times*, Nov. 19, 1966.

"Mike Connolly Dies; Film Columnist," *Chicago Tribune*, Nov. 19, 1966.

"Mike Connolly Dies Following Heart Surgery," *Daily Variety*, Nov. 21, 1966.

"Mike Connolly Dies; Showed Newsman's Talent as DI Editor," *Champaign-Urbana Courier*, Nov. 19, 1966.

"Mr. Kazan's Good Example," *N.Y. World Telegram*, Apr. 15, 1952; reprinted in the *Hollywood Reporter*, Apr. 18, 1952.

"Mistrial Verdict for Confidential; Foreman Tells Judge Jury is Hopelessly Split 7 to 5 in Libel Conspiracy Case," *N.Y. Times*, Oct. 2, 1957.

Mitchell, Sean. "The Oscar Plunge: The Glory Days; Reporting About the Movies Used to Be Lightweight and Fun, But Big Money and Big Business Put a Different Spin on Hollywood News," *Los Angeles Times*, Mar. 24, 1991.

"Movie Columnist Mike Connolly, 53, Dies After Surgery," *Chicago Sun-Times*, Nov. 19, 1966.

Muir, Florabel. "Spat Takes Franchot to Court," *N.Y. Daily News*, Oct. 31, 1951.

_____, and Theo Wilson. "Clark Gable Linked to Mag's Party Girl by Scandal Witness," *N.Y. Daily News*, Aug. 13, 1957.

_____, and _____. "Court Hears the Story of Maureen O'Hara as the Girl in Row Thirty-Five," *N.Y. Daily News*, Aug. 17, 1957.

_____, and _____. "Stars Shine in Bedtime Stories at Trial of Mags," *N.Y. Daily News*, Aug. 15, 1957.

O'Brien, John A. "America and War," *Daily Illini*, July 10, 1937.

_____. "The Noblest Work," *Daily Illini*, Jan. 16, 1938.

_____. "On Being Profane," *Daily Illini*, Jan. 23, 1938.

"O'Brien Praises Mass Meeting," *Daily Illini*, Feb. 26, 1939.

O'Flaherty, Terrence. "Baked Alaska," *San Francisco Chronicle*, Dec. 27, 1956.

_____. "The Eskimo Pie," *San Francisco Chronicle*, Dec. 28, 1956.

_____. "Giving Up Hope," *San Francisco Chronicle*, Jan. 1, 1957.

_____. "Jayne Mansfield, Hit or Myth?" *San Francisco Chronicle*, Dec. 31, 1957.

_____. "Where There's Life There's Hope," *San Francisco Chronicle*, Dec. 28, 1956.

_____. "With Jayne, There's Hope," *San Francisco Chronicle*, Dec. 30, 1957.

O'Hehir, Andrew. "Waiting for O'Lefty," *N.Y. Times Book Review*, Feb. 24, 2002.

O'Neil, Paul, "Great Tell-It-All Ghost," *Life*, June 29, 1959.

"Ordinance Recommended to Fight Social Disease, Prostitution in Twin Cities; Hygiene Committee Endorses Proposal After Months of Study; 'No Houses in Urbana,'" *Daily Illini*, Apr. 30, 1936.

"Pansy Parlors: Tough Chicago Has Epidemic of Male Butterflies," *Variety*, Dec. 10, 1930.

Pareles, John. "Millard Lampell, 78, Writer and Supporter of Causes, Dies," *N.Y. Times*, Oct. 11, 1997.

"Peer Escort Loses Miss Mansfield," *London Daily Telegraph*, Sept. 26, 1957.

Petersen, James R. "Playboy's History of the Sexual Revolution: Something Cool, Part VI: 1950–59," *Playboy*, Feb. 1998.

Pryor, Thomas M. "No. 2 Open End News-Front Winds Up a Wide-Open Rhubarb," *Variety*, Sept. 7, 1960.

_____. "Soviet Seeks Tie with Hollywood: Russian Cultural Official, on Visit to Coast, Announces Plans for Joint Movie," *N.Y. Times*, Aug. 22, 1956.

_____. "Todd Summarizes Moscow Mission; Producer to Confirm Deal on First Soviet–U.S. Movie Co-Production Venture," *N.Y. Times*, May 12, 1956.

"Putting the Papers to Bed," *Time*, Aug. 26, 1957.

Quirk, Lawrence J. "Fan Mags: The Pros and Cons," *Variety*, Jan. 9, 1963.

Rasmussen, Cecilia. "L.A. Then and Now: D.A. Fitts Was Good Match for Scandalous '30s," *Los Angeles Times*, Sept. 19, 1999.

_____. "The Man Behind the Sunset Strip," *Los Angeles Times*, Dec. 7, 1997.

Raymond, Jack. "Russians and Todd Are Planning to Produce Five Films in Soviet," *N.Y. Times*, May 6, 1956.

Rau, Neil and Margaret. "Bogie vs. the Fourth Estate," *Pageant*, Feb. 1956.

Reed, Cecelia. "They're Sleazy, Sensational and of Historical Interest," *Advertising Age*, Oct. 5, 1987.

"Reshuffling Chi Clearance After Jackson Park Edict," *Variety*, Mar. 20, 1946.

Richards, Dick. "20th Hires Lord Kilbracken," *Variety*, Oct. 2, 1957.

Rosenfield, Paul. "Where Did All the Gossip Go?" *Los Angeles Times*, Dec. 14, 1986.

Rushmore, Howard. "Movie Star Rory Calhoun: But for the Grace of God Still a Convict!" *Confidential*, May 1955.

Rutledge, J. Howard. "Gossipy Private Peeks at Celebrities' Lives Start Magazine Bonanza: Confidential's Racy Exposes Crack Newsstand Records; Lowdown Whispers Secret; Rise of a Pin-Up Publisher," *Wall St. Journal*, July 5, 1955.

Scharper, Al. "Hope Grins and Bears It," *Variety*, Dec. 26, 1956.

"Services Tomorrow for Mike Connolly, 'Rambling Reporter,'" *Hollywood Reporter*, Nov. 21, 1966.

"Seventeen Major Chi Clubs Operating Sans Licenses Due to Code Infractions," *Variety*, Apr. 3, 1946.

Severo, Richard. "Igor Cassini, Hearst Columnist, Dies at 86," *N.Y. Times*, Jan. 9, 2002.

_____. "Ring Lardner Jr., Wry Screenwriter and Last of the Hollywood Ten, Dies at 85," *N.Y. Times*, Nov. 2, 2000.

"Sewer Trouble," *Time*, Aug. 1, 1955.

"Shirley Slugs Male Scribe," *Newark [N.J.] Evening News*, June 11, 1963.

"Shoe-Leather Newsmen," *Newsweek*, Jan. 23, 1961.

"Shoe-Leather School," *Newsweek*, Jan. 4, 1965.

Simonson, Robert. "Foundry Theatre's Legacy Series Passes on the History of Theatre," *Back Stage*, Dec. 6, 1996.

Slade, Brian L., and Mark Miller. "Rock Hudson's Hollywood," *Harvard Gay and Lesbian Review*, Apr. 30, 1996.

Slide, Anthony. "Hedda Hopper: The Queen of the Gossip Columnists Had a Strange Love-Hate Relationship with the Gay Men and Women of Hollywood," *Stallion*, June 1986.

"Small-Screen Hollywood," *Newsweek*, Dec. 16, 1957.

Solberg, Winton. "The Catholic Presence at the University of Illinois," 76 *Catholic Historical Review* No. 4, Oct. 1990.

Spindler, Amy M. "The Hills Were Alive with the Sound of George Cukor's Parties: A Tribute to Hollywood's Most Sociable Director," *N.Y. Times Magazine*, Nov. 19, 2000.

Steinberg, Neil. "A Century of Gay Life on Exhibit at U. of C.," *Chicago Sun-Times*, Sept. 17, 2000.

Strong, Lester. "L.A. and 'Lily Law': A Talk with David Hanna," 2 *Journal of Gay, Lesbian, and Bisexual Identity* 173–186, 1999.

_____, and David Hanna. "Hollywood Watering Holes, 30s Style," *Harvard Gay and Lesbian Review*, Summer 1996.

"Surprising Spin for Shirley," *Life*, June 21, 1963.

"Third from the Right," *Time*, Mar. 10, 1952.

"Todd Linked to Article; Attorney Says Producer Gave Facts to Confidential," *N.Y. Times*, Aug. 29, 1957.

"Todd to Film in Soviet: Culture Aide Flying Here to Complete Negotiations," *N.Y. Times*, Aug. 9, 1956.

"Two Magazines Guilty in Obscenity Case," *N.Y. Times*, Dec. 19, 1957.

"U. of Illinois Joins Student Paper's Anti-Syphilis Fight," *Chicago Tribune*, Oct. 23, 1937.

Varadarajan, Tunku. "Outside In: Gay Themes, Mainstream Press," *Wall St. Journal*, Mar. 15, 2002.

"Wanna Curl Up in a Theatre Lobby with a Good Book?—Chi Started It," *Variety*, Apr. 18, 1945.

"Warmth, Loyalty Marked Wald, Mourners Told," *Variety*, July 18, 1962.

Wechsberg, Joseph. "The Loves of Hoffman," *Esquire*, Aug. 1953.

Weinraub, Bernard. "Blacklisted Screenwriters Get Credits," *N.Y. Times*, Aug. 5, 2000.

_____. "For the Blacklisted, Credit Where Credit Is Due," *N.Y. Times*, Oct. 1, 1997.

_____. "High Noon, High Dudgeon," *N.Y. Times*, Apr. 18, 2002.

_____. "Papers Battle to Control Hollywood's Buzz," *N.Y. Times*, May 3, 1999.

_____. "Three Journalists Resign in Clash of Old and New in Hollywood," *N.Y. Times*, May 14, 2001.

"Why They Love Kup," *People Today*, Mar. 25, 1953.

"Why You Guys Should Be Satisfied with Whatever Hat the Wife Wears," *Variety*, Feb. 13, 1946.

Wilgoren, Jodi. "For Chicago's 'Town Crier,' the Stories Linger," *N.Y. Times*, Aug. 14, 2002.

Wilkerson, William R. "Give It the Right Name," *Hollywood Reporter*, Aug. 26, 1946.

_____. "More Red Commissars!" *Hollywood Reporter*, Aug. 22, 1946.

_____. "Red Beach Head!" *Hollywood Reporter*, Aug. 20, 1946.

_____. "The Six Hundred Dollar Question?", *Hollywood Reporter*, Aug. 27, 1946.

_____. "A Vote for Joe Stalin," *Hollywood Reporter*, July 29, 1946.

_____. "The Writers' 'Authority,'" *Hollywood Reporter*, Aug. 23, 1946.

Wilkerson, William R., III. "Writing the End to a True-to-Life Cinderella Story," *Los Angeles Times*, July 1, 1995.

"William Parker, 1902–1966, Police Chief, Los Angeles (1950–1965)," *California Journal*, Nov. 1, 1999.

Williams, Gordon. "The Queen Bee and the Stork Club: Hedda Hopper's Hollywood," *North Coast X-Press [Sonoma Co., Calif.]*, July 1993.

Wilson, Earl. "The Best Laughs for the First Half of '52," *N.Y. Post*, July 6, 1952.

"Witnesses Rebut Blackmail Story; Defense in Confidential Trial Attempts to Break Down Producer's Charge," *N.Y. Times*, Aug. 28, 1957.

Wolfe, Thomas K. "Public Lives: Confidential Magazine; Reflections in Tranquility by the Former Owner, Robert Harrison, Who Managed to Get Away with It," *Esquire*, Apr. 1964.

Wolff, Michael. "Strange Bedfellows," *New York*, June 18, 2001.

"You Can't Call Verce's Fans Morons; Sinatra Swings Back at Stevens," *Variety*, May 22, 1946.

Index

Kaye, Danny 150*n7*
Kazan, Elia 6, 104–105
Keith Circuit 52
Keller, Father James 42
Kelly, Orry *see* Orry-Kelly
Kelly, Patsy 79–84
Kennedy, George H. 91, 93, 95, 105–106, 118
Kennedy, John F. 50, 59, 76, 129–137, 142, 143
Kennedy, Joseph P. 130, 132–133, 161*n11*, 161*n16*, 161*n21*
Kennedy, Rose 133
KFAC 107
KFWB 107
Khan, Aly 8
Khrushchev, Nikita 58, 109, 113, 122, 132
Khrushchev, Nina 113
Kilbracken, Lord 141
King, Charley 56
King, Hal 120
King, Peggy 119
King Brothers Productions 106
Kinsey, Dr. Alfred 1, 81–82, 156*n25*
Kipling, Rudyard 53–54
KLAC 107
KMPC 107
Knickerbocker Hotel (Los Angeles) 44
Knight, Gov. Goodwin 133
Korda, Alex 45
Kupcinet, Irv 17, 24, 46–47, 80, 106, 124, 145, 153*n27*

Lady Godiva 55
L'Aiglon 90
Lake Minnetonka 98
Lake Tahoe 132
LaMarr, Don 17, 26, 83, 86
Lanza, Mario 99, 109
Lardner, Ring, Jr. 114
LaRue 89–90
Las Vegas 4, 31, 44, 48, 90, 93, 132, 134
Lasky, Victor 137
The Last Hurrah 57
Laurents, Arthur 11, 103, 150*n6*
Lawford, Peter 129–133, 135–137
Lawrence, Carol 136
Lawrence, D. H. 5
Lawrence, Marc 107, 159*n15*
Lawson, John Howard 122

Lee, Doris 96
Lee, Gypsy Rose 67, 85
Leisen, Mitch 11, 150*n6*
Leitzel, Lillian 52
Lennon Sisters 79
Leo, Dr. Sidney 143–145
LeRoy, Mervyn 23, 133
Les Brown's Band of Renown 142
Leslie, Amy 53
Levant, Oscar 17
Levy, Ralph 15
Lewis, Jerry 40, 130, 134, 141, 161*n8*
Lewis, Lloyd 53
Liberace 151*n14*
Liberman, Frank 97, 119–120, 146, 151*n6*
Liberman, Pat Harris 97
Libott, Robert Yale 123
Life magazine 41
Lillie, Beatrice 19, 56
The Little Show 56
Lizzo, Sam 55
Loesser, Frank 107, 159*n15*
Logan, Ella 17
Logan, Joshua 23, 142
Lollobrigida, Gina 100
London, Julie 49
Lopez, Trini 8, 79
Loren, Sophia 3
Loretta Young Show 19
Los Angeles County District Attorney 27
Los Angeles Police Dept. 25, 37
Los Angeles Times 46, 134
Love Me or Leave Me 117
Lowdown magazine 27
Lustgarten, Edgar xiv–xv, 109, 112
Lyles, A. C. 45, 96
Lyles, Lee 77, 156*n10*
Lyon, Herb 80

Mabley, Jack 64–72, 75
MacArthur, Charles 53, 85
MacLaine, Shirley 125–127, 160*n35*
Macmillan Publishers 137
Madison, Guy 19–20, 22
Mahoney, John xiv
Magnani, Anna 98
Magnificent Obsession 142
Maizish, Harry 107
Maltz, Albert 131, 161*n11*
The Man from U.N.C.L.E. 123